Desmot & Lou

Hope you enjoy the
tales

Best wishes

Jim

Liverpool VCs

For

23127264 Trooper James Ronald Flynn, 15/19 Royal Hussars

and

PO63276D Marine Patrick Dominic Murphy, Royal Marines.

Liverpool VCs

James Murphy

JAMES MURPHY

Foreword by
Lord Derby

Pen & Sword
MILITARY

First published in Great Britain in 2008 by
Pen & Sword Military
an imprint of
Pen & Sword Books Ltd
47 Church Street
Barnsley
South Yorkshire
S70 2AS

ISBN 978-1-84415-780-8

A CIP catalogue record for this book is available from the British Library.

Typeset in 11/13 Ehrhardt by Concept, Huddersfield, West Yorkshire
Printed and bound in England by CPI UK

Pen & Sword Books Ltd incorporates the imprints of Pen & Sword Aviation,
Pen & Sword Maritime, Pen & Sword Military, Wharncliffe Local History,
Pen & Sword Select, Pen & Sword Military Classics, Leo Cooper, Remember When,
Seaforth Publishing and Frontline Publishing

For a complete list of Pen & Sword titles please contact
Pen & Sword Books Limited
47 Church Street, Barnsley, South Yorkshire, S70 2AS, England
E-mail: enquiries@pen-and-sword.co.uk
Website: www.pen-and-sword.co.uk

Contents

For Valour

Thus saith the Queen! 'For him who gave
His life as nothing in the fight,
So he from Russian wrong might save
My crown, my people and my right;
Let there be made a cross of bronze
And grave thereon my queenly crest,
Write VALOUR on its haughty scroll,
And hang it on his breast.'

Thus saith the Land! 'He who shall bear
Victoria's cross upon his breast,
In token that he did not fear
To die, had need been, for her rest;
For the dear sake of her who gives,
And the high deeds of him who wears,
Shall, high or low, all honour have
From all, through all his years.'

Edwin Arnold, February 1856

Introduction

The Victoria Cross is a potent symbol of courage and heroism and is Britain's, and arguably the world's, most prestigious award for gallantry. It is also an emblem of our humanity, amid the thunder and crash of man's most inhuman of endeavours, war: in moments of crisis on the battlefield, some men find extra reserves of strength and courage to renew the challenge and go forward to offer their own lives so that others might live. Those who display such altruism, such 'conspicuous bravery, or some daring or pre-eminent act of valour or self-sacrifice or extreme devotion to duty in the presence of the enemy', are the bravest of the brave and merit the honour of the Victoria Cross.

The award was instituted by Royal Warrant signed by Queen Victoria in 1856, and was made retrospective to the opening forays of the Crimean War in the summer of 1854. This conflict, the first major campaign Britain had fought in forty years, witnessed extraordinary bravery on the part of the men in British uniforms not only in the face of the enemy but also in the face of incompetent leadership at the highest levels, which resulted in five times the numbers of casualties off the battlefield as on it. The war was a success for British and French force of arms, and in recognition of the astonishing courage displayed by her troops under such adverse conditions, the young Queen sought to honour the bravest, irrespective of rank, with the grant of her new honour.

The official announcement of the first awards of the Victoria Cross was made in the *London Gazette*, and the first to be honoured was Charles Lucas, an Irishman from Armagh, serving with the Royal Navy. Together with sixty-one other veterans of the Crimea campaign, he attended the initial presentation at Hyde Park on 26 June 1857. For the navy, the medal was dressed with a blue ribbon, for the army, crimson. But, since the formation of the Royal Air Force in the latter months of the First World War, all awards have been made with crimson ribbons.

Under Rule 13 of the warrant, a serviceman could be elected to the award by his comrades. Amendments have been made to the original warrant over the years: originally it bestowed a pension or annuity of £10 per annum on the recipient; this has now risen to £1,495; and the award is now open to all men and women, irrespective of nationality, serving under British command. Since 1920, the posthumous grant of the honour has been officially allowed, and the award is no longer forfeited by the holder after conviction for a criminal offence. The Victoria Cross has been granted on only 1,357 occasions in its

154-year history, and three men have been honoured twice, Captain Surgeon Arthur Martin-Leake, Captain Noel Chavasse and Captain Charles Upham.

This volume chronicles the lives and times and gallant deeds of a small contingent of Victoria Cross holders, twenty-three men of Liverpool who covered themselves in glory on foreign battlefields while the city was growing up. Eighteen were 'Dicky Sams', native-born Liverpudlians, and five made a home in the city and are buried within its boundaries. They came from a variety of backgrounds and walks of life – labourers, clerks, tradesmen, servicemen, volunteers and professional soldiers. Some were rich, some knew only poverty; three were rascals, the remainder angels; a few were illiterate, but most could read and write. However, the battlefield is a great leveller, and the courage and equanimity these men showed in the face of the enemy made them equals. Five died bravely in battle, four returned home unnoticed to a last resting place in a pauper's grave, some were buried with full military honours, while others declined that reward. All the survivors had in common a quiet dignity and an abiding modesty, and would not permit themselves to be singled out and lionized for what they had accomplished to aid their comrades under fire.

There has been renewed interest in the deeds of the Victoria Cross heroes of Liverpool, mainly because of the industry and dedication of Denis Rose and the late Sid Lindsay. Some of the men herein may be unfamiliar to the reader, others may not, but the stories of two men who are usually associated with the city, Patrick Mylott VC and Charles Anderson VC, have been omitted. The reasons are given in the Appendix. A third hero is also missing, a man whose name is synonymous with Liverpool and Victoria Cross – Noel Chavasse, dual winner of the honour.

Born in Oxford in 1884, Noel Chavasse came to Liverpool in 1900, and during the First World War served as a medical officer attached to 10th Battalion, the King's (Liverpool) Regiment, the Liverpool Scottish. His first honour for heroism came on the Somme in 1916, the second during the Third Battle of Ypres in 1917, when he died of wounds sustained attending the wounded. He is buried at Brandhoek New Military Cemetery, Belgium. Much has been written about this brave man, and though seen by many as a Liverpool hero, since he was neither born nor buried in the city, he does not fulfil the criterion for this series of narratives. However, his heroism is a thread which runs through and connects the tales of several of the Liverpool heroes who fought on the Western Front.

It is hoped that this book will maintain the revival of interest in the Victoria Cross heroes of Liverpool. They witnessed the days when commerce, progress and growth elevated Liverpool to become the most cosmopolitan city of Britain and 'gateway' to the British Empire. Much has changed in the city since their time, but the honour they carried from foreign battlefields to the city is forever woven into its history and heritage.

Acknowledgements

In researching this book, I had the great good fortune at an exhibition to hold in my hand a Victoria Cross. It is a most understated honour, a cross pattée measuring only 1.61 × 1.42 inches (41 × 36 mm) and weighing, together with the suspender bar, just 0.87 troy ounces (27 grams). It does not glisten or shine, being cast from gunmetal and chased and finished by hand before a chemical wash is applied to render a dull, brown-gold colour. The obverse of the medal holds the royal cypher and two words, 'For Valour', and the bar is adorned with laurel leaves, the ancient Roman award for a hero. But every medal is unique: on the reverse, the bar gives the name, rank and regiment of the recipient and the medal itself is inscribed with the date of the gallant deed. Each medal has its own particular story to tell.

Some of the stories could not have been told but for the children, nephews and nieces, great, great-great and greater still, of the Liverpool heroes, who came to my assistance by granting me access to family histories, memories, legends, sagas and anecdotes, and to whom I am most grateful. They are Thomas White, Frank Wilson, Shirley Ross, Patricia Heaps, Ian and Elizabeth Stuart, John and Bernadette Doolan, Peter Nurse and Sue Sayers.

No study of Victoria Cross winners from Liverpool or Merseyside can be made without reference to the work of Denis Rose and his late colleague, Sid Lindsay, two local historians, who, for many years, have devotedly and enthusiastically compiled their life stories from countless sources. Denis Rose supplied many insights into their lives and was always willing to give his time and energies to the project. Many thanks.

Regimental Museums and their curators have provided service records and addenda for some of the heroes, and I am indebted to Major Ian Riley and Dennis Reeves, Liverpool Scottish Museum; Major W. White, Duke of Cornwall Light Infantry Museum; David Murphy, Royal Scots Museum; Joe Devereux, King's Liverpool Regiment Museum; the South Lancashire Regiment Museum, 1st The Queen's Dragoon Guards Museum and the Highlander Regimental Museum.

I would like to thank also, for their assistance and patience, Dr Cormac Murphy, Dave Walker, Ian Warner, Neil Clark, Len Smith, Chris Baker, Christine Collins, Margaret Kane, Brian Best, Paul F. Wilson, Elizabeth Murphy, Jeff Birch, Peter Gallagher, Elizabeth Talbot-Rice, David Maw and Jim Bowman. Needless to say, any errors in the narratives are entirely the fault of the author.

Foreword

It is with enormous humility that I set about writing a foreword to a book about Liverpool Victoria Cross holders. When almost any of us see those famous letters, VC, after someone's name, it makes us instantly take notice and contemplate what extraordinary deed of heroism they carried out on the battle field.

That less than 1,400 have been issued in its 150 year history adds to the mystique of the medal. The Victoria Cross is awarded for the 'most conspicuous bravery, or some daring or pre-eminent act of valour or self-sacrifice, or extreme dedication to duty in the presence of the enemy'. This sadly means that a great many have been awarded posthumously.

Liverpool lads have won more than their fair share of VCs reflecting the long-established reputation of Liverpool for producing many brave servicemen. Victoria Cross holders went about their actions in the knowledge that death was probable and not just possible.

This book is a very welcome tribute to the Liverpool holders. Whilst I have read citations or obituaries in the past I have never had the chance to learn so much about the individuals, their family lives and backgrounds before. I am stunned by the accounts of extraordinary and selfless bravery of these remarkable citizens of Liverpool.

The Earl of Derby DL
Knowsley Hall

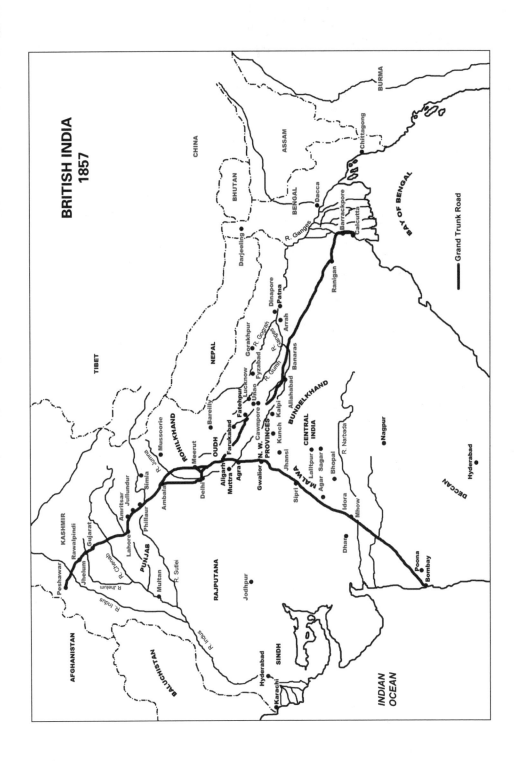

BRITISH INDIA
1857

—— Grand Trunk Road

THE WESTERN FRONT
1914–1918

NORTH SEA

HOLLAND

Zeebrugge
Ostend
Bruges
Ghent
Nieuport
Dunkirk
Calais
St Omer
Hazebrouck
Ypres
Passchendaele
Messines
Ploegsteert
Laventie
Lille
Brussels

BELGIUM

Boulogne
Etaples
Neuve Chapelle
Givenchy
La Bassee
Montreuil-sur-Mer
Loos
Lens
Douai
Mons
Vimy
Valenciennes
Maubeuge
Arras
Cambrai
Le Cateau
Landrecies
Abbeville
R. Somme
Baupaume
Albert
Peronne
St Quentin
Sedan
Amiens
Noyon

F R A N C E

Soissons
Rheims
Verdun

────	: Armistice Line 1918
━ ━ ━	: Western Front 1916
─·─·─	: Borders

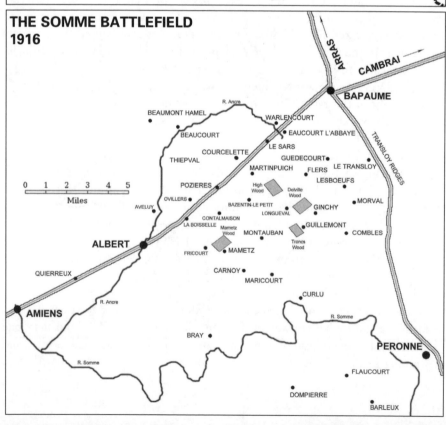

THE SOMME BATTLEFIELD
1916

ARRAS
CAMBRAI
BAPAUME
R. Ancre
BEAUMONT HAMEL
WARLENCOURT
BEAUCOURT
EAUCOURT L'ABBAYE
LE SARS
COURCELETTE
THIEPVAL
GUEDECOURT
TRANSLOY RIDGES
MARTINPUICH
FLERS
LE TRANSLOY
POZIERES
LESBOEUFS
High Wood
Delville Wood
OVILLERS
AVELUY
BAZENTIN-LE PETIT
LONGUEVAL
GINCHY
MORVAL
CONTALMAISON
LA BOISSELLE
Mametz Wood
MONTAUBAN
GUILLEMONT
COMBLES
ALBERT
FRICOURT
MAMETZ
Troncs Wood
QUIERREUX
CARNOY
MARICOURT
CURLU
R. Ancre
R. Somme
AMIENS
BRAY
PERONNE
R. Somme
FLAUCOURT
DOMPIERRE
BARLEUX

| 0 | 1 | 2 | 3 | 4 | 5 |

Miles

Joseph Prosser VC
(1828–67)

At the end of October 1843, the right wing and headquarters staff of the 2nd Battalion, Royal Regiment of Foot, en route to a new station in Barbados, boarded the troop-ship HMS *Premier* at Quebec and sailed down the St Lawrence river, heading for the Atlantic. More than 350 officers and men, wives and children were embarked, and a joyful mood of celebration swamped the decks: all were relieved to be leaving behind the harsh winters of Canada and delighted in the prospect of service in the warmth of the West Indies. But the Canadian winter was reluctant to let them go. In the early hours of 4 November, as she hugged the coast during a blinding snowstorm, the vessel struck a reef of rocks near Cap Chat, lost her rudder, was holed in the bow and driven on to a sandbar.

Passengers and crew on the stricken vessel endured a long and terrifying night at the mercy of the storm. But discipline was maintained: the women and children were cared for, and soldiers and sailors together battled the elements to rig lines to the shore. By ten o'clock in the morning, a crew member finally secured a cable to dry land; and, over the next ten hours, the perilous evacuation of HMS *Premier* was completed. Swinging hand over hand along the rope dangling above the raging surf, the men, women and children carried themselves to safety. They found refuge at St Ann's, a small fishing village five miles further along the coast, and there lived a bare existence in the winter cold for three weeks until rescue came.

On hearing of the incident the Duke of Wellington and Queen Victoria warmly complimented the officers and men of the regiment for their discipline and courage under such adverse conditions and for rendering safe the lives of all the women and children. Among the rank and file on board HMS *Premier* was a young drummer boy, Joseph Prosser. Twelve years later, he would receive further acclaim from his monarch when he won the regiment's first Victoria Cross during the Crimean War.

Joseph Prosser was a 'slip of a lad', as the Irish would say, short and scrawny with hardly an ounce of weight to him. Fully grown he barely reached 5 feet 5 inches, a skinny bantamweight, but, by all accounts, a fierce and fiery one when roused. A good head of brown hair above a pair of sparkling blue eyes and a winning smile completed the picture. He was born on 11 January 1828 in

County Offaly, Ireland, in the village of Moneygall, a small farming community of less than 300 inhabitants situated close to the Tipperary border, thirty miles north-east of Limerick.

Nothing is known of his early life, his parents or his education, except that he had an elder brother, John. On his fourteenth birthday he enlisted as 1672 Private Joseph Prosser in the 2nd Battalion, Royal Regiment of Foot, at Kinsale Barracks, County Cork. At the time, it was not unusual for boys of his age to enlist and sign on, like their elders, for life. The misgovernance of Ireland had pushed the majority of the rural population into dire poverty and a stark, hand-to-mouth existence. The potato was the staple diet, but small-scale failures of the crop occurred annually and hunger stalked the land. Consequently, Irishmen were over-represented in the British army of the day – 'Jack Frost and an empty belly . . . are the best recruiting sergeants' it was said – and, more than likely, Joseph Prosser enlisted to escape the poverty, to put warm food in his stomach, clothes on his back and a roof over his head.

Not a soldier on full pay until the age of 18, he was assigned to the band as a drummer boy, under the watchful eye of the drum major, the sergeant drummer. He learnt the various drum cadences which set the marching pace for the battalion and kept up the morale of the troops on the battlefield, and also the ominous drum rolls which preceeded punishments. One of the 'old sweats' of the battalion would have taken him under his wing to teach him his drill and the care of his uniform, in particular how to apply the pipe clay to whiten his gaiters, belt and webbing. A young country boy, he would have been impressionable and easily led; and he would have to learn very quickly how to survive and stand up for himself. Fighting, arguing, complaining and taking comfort in the demon drink, as in every barrack room, in every soldier's army, would have been his lot.

His first station was Canada, and he spent almost two years on garrison duty in London, Ontario and Toronto before the ill-fated journey aboard HMS *Premier*. Following the rescue, the right wing of the battalion was stationed at Halifax, Nova Scotia, for several months awaiting transportation to the West Indies, followed by sixteen months in the sunshine of Barbados, with minimal duties and plenty of free time. And it was during this period, as he neared manhood, that Joseph Prosser made a name for himself as a trouble-maker – overindulging in the local poteen, he was inspired to take on the world with his fists. But, it was not until his return to England in 1846 that his behaviour merited punishment beyond a reprimand: at Aldershot barracks, he was sentenced to twenty-eight days' confinement in the cells. More was to come.

The following year, the battalion went on station in Ireland, and remained there for five years. Bleak though the country had been when he left five years earlier, it was now devastated by the potato famine, known to the Irish as *An Gort Mohr*, the Great Hunger. During his time in Ireland, one million inhabitants died of starvation and disease, and a further two million emigrated to escape the horror, many of them crossing over to Liverpool, where some remained, while others ended their ordeal in North America.

Whole communities perished or were forced to disperse to wander the land in sickly, skeletal bands in search of sustenance. Joseph Prosser's birthplace was no exception: Moneygall ceased to exist. There can be no doubt he was deeply affected by the appalling conditions; and his conduct within the battalion reflected this. A family story relates he was desperate to obtain compassionate leave to visit his family. His request denied, he nevertheless tried to make his way home, but was arrested and returned to the barracks; and in August 1847, he served twenty-eight days in the cells for being absent without leave. The following year, he was labelled a deserter. On 26 April 1848, he went absent without permission again, and this time managed to reach Moneygall. But he was met by devastation. The village was abandoned, and his family had disappeared. It took him several weeks to discover that his brother John had survived and was living in Liverpool. There was nothing he could do.

He returned to the battalion voluntarily on 13 June, and was charged with desertion. At his court martial, he was found guilty and sentenced to eighty-four days' imprisonment. In addition, he forfeited all his time with the colours, two years and two months, since his eighteenth birthday. This long period of confinement cooled him down and he became a model prisoner, earning a day's remission to the sentence. On release, he kept out of serious trouble until September 1851, when he again found himself in the cells, this time for forty-two days, for taking one too many drinks. However, this was his last incarceration: from that time onwards, he was on his best behaviour and was even in receipt of good conduct pay. He was never promoted, remaining a private all his days, and family history says he was offered, but refused, rank: he continued to play in the band throughout his enlistment, preferring to remain one of the *bhoys* rather than accept promotion.

By 1853, the worst of the famine was over, though its effects would be felt in Ireland for generations to come; and for Prosser, it was time for new horizons. He spent the next two years basking in the 'Old McCormac', soldier slang for the sun, on the island of Cephalonia, in the Ionian Sea. Duties were light and he had plenty of time on his hands to enjoy himself. But he did not lapse into his old, troublesome ways, and kept his nose clean: the British Empire was at peace, and so was Joseph Prosser. However, that was about to change. The ambition of Czar Nicholas I to challenge the British and French in the Mediterranean from his naval base at Sebastopol on the Crimean peninsula signalled an end to his idyll in the sun, and placed him on a battlefield for the first and only time in his life: war was declared against Russia in March 1854.

The opening round of the Crimean War, the Battle of the River Alma, in September 1854 saw the Russians soundly beaten, and should have brought the war to an end. But, the legacy of the greatest military commander the world has ever seen, the Duke of Wellington, was about to be trodden under foot by the supine incompetence of his successors, the Duke of Cambridge and Lord Raglan: the Czar's forces were allowed to fall back unhindered on Sebastopol, and the campaign laboured disastrously into siege, which was to cost the lives of thousands of British fighting men.

In May 1855, Prosser and the 2nd Battalion sailed to the Crimean port of Balaclava and marched up to the lines at Sebastopol the following month. When he arrived, only 11,000 British troops were fit for duty. Cholera, dysentery and malaria had ravaged the Expeditionary Force in transit the previous summer, and in the harsh winter which followed thousands of men perished in the trenches before Sebastopol from hunger and exposure because of lack of supplies. Now, 23,000 sick and wounded suffered in dank, dark hospital wards at Balaclava and Scutari.

The French had fared much better throughout the campaign and had 90,000 fighting men in front of Sebastopol. They took over most of the trenches, and all the decision-making, while the British were to be found cramped and sand-wiched between their lines, facing the Great Redan, which jutted out towards the British positions like a giant wedge. Protected by a wide, deep ditch, it stood atop a bare slope surrounded by an *abattis*, a rampart of felled trees bound together and bristling with cannon which covered all approaches.

Preparations were already afoot for the storming of the Great Redan when Joseph Prosser and his comrades went forward into the trenches. The key to the taking of Sebastopol was the Malakoff, a huge stone tower which domin-ated the southern sector of the city, whose fortified base guarded the way into the city. It lay within the French area of responsibility, and the British attack on the Great Redan was to be no more than a sideshow to a French assault on the Malakoff, which was to open the way into Sebastopol and end the war.

Joseph Prosser's baptism of fire came earlier than he anticipated. His bat-talion was one of the freshest at the front, and when the Allies decided to bring their big guns in closer to the city to batter the defences, plans were made to capture two Russian outposts where the guns could be repositioned. On 6 June, the third bombardment of Sebastopol began; and under cover of the barrage, British troops, among them the 2nd Battalion, swept down on the Russian outpost known as the Quarries. In a short, fierce engagement, the Russians were overrun and the outpost secured, as was another, the Mamelon, which French forces stormed. Joseph Prosser came through his first fight unscathed.

The British and French troops and their commanders were greatly heart-ened by these two easy successes, the first positive movement forward in eight months of siege; and with the heavy bombardment continuing for a further three days, all boded well for the twin assaults on the Great Redan and the Malakoff. The date set for the attacks was auspicious, 18 June, the fortieth anniversary of the Battle of Waterloo.

Joseph Prosser and the battalion moved up into the forward lines and began final preparations for the attack. Anticipating that something was afoot, but not knowing when it would commence, the Russians kept up a relentless fire on the Allied lines to hinder any build-up. On the night of 16 June, while standing guard, Joseph Prosser spied a British soldier desert his own lines and make his way stealthily under cover towards the Russian defences. Without a thought for his own safety, he climbed from his trench into no man's land; and, dodging and weaving through the intense, Russian crossfire, chased after the man. He apprehended and arrested the deserter and hauled him back to the British lines.

It is not known who the soldier was, nor from what unit he came. But the penalty for desertion in time of war was summary execution. Prosser himself never spoke of his deed. But he, like all the rest of his comrades, knew enemy resistance would have been stiffened considerably with the knowledge not only of the timing of the attack, but also of British troops eager to desert. Fore-warned, the Russians would have put up a formidable defence. Prosser's act of bravery under fire in apprehending the deserter and preventing vital inform-ation falling into the hands of the foe was duly noted by his superiors.

The assaults on the Malakoff and Great Redan were to commence at dawn, but in the chaos and confusion which arose when the huge attacking force moved forward and filled, and then overflowed, the narrow trenches at the front, the French jumped the gun. Charging forward against the Malakoff, they alerted the Russians before the British were prepared, and were chopped down in ranks for their presumption by the devastating fire from the defenders. By daybreak, it was obvious to Lord Raglan that the French had failed. Fearing criticism for not supporting the French, Raglan needed a body count, and ordered his men forward into the jaws of death.

British troops, including both the 1st and 2nd Battalions of the Royal Regiment of Foot, dashed across the ditch at the base of the Great Redan and up the steep incline of the glacis beneath a withering barrage of grapeshot and musketry. But they failed. By the time the doomed attacks were called off, 1,500 British troops littered the slope, and 3,500 Frenchmen lay dying under the ramparts. Shattered and demoralized, Joseph Prosser stumbled back to the lines. Again, he came through the fight unhurt. In fact, his service record indicates that he was never wounded or injured in combat. He was to be tested once more in battle, in another desperate slaughter, before he was released from the Crimea.

Between June and September, British sappers dug trenches and parallels to bring the British lines closer to the Great Redan in preparation for a second assault. The sappers were constantly harassed by enemy musketry and artillery fire, and their parties were defended by fighting patrols returning fire on the Russian defenders. On 11 August, Prosser was in a forward trench, sniping into the Russian lines. He saw a soldier of the 95th Regiment fall severely wounded. As before, he unselfishly exposed himself to a heavy enemy crossfire, climbing out of the trench and making his way into no man's land to attend the wounded man. With all the strength in his slight frame, he pulled and dragged the wounded man to safety, with the help of a comrade.

For bravery in apprehending the deserter, and for helping to save the life of a wounded man, both deeds carried out under fire, Joseph Prosser was awarded the Victoria Cross. On 24 February 1857 the announcement of his award was made in the *London Gazette*. The citation reads:

> 2nd Battalion 1st Regiment. Number 1672 Private Joseph Prosser. 1st – On 16 June 1855, when on duty in the trenches before Sebastopol, for pursuing and apprehending (whilst exposed to two crossfires) a soldier in the act of deserting to the enemy. 2nd – On 11 August 1855, before Sebastopol, for leaving the most advanced trench, and assisting to carry in a soldier of the 95th Regiment who lay severely wounded and unable to move. This gallant and humane act was performed under a very heavy fire from the enemy.

On 8 September 1855, in what is believed to be the first attack coordinated by timepiece, and under a heavy artillery bombardment, British troops went forward to attack the Great Redan while the French assaulted the Malakoff. Within ten minutes, the French had forced the Malakoff and held it against a fierce Russian counter-attack. But the British forces fared disastrously. Having crossed the ditch and fought their way up the glacis and onto the *abattis*, they were confronted by increasing numbers of Russian reinforcements and found themselves lacking in both ammunition and support.

Amid a cacophony of roaring cannon, crackling muskets, clashing steel, furious yells and gasping groans, and with the men choked by a swirling cloud of dust and smoke, the attack faltered and then broke. The troops tumbled and fell from the *abattis* and down the slope, slippery with the gore of fallen comrades, towards their own lines; and the Russians surged forward and poured volley after deadly volley into the backs of the retreating men. With the luck of the Irish, Joseph Prosser once more escaped unharmed to safety. In just two hours of fearsome fighting British losses were 2,500 killed and wounded. The attack on the Great Redan was of no strategic value whatsoever, and was a terrible waste of lives: that night, with the Malakoff in French hands, the Russians abandoned Sebastopol through the northern sector, and the Crimean War was all but over.

The 2nd Battalion recuperated in the Crimea until August 1856, while peace negotiations between the belligerents were under way. Then it was shipped off for a year of garrison duty in Malta. Because of his station, Joseph Prosser could not receive his Victoria Cross from the hand of Queen Victoria at the inaugural Victoria Cross investiture at Hyde Park on 26 June 1857. Instead, a letter of commendation and his Victoria Cross were fowarded to Malta, where he received both from his commanding officer, Colonel Sir Edward Blakeney, while the battalion paraded. He also received the British Crimea Medal with Sebastopol clasp and the Turkish Crimea Medal. In addition, in a letter from the War Office to the battalion in March 1858, his service record was restored: the two years and two months he had forfeited on conviction for desertion would be counted as time served with the colours and contribute to his pension entitlement upon discharge.

After Malta, the battlion spent eleven months at ease in Gibraltar, but in 1858 was called on again to defend the empire. At that time, Britain was engaged in the Second Opium War, skirmishing with the Chinese to maintain the lucrative and legal opium trade. However, Prosser would do all his fighting in bed: landing in Hong Kong, he was found to be suffering from hepatitis and was confined to the hospital. For several months he was seriously ill, but was nursed back to health by a young Irish woman from County Cork, Katherine Riddle, one of the new breed of carers trained in the methods of Florence Nightingale and Mary Seacole.

It is not known for certain when the couple married, but in 1860, Katherine Riddle Prosser gave birth to a daughter, Ellen. The following year, Joseph, his wife and daughter were returned to England. They lived for a time in married quarters in Aldershot, but Joseph's fighting days were over. The hepatitis continued to plague him, and on several occasions, he was confined to the Royal Victoria Hospital, Netley, for treatment and was unable to perform his duties.

During his last confinement there in June 1863, a regimental board sat at Aldershot to consider his case. The board concluded that Prosser was incapable of further service in Her Majesty's Army, and that he should be dismissed, never to be recalled, being medically unfit with chronic hepatitis. The Chelsea Commissioners granted him a pension of one shilling a day because of his ill health. He left the army on 30 June 1863, aged 35, having given almost twenty-one years as boy and man to the regiment. On discharge, he was in possession of two Good Conduct badges, despite his name appearing forty-three times in the Defaulters Book and having stood before a court martial on four occasions.

The only known likeness of Joseph Prosser is a daguerreotype made following the birth of his second daughter in 1863. It shows a handsome man in dress uniform, glancing shyly at the camera, a smile, perhaps of devilment, forming on his lips. His cheeks are encased in a set of fashionable 'Dundreary weepers', made fashionable by the Liverpool-born actor Edward Askew Sothern. But his eyes, eyes that could laugh, that could plead, that could turn to blue steel, as the occasion demanded, appear uncertain, as if he is peturbed by all the to-do. Like many Victoria Cross winners, he did not understand, nor would he countenance, the fuss and bother which the award sometimes brought.

The next port of call for Prosser was Liverpool, where his brother John lived. John had settled in the city, married and was bringing up a family. Like many Irishmen, he found work on the docks, and would have been well positioned to help his brother find a home and work. However, Joseph's illness and his debilitating condition precluded labouring as a docker, and he searched for, and found, easier work. He set up home at 8 Lancaster Street, Kirkdale, where a second daughter, Katherine Victoria, was born in August 1863. A son, Joseph William, was born on 4 June 1865 when the family was living at 96 Gordon Street, off Great Homer Street.

Prosser was employed on the docks by HM Customs and Excise as an out door officer (ODO), checking for contraband among the cargoes and the passengers of the many vessels that tied up at the quays. The work was not difficult, but he spent many long hours on his feet in all kinds of weather, which would not have helped his chronic medical condition. As a soldier, he had been a toper, and had indulged himself liberally with his friends whenever possible, often, as was the case in those days, resorting to illicit and somewhat poisonous brews such as poteen, which probably had weakened his liver and left it susceptible to infection. But, in Liverpool, he led a decent and hard-working life and was a good husband and devoted father to his children. Time was not on his side, however, and he had precious few years in which to show his true colours.

When Katherine Prosser became pregnant again, Joseph moved the family to 26B Birchfield Street, just off Islington in the city centre: a third daughter, Mary, was born there on 10 March 1867. His condition continued to deteriorate, and in great pain he would try to drag himself to work. Doctors found he was afflicted also with tuberculosis, what was then commonly known as consumption or pulmonary phthisis. A contributing factor to the illness can be typhoid fever, which was prevalent in the Crimea at the time he was there and was also rife in Cephalonia and Hong Kong.

At Birchfield Street, on 10 June 1867, three months after the birth of Mary, Joseph Prosser VC passed away, aged 39. He died not from the hepatitis but from pulmonary phthisis. He was buried three days later in a quiet family ceremony in the Church of England section in Liverpool's Anfield Cemetery. There were no military honours to mark the passing of this brave man, no melancholy bugle call sounding the 'Last Post', not even a headstone to mark his final resting place. 'The Land', which the poet Edward Arnold commended to honour such a hero as Joseph Prosser VC, had forgotten him.

The death of her husband meant financial disaster for Kate Prosser: she lost not only her husband's weekly salary, but also his Chelsea and Victoria Cross pensions, and she had to go back to work to support her young family. She moved to London with her children, and lodged for some time at Charing Cross with her sister, Ellen, who had married a former soldier, Thomas O'Connor. There is a family story that at this time the Prosser children were placed in a home or an orphanage: and the records show that Ellen, then aged 11, and Kate Victoria, aged 7, were admitted to Royal Victoria Patriotic Asylum for Girls, in Wandsworth. This institution, despite its name, was a school, probably one of the ragged schools which opened during that era to care for children whose parents could not afford to provide for them. Meanwhile, Joseph William and Mary continued to live with their mother.

Kate worked in several jobs in the city, as a cleaner and as a servant, until in May 1871 she secured work as a nurse at the Chelsea Hospital. She nursed at the hospital for two years until she resigned at the end of September 1873 to marry an Irishman, Hugh Lunny, a former soldier and Chelsea pensioner. The couple set up home at 9 Pennington Buildings, Tower Hamlets; and all four children lived with their mother and their stepfather. Ellen and Kate Victoria later left home and were employed as live-in housemaids in Kensington; and Joseph William secured employment as a clerk.

Kate's second marriage was childless; and Hugh Lunny passed away in June 1890 at the age of 59. By 1891, Kate Prosser Lunny was living on her own means with her son Joseph William at 70 The Grove, Lambeth. Joseph William worked as a clerk, but he taught shorthand and the banjo, the talent for music coming from his father, perhaps. By 1901, he was living in Mosside, Manchester, with his mother at 10 Sewerby Street, and working as a cashier's clerk. It is believed that Mary Prosser died the age of 18 in 1885; and that Kate Victoria died in London in 1883. No records have been found of Ellen Prosser after 1881.

Kate Prosser Lunny died at the age of 69 in Chorlton, Manchester, in the spring of 1905; and in July of that year, Joseph William Prosser married Catherine Eleanor Ball. There were two sons from the marriage, Charles Hugh and Joseph Cyril, and their descendants live in the Manchester area today. The Liverpool branch of the Prossers, established by John Prosser, who had two sons and two daughters, is noted for the exploits of John's eldest son, William Henry Prosser, a remarkable man who made it his vocation to save lives.

On 18 July 1927, two young boys were bathing off Egremont Pier on the Birkenhead side of the River Mersey when they found themselves in difficulties. William Prosser, hearing their cries for help, threw down a lifebuoy and jumped from the boulevard into the river, grabbing hold of the boys and supporting them in the water until they could be pulled to safety. What is notable about this rescue is that William Henry Prosser was 75 years of age at the time; and that this was the seventeenth recorded occasion he had saved someone in danger of drowning.

Born in 1853 in Chaucer Street, William Prosser, like his father, worked all his life on the Liverpool Docks. Many of his life-saving feats led to the rescue of working dockers who fell or were knocked from vessels or quaysides into the River Mersey. He was still working on the docks aged 72 when he effected his penultimate rescue, in the Langton Dock. For his seventh rescue in August 1887, he was awarded the Liverpool Shipwreck and Humane Society's second highest honour, the silver Marine Medal. Subsequent rescues earned him nine silver clasps to this award.

William Prosser never married. He lived for a time with his brother, Thomas, in Tillard Street, off Fountains, close to where William Dowling VC lived. He lodged also in Skervington Street and Lambeth Road. He died on 9 December 1934 aged 82, and was buried, like his uncle Joseph, in Anfield Cemetery.

Joseph Prosser's Victoria Cross was purchased by his regiment when it was put up for auction at Sotheby's in 1954 by his grandson, Charles Hugh Prosser, and is now in the Royal Scots, The Royal Regiment Museum, Edinburgh Castle. In 1995, a headstone to honour his final resting place in Liverpool was erected in Anfield Cemetery.

John Kirk VC
(1827–65)

Private John Kirk won his Victoria Cross during the Indian Mutiny, in June 1857. With the assistance of Sergeant Majors Peter Gill and Matthew Rosamund, he effected the rescue of a family besieged and threatened with death by a band of mutineers. The two Sergeant Majors won Victoria Crosses also, which were gazetted in 1858. However, John Kirk's award was not gazetted until 20 January 1860, eighteen months after the end of the Mutiny. Had notification of his award been made earlier, perhaps he would have been spared the great pain and humiliation inflicted upon him on 12 April 1858 following a regimental court martial, when, 'drunk on the line of march', he was sentenced to be flogged, fifty lashes with a cat-o'-nine-tails.

The regiment would have been paraded and formed up into a square to witness the punishment. Stripped to the waist, John Kirk would have stood in the centre, his hands strapped above his head to a triangle of poles, while two burly blacksmiths laid on the cat-o'-nine-tails across his back. The regimental drummer would have beat out the hollow rhythm, and a senior, non-commissioned officer, armed with a stick with which to beat the floggers should they flag, would have ensured that the beating was applied vigorously. The whole proceeding would have been overseen by a senior officer who would count off the strokes, and a doctor to monitor his condition.

After the flogging, he was cut down and his torn and lacerated flesh washed over in salt water. This would have caused him further, excruciating pain, but the salt acted as a crude antiseptic and would have helped to prevent infection. The scars would remain with him for life. John Kirk was excused duty for three days to recover, after which he stood in the square alongside his mates and faced the last of the rebellious sepoys in the north-east of India.

It could be said that John Kirk was his own worst enemy: the demon drink and women were his downfall. His disciplinary record was appalling and he appeared fifty-six times in the regimental defaulters book during his eighteen years with the colours, which included six appearances before a regimental court martial, and he was described as a 'bad soldier' in his discharge papers. But a soldier's job is to fight in battle, and Kirk fought many actions in India, and fought bravely, as his Victoria Cross attests. It was in the intervening periods, between the fighting, at ease in the barrack room, the canteen and the bazaar, on parade and on review, that the indisciplined, 'bad soldier' side of him was manifest. But the military culture prevalent in India during his thirteen years' service there actively encouraged his dissipation. Work hard, play hard, could well have been his motto, as it was for so many servicemen of the time.

When he enlisted in the 10th (North Lincolnshire) Regiment of Foot at Liverpool on 27 January 1846, he gave his place of birth as Liverpool, his occupation as a labourer and his age as 18 years and 6 months. His date of birth can be calculated as July 1827, but who his parents were, and in what part of the city he was born and brought up, are unknown. Rumour and speculation attend his early years.

The first national census was recorded in 1841, and shows only one Kirk family registered in Liverpool, living at 24 Ormond Street, off Oldhall Street in the city centre: William Kirk, an ostler, and his wife Elizabeth, and two sons, John, aged 13, and George aged 10. Perhaps this is John Kirk and his family. However, there may have been other Kirk families in Liverpool at the time, hidden from the prying eyes of the census officers in the many slums and cellars of the city, suspicious of officialdom and not wanting to be found.

According to Sid Lindsay, the Liverpool historian, there was information that Kirk could have been born in the Liverpool Workhouse on Brownlow Hill, where the poor and destitute were confined, or entered that institution at an early age; and that his name was not his own but was given to him by the workhouse keepers.

There were several John Kirks whose birth years were 1827 or thereabouts living without families and working around Liverpool on farms in 1841; and in the 1861 census, John Kirk VC, stationed at Aldershot Barracks, stated his former occupation was farm servant. If he had indeed been brought up in a workhouse, he would not have remained there beyond the age of 10 if he was fit and well: when labour was in short supply, healthy workhouse children were sold by their keepers as pauper apprentices to work in factories, mines and on farms. He may have been sold or he may have been sent out to earn his keep wherever work could be found. If John Kirk was an inmate of a workhouse in his formative years, then his life was to come full circle: he was to die in such an institution fifteen months after his discharge from the army.

Whatever his antecedents, the first definite and unequivocal record of him is when he took the Queen's shilling as 2359 Private John Kirk in the 10th Regiment of Foot in 1846. He was described as 5 feet, 7½ inches tall, with a fresh complexion, blue eyes and brown hair. The only known likeness of him was taken after he had received his Victoria Cross, when he is wearing the award, together with the Mutiny Medal, on his dress uniform. He looks a no-nonsense type of man who had fought a few rounds, his nose is broken, and signs of the dissipation which blighted his life are beginning to show in his features.

The 10th Regiment had been in India since 1842, and John Kirk entered its ranks at Fort William, Calcutta, in the summer of 1846. A whole new world opened up to him in India, one in which, after a tenuous start, he was to indulge himself liberally. He was kitted out in his new uniform, white tunic and white trousers and helmet, which was fitted with a pagris, a square of white cotton that fell over the neck to protect it from the sun.

At the time, India was administered by 'John Company', the Honourable East India Company (HEIC). The major cities, Delhi, Lucknow and Benares, which were to figure prominently in the Indian Mutiny, were patchworks of segregation and separation. In each city, at the top of the social ladder was the Civil Commissioner, the Resident, who governed the region for the HEIC. The Residency, where he lived, and its immediate environs, where lived and worked the governing and administrative elite, stood apart from the native section of the city which in turn was segregated and divided by class and caste.

Separated from both was the military cantonment. Here was quartered the garrison. The HEIC had three mercenary armies, made up of British-recruited and native Indian regiments, under the command of British officers; and their strength was supplemented by regular British army units. The lines of the regular army regiments were separated from the HEIC British units, which in turn stood apart from the native contingents. British officers lived in bunga-lows, pampered by servants; the British rank and file lived in barrack rooms and were catered to by *wallahs*, and the sepoys, native infantrymen, and the *sowars*, native cavalrymen, lived in straw huts.

The British soldiers in their cantonments had their own canteens and dedicated bazaars, drinking dens and brothels. At the time of John Kirk's arrival in India, it was a time of peace, and military duties, especially during the oppressive heat of the summer, were minimal. Neither the officers nor the men were inclined to exert themselves, and the troops were left to their own devices. Rarely did a day go by when the canteens, the bazaars and brothels and drinking dens were not swarming with soldiers looking for pleasure. 'The trouble was there was not enough to occupy the men in their long leisure time. ... After morning parade, breakfast. ... Then there was nothing to do until one o'clock when it was time to go to dinner ... throughout the long afternoon the men turned into bed and slept ... or drank their cheap arrack.'

The canteen was open all day and every day, and the arrack or rum, which the soldiers called 'billy-stink', was readily available, overproof and deadly: 'you could have as much as you liked to drink ... there was men dying every day from the effects of drink [which] did more for death than fever. ... Drink was the rage in India.' Drink was smuggled out of the canteens against regu-lations by the men in their 'bishops' (pigskin pouches), and were usually filled with 'billy-stink' before a march; and replenished en route from village stills, the villagers being always ready to accommodate the *firinghis*, the infidels in uniform.

And when they tired of drinking, the men could be found in the Lol–Bibbees Bazaar, where their own private supply of prostitutes plied their trade 'The women there wore pantaloons, their breasts exposed, rings and bangles all over their arms and legs', and were always available to the men. Prostitution was regulated: the women were shipped in and housed by the authorities, and standard rates were charged. Business was always brisk. But venereal diseases were rife, and about a quarter of the patients in British military hospitals of the time suffered from such infections, typically syphilis.

Drink and women, amid the hustle and bustle of barrack room and bazaar, beneath a scorching sun, day in and day out, was the world John Kirk entered at the age of 18, fresh-faced and innocent from his labours on the farm. It is no wonder he succumbed to temptation when all around him indulged and when very little was done by those in authority to exercise any control. Awarding soldiers good conduct pay of a few extra pence per day and good conduct badges were the standard means of inducing and encouraging decent behaviour. Kirk was never in receipt of this extra pay or badges, but his disciplinary record was no worse than that of many hundreds of other soldiers in service in India at the time.

He first saw action when the 10th Regiment fought at the siege of Multan during the Second Anglo-Sikh War. Throughout the autumn and winter of 1848, he was engaged in several fierce, hand-to-hand encounters against the war-like Sikhs; and when the city surrendered in January 1849, the regiment pursued the rebels towards Lahore. At the Battle of Gujarat in February 1849, the Sikhs were defeated finally, and their kingdom was annexed by the HEIC. Kirk received the Punjab Medal and two clasps, Multan and Gujarat, for his doughty service against the Sikhs.

From 1849 until the beginning of the Indian Mutiny in 1857, peace prevailed in the sub-continent. The 10th Regiment was garrisoned at various outposts throughout India, and John Kirk settled into the routine of minimal duty and long leisure hours. Until 1850, he appears to have been reasonably well behaved and had no serious disciplinary problems. But the strain of enjoying himself began to tell, and while stationed at Govindpur, near Calcutta, he made his first court martial appearance in June of that year, charged with being drunk and cheeking an officer, for which he received thirty days' detention.

Other minor infringements occurred, and in August 1855, he received a further thirty days' detention, on this occasion for being drunk on evening parade. By that time, he had also been, like many of his comrades, hospitalized with syphilis. There was no cure for the disease, which, in the long term, could be fatal if progressing through to the third or tertiary stage of infection. Unfortunately for John Kirk, his infection did reach this terminal phase, and was to kill him.

When the Indian Mutiny broke out in the second week of May 1857, the 10th Regiment was on station at Benares, the holy Hindu city on the River

Ganges in the south of Oudh, 500 miles south-east of Delhi. The military cantonment of Sikraul and the European quarter at Sikra were to the west of the native town, along both banks of the River Banra, which ran into the Ganges. Also on duty there were the 15th Loodiana Sikh Regiment, the 37th Bengal Infantry and elements of a native cavalry regiment.

As the mutiny spread from Meerut, instructions were received at Benares at the beginning of June to disarm any sepoy contingents suspected of disloyalty. Matters were particularly sensitive in Benares: many state prisoners and members of the Moghul royal family lived in discontented idleness in the city, and it was thought that they might exploit any signs of infidelity among the sepoys there.

At first, the garrison commander, Brigadier Ponsonby, dithered and did not disarm his native troops immediately, and brooding sepoys and *sowars* of the 37th Bengal and the irregular cavalry units roamed their lines intent on trouble. Then, on 4 June, Ponsonby ordered all the sepoys and *sowars* to parade, including the Sikhs of the 15th Loodiana Regiment. Under artillery cover, and with the 10th Regiment standing by with fixed bayonets, Ponsonby ordered the native soldiers to disarm. The reluctant contingents began to stack their weapons. But when a shout went up among their ranks that they would be fired upon once they had relinquished their muskets, the troops panicked, broke ranks, rearmed themselves and began shooting at their officers. The Sikh regiment stood firm and remained loyal.

In the confusion that followed, the artillery opened up blindly on the ranks of the sepoys, but some of the shells landed among the loyal Sikhs, who immediately took flight. The 10th Regiment moved forward to quell the revolt, but the rebels quickly dispersed amid the ensuing chaos and went on the rampage.

The insurgents raged throughout the Sikraul cantonment, firing buildings and looting, and killing anybody who tried to stop them. John Kirk and the regiment were in hot pursuit, desperate to prevent the mutiny spreading into the European quarter of Sikra. What drove on the pursuers were the lurid tales of massacre: muntinous sepoys in other towns and cities had not only killed their officers but had resorted to murdering all *firinghis*, men, women and children, wherever they could be found. There was a determination to prevent this happening in Benares. European families were escorted from danger, sometimes under fire, before the rebels could get to them; and the sepoys were contained within the cantonment and slowly weeded out, street by street, by the 10th Regiment and loyal native troops, including the Sikhs. It was during this phase of the Benares mutiny that John Kirk won his Victoria Cross.

News came down the line to the regiment that rebels were burning and looting the officers' quarters, and that Pension Paymaster Captain Brown and his wife and young daughter, who had hidden away in their own bungalow waiting to be taken away to safety, had been discovered by the mutineers, and were trapped inside, in danger for their lives. John Kirk volunteered immediately to go to their rescue.

By all accounts, he set off alone to rescue Brown and his family. Why he did so, and why other members of the regiment did not offer to assist him, is not known. On the way, as he dodged the incessant fire of the rebels and hid from marauding bands, he met Sergeant Majors Gill, 15th Loodiana Regiment, and Rosamund, 37th Bengal Infantry, who were also seeking to help the captain. By the time the three men reached Brown's bungalow, it was surrounded by rebels. Fire was raging through the roof thatching and Captain Brown, desperately holding back the enemy with his revolver, was about to be overwhelmed.

Kirk, Gill and Rosamund drew up a plan of attack: they opened fire on the sepoys and charged through their lines to reach the bungalow. Once inside, they checked that Brown and his family were uninjured before they organized themselves into a firing party and started to bring down the rebels as they crept forward. Their fire was so accurate and effective that the rebel assault faltered. When the sepoys began to fall back under this intense fire, Kirk, Gill and Rosamund rushed Captain Brown, his wife and daughter from the bungalow just before the raging conflagration above their heads brought down the roof. Under continuous fire from the sepoys, the party fought its way through to the safety of the lines set up by the 10th Regiment.

For gallantry in the face of the enemy, John Kirk was awarded the Victoria Cross. His citation reads:

> John Kirk, Private, the 10th Regiment. Date of Act of Bravery: 4 June 1857. For daring gallantry at Benares, on 4 June 1857, at the outbreak of the mutiny by the native troops of that station, in having volunteered to proceed with two non-commissioned officers to rescue Captain Brown, Pension Paymaster, and his family, who were surrounded by rebels in the compound of their house, and having, at the risk of his own life, succeeded in saving them.

The rebellion at Benares was suppressed quickly that day. The mutinous sepoys and *sowars*, outnumbered by loyal troops and the 10th Regiment, were overcome in a couple of hours and disarmed. Gallows were set up on the parade ground and scores of mutineers were strung up by the neck. Some local youths, who, for fun, had donned rebel colours and danced and sang in the streets, were similarly dispatched.

From Benares, the 10th Regiment marched to Dinapore to suppress the revolt there, and on to Arrah, where a third rebellion was suppressed, and for the next twelve months, was constantly on the move, mopping up pockets of resistance. The only major engagement in which Kirk fought was the relief of Lucknow, where the Residency had been besieged from the early days of the Mutiny. The city was first relieved in September, but the following month was abandoned to the rebels. It was not until March 1858 that the city was retaken, when Sir Colin Campbell marshalled his avenging army to drive out the mutineers.

The city was bombarded for several days with heavy guns before Campbell unleashed his foot soldiers. Though greatly outnumbered by the insurgents, the British forces, thirsting for revenge, made short work of the rebels. Mutineers who surrendered were killed where they stood; those captured were executed in batches, by bullet and bayonet and the rope. And the slaughter spilled beyond the battlefield into the houses and homes of the city dwellers, when the troops went on the rampage and grabbed anything of value, killing anybody who resisted their depredations. All discipline disappeared and the troops ignored their officers, some of whom were too busy looting to care. Besides gold and silver and jewels, beer, wine and spirits were liberated in vast quantities, and fuelled an insane orgy of death and destruction for several days. William Howard Russell, *The Times* reporter of Crimea fame, noted that 'these men were wild with fury and lust for gold ... literally drunk with plunder.' By the time the havoc was curtailed, the city lay in ruins, and bloated bodies littered every walkway, every passageway and every street.

Kirk more than likely had his fill of slaughter and plunder. But he would return from India a poor man. Like many others of the rank and file, it was the demon drink and immediate gratification he sought. Russell met a soldier who had stolen 'an armlet of emeralds and diamonds and pearls' worth thousands of pounds, but who was prepared to accept two *mohurs*, two gold coins issued by the HEIC, and a bottle of rum for the bauble. The man could have been John Kirk.

He saw out the Mutiny as part of the Azimghur Field Force, a mixed force of cavalry and infantry. Azimghur, fifty-six miles north of Benares, had become the centre of a second rebellion, following the withdrawal of troops to fight in Oudh. A guerrilla campaign was launched by the rebels in the jungles and forests of the region, which ran the British ragged. And while tramping south from Lucknow to Azimghur, Kirk was found to be 'drunk on the line of march', and punished by fifty lashes with the cat-o'-nine-tails. Despite the flogging, he took part in the relief of Azimghur on 15 April. He saw action near Arrah again, and took part in the pursuit of the rebels through to the beginning of June, when the region was declared pacified.

The 10th Regiment returned to England in 1859 and went into barracks at Plymouth. But Kirk was not cut out for home duty. After thirteen years on the Indian sub-continent and ready access to 'billy-stink', being confined on an army base with few opportunities to indulge what had now become an addiction to alcohol, proved too much for him. Hardly had the dust settled beneath his feet before he was in trouble again. In October, for being drunk on parade, he was sentenced to twenty-eight days' hard labour.

Notification of his award of the Victoria Cross was published in the *London Gazette* of 20 January 1860. It would appear that his new celebrity temporarily curbed his enthusiasm for the drink, and he did not transgress for almost a year. It is believed he received the honour from the hands of his sovereign in November 1860.

The regiment went on station at Aldershot, and it was there that the incorrigible John Kirk VC resumed his old ways: in July 1861 he was sentenced to forty-eight days' hard labour and sixty-eight days' forfeiture of pay for habitual drunkenness. He was also confined to the barrack cells on several other occasions for absence without leave; and he broke out of the cells during one incarceration and made his way into the town, where he was apprehended in a drunken stupor.

The following year, the 10th Regiment was posted to Kilkenny, Ireland. Kirk was now suffering more and more from the effects of his dissipation. The syphilis had spread through his body, and he was wracked with rheumatism to such an extent that some days he was unable to walk. On 8 April 1864, he came before a regiment board in Kilkenny and was found unfit for further service, the surgeon noting that 'syphilis is the primary cause of his incapacity ... [and was caused] ... in the service but not by the service.' Therefore he was not eligible for an army pension, having been with the colours for only eighteen years, his inability to continue as a soldier to twenty-one years of pensionable service being of his own making. The surgeon also appended a helpful note to his diagnosis: 'He may be able to ... gain a livelihood.'

On 10 May, his discharge from the army was confirmed; and at the age of 37, he left the barracks, his friends and the only life he had ever really known, sick, incapacitated and washed up. He was a product of a system in which he could no longer function, and the system held up its hands and dismissed him: no allowances would be made for a man who possessed the honour of a cross pattée of bronze with crimson ribbon. 'The Land' washed its hands of Private John Kirk VC, and in fifteen months he would be dead.

He came home to Liverpool to die, to a city much changed in his absence. Additional docks, Stanley, Sandon and Wapping, had been built, and the Herculaneum was under construction. The starving Irish who were landing on the quays when he joined the colours had stayed and survived in the crowded courts and cellars along Vauxhall and Scotland Roads: they now worked as dockers, crewed the vessels which jammed the port and laboured on building sites alongside Italian artisans. New suburbs were sprouting up to accommodate the rising population, and the city planners were marking out Stanley Park, which was to become the lungs of the city.

But beneath the boom loomed the same dire poverty, disease and rat-infested slums from which he had escaped as a youth. What few services existed to cope with, and alleviate, the suffering of the poor were overwhelmed, and the health and welfare of the city suffered. For the destitute, the homeless, for those too old or too young, too ill or too broken to earn a living, the workhouse was the only recourse.

Under the Poor Law, workhouses were instituted and overseen by Poor Law Guardians and the local authorities to provide relief and a roof over the heads of the destitute. They provided a bed in a dormitory and a very basic diet, in conditions which are unimaginable today. The sick and the feeble languished uncared for in the dark, draughty dormitories or on the sick ward, and those scarecrow inmates capable of work were sent out to earn a wage, from which was deducted the costs of the bed and food supplied. For John Kirk, homeless, friendless and incapitated, the workhouse beckoned. He was admitted to the Liverpool Workhouse on Brownlow Hill, where now stands the Liverpool Metropolitan Cathedral of Christ the King, the city's Roman Catholic Cathedral. However, he was fortunate, if he could be so described, to have entered that particular institution, at that particular time.

William Rathbone, a wealthy Liverpool merchant and a great benefactor to the city, was working to relieve the distress of the less fortunate of the city. He pioneered the use of trained nurses in workhouses with the help of Agnes Elizabeth Jones. In the Brownlow Hill Workhouse infirmary, he funded the placement of twelve nurses, educated and trained at the Nightingale School, who were assisted by eighteen probationers, and helped further by a group of able-bodied female inmates who received some training and a small salary. For the first time in Britain, the needy, the destitute, the sick and the poor, were comforted and cared for within the confines of a workhouse. And Rathbone's innovation was taken up by other institutions throughout the country.

John Kirk VC died at the age of 38 in the male infirmary of Brownlow Hill Workhouse on 31 August 1865. It can be surmised that he passed away under the care of Agnes Elizabeth Jones and the dedicated Nightingale staff, and that he was comforted and nursed in his final hours. The death certificate gave the cause of death as phthisis, consumption, what is now known as tuberculosis, and no mention was recorded of syphilis. Tuberculosis most commonly attacks the lungs, and in addition to the symptoms of a bloody cough, fever and a general wasting away, it also presents oral and oralfacial growths, small, lobed nodules known as granulomatous lesions. Tertiary syphilis presents similar lesions, and it is possible that the attending physician took them as tubercular, rather than syphilitic, in origin, and signed off accordingly.

He was buried in a pauper's grave in Anfield Cemetery, without any fanfare, without recognition of the great service and great sacrifices he had made for the country. His life was short, and, to a large extent, brutal, a life passed without love and drowned in alcohol and the pursuits of the flesh beneath the harsh discipline of the army. No one mourned him. The grave, which was re-opened several times after his burial, was unmarked and eventually lost. But in the 1980s, it was found again by Bob Halliday, who works at the cemetery; and a stone was purchased by the city council and erected above the grave to commemorate this brave but incorrigible son of Liverpool.

The 10th Regiment of Foot became the Lincolnshire Regiment in 1881, and Arthur Evans VC would serve in its ranks during the First World War. Kirk never married, and as far as it is known he had no living relatives in Liverpool at the time of his passing; his Victoria Cross and campaign medals disappeared from sight following his death. In 1946, the Lincolnshire Regiment was renamed the the Royal Lincolnshire Regiment; and some time later it acquired John Kirk's Victoria Cross. In whose ownership it had been in the interim is unknown. The trustees of the regiment own the honour, and it is on display in the Regimental Collection at the Museum of Lincolnshire Life, Lincoln.

Alfred Stowell Jones VC
(1832–1920)

Doctor Edmund Alexander Parkes began his army life as assistant surgeon with the 84th Regiment of Foot in India. On his initial posting to Madras in 1842 he fought several epidemics of cholera and dysentery, which decimated the ranks of the regiment. Further experience with the same diseases in Moulmein, Burma, and in the Crimea underwrote his famous tome, *Military Hygiene*, in which he set out the principles of maintaining a healthy environment for the troops, most notably through the proper siting and use of latrines and the treatment and safe dispersal of sewage. Parkes was rightly of the belief that inadequate sanitation was a major contributory factor in the development and spread of these fatal fevers. He became the first Professor of Military Hygiene at the Army Medical School, and was at the forefront of public health reforms to make the cities of Britain healthier places in which to live. During the Indian Mutiny, his teachings were to find a convert in Alfred Stowell Jones.

The Mutiny erupted at Meerut on 10 May 1857. The following day, rebellious sepoys captured the city of Delhi, capital of the former Mughal Empire, and massacred hundreds of European inhabitants. In response, General George Anson, Commander-in-Chief, India, set out from his headquarters at Simla with a column of troops to retake the city, supported by a second force under Major General Hewitt. Alfred Stowell Jones was a young lieutenant in the 9th (Queen's Royal) Lancers, one of the most prestigious cavalry regiments in the British Army. The march on Delhi was his first campaign. It was also his road to Damascus.

At the age of 25, and with five years of service under his belt, Alfred Jones, the son of a clergyman, typified the vainglorious, frivolous, cavalry 'rupert' of his day, swanking in his posh uniform and ever mindful of the elitist tradition and ethos of his regiment. He and his fellow officers filled their days on the sub-continent in daily rounds of sporting contests, good food and plenty of drink, and saw themselves a very large cut above the rest, disdainful of other cavalry units and derisive of the cannon fodder, the officers and men of the infantry. For the likes of Jones, duty and service was primarily to his own class and his regiment, and everything else came a very poor second.

But on the trail his eyes were opened to the realities and horrors of warfare and what service in the army truly entailed. In the heat of the high summer, poor and hasty provisioning, bad water and non-existent sanitation took their toll of the relieving columns: virulent diseases arose and thrived, thinned the ranks and undermined fighting capabilities. Officers and men alike suffered, as did the horses and draught animals. General Anson, one among many, contracted cholera and died. And the situation was exacerbated when the two disease-ridden and debilitated columns arrived before the city.

The siege of Delhi took place at the height of the summer. The city was enveloped in an atmosphere rank with the weighty stench of decay and decomposition as the 'Old McCormac' brewed a toxic environment from rotting corpses and vegetation infested with rats, bloated flies and buzzing mosquitoes, washed over by streams and rivulets of human waste. Every aspect of life was polluted, and contaminated food and water engendered red and white fluxes, bacillary and amoebic dysentery, which proved more lethal than the fire from the muskets and cannons of the sepoys. Sweating heavily in their uniforms under the harsh sun, the troops were further dehydrated when the dysentery triggered continual, violent attacks of vomiting and diarrhoea, resulting in the depletion of vital body salts. Excessive loss of potassium salt affected brain function and compromised cardiac function, leading to death.

Jones was given a copy of Parkes's book by Dr Clifford, the regiment's assistant surgeon, after making urgent enquiries as to how to fend off the sicknesses plaguing the army. After so many deaths, he was struck by the realization that if he was to serve his Queen and country, he must, first and foremost, look to the well-being of his men, and not just of the troops of his own regiment: dysentery and cholera did not recognize regimental boundaries, rank or privilege. An army of sick men served no one but the foe: combatting simultaneously two enemies, on two different fronts, could only end in disaster in the long term. Parkes's book became his Bible, and he set out to apply and implement practically the basic principles of good sanitation under campaign conditions. As events were to unfold, he would spend many years fighting disease and digging latrines and barely five months on the battlefield.

When the relieving colums neared Delhi, the sepoys attempted to intercept and impede them. Two fierce battles were fought at the beginning of June, when, despite the weariness and poor health of the British forces, the sepoys were driven back into the city. On Monday, 8 June 1857, under the command of General Sir Henry Barnard, Anson's successor, the 9th Lancers were part of a force ordered to attack a strategic group of buildings known locally as Badli-ki-Serai, five miles north-west of the city. The position, which overlooked the native quarter, was heavily defended by the mutineers, and as the British approached, the sepoys 'fired musketry, round shot, shell and every other thing they possibly could ... they had no end of heavy guns in position ... the grape rattling in among [us] like a hailstorm.'

It was a desperate struggle against a determined enemy during a long, hot day, and casualties on both sides were high. But, gradually, Barnard's men pushed up against the sepoys and drove them from the buildings. And as the defenders began to fall back, the rebel artillerymen limbered up their guns and made off across the plain to the safety of the city. The retreating gunners were spotted by cavalry scouts, however, and the 9th Lancers, under Colonel Yule, were sent to intercept them.

Lieutenant Jones was leading the right troop of the 4th Squadron of the regiment, the troopers resplendent in their blue tunics and white turbans, their pennons flapping in the wind, as they galloped in line in pursuit of a swirling cloud of dust which had been identified as the enemy guns. As the line advanced, Jones spotted on his left six enemy gunners driving a team of horses hauling a limber with a 9-pound cannon attached. Pulling up short, he set off after the gun, urging on his Arab steed. The drivers, seeing Jones in pursuit, whipped and flogged their horses to greater effort. Meanwhile, the squadron maintained its course, unaware at first of Jones's lone dash.

Drawing alongside the limber, Jones drew his sabre and slashed down at the lead driver, cutting him across the shoulder, and causing him to tumble from his mount and fall beneath the wheels of the carriage. Guiding his own horse with his knees, Jones stretched across the neck of his mount to gather up the traces, and brought the galloping team to a jolting halt. The other five drivers could not keep their seats as the horses panicked and reared, and were thrown beneath the wheels and the stamping hooves of their mounts. Jones was then joined by Regimental Sergeant Major Thonger who had seen him charge off after the gun, and had followed with three troopers to render assistance. Jones ordered the sergeant major and his men to dispatch the injured sepoys with their lances, while he set about rendering the gun inoperative by spiking the exhaust vent. Within minutes, the rest of the squadron, having failed to over-take the dust cloud, arrived at the scene, quickly followed by Colonel Yule and the rest of the 9th Lancers.

Several shells were discovered on the limber carriage and Colonel Yule ordered Jones to remove the spike and make the gun operative again. The cannon was loaded and trained on a fortified village in the distance. Several rounds were fired and the defending mutineers, surprised by the bombard-ment, quickly abandoned the village, leaving it open to the advancing British.

Explaining his act of bravery, Jones reported he believed that he could not halt the squadron in its gallop and turn it in pursuit of the gun, which he alone saw from his position on the extreme flank. 'It is questionable,' he later noted, 'if the VC does not interfere with discipline, which might have demanded a trial by court-martial if I had been riding a slower horse, and so had failed to reach my prey.'

Major General Hope Grant rewarded Jones for his initiative, not only for the capture of the gun but also for his labours to improve sanitation, by making him deputy assistant quartermaster general of the cavalry for the Delhi Field Force during the siege, which was to continue until the insurgents finally abandoned the city on 18 September. During that time, Jones was able to put into practice on a very limited scale what he had gleaned from Parkes's *Military Hygiene*: he oversaw the digging of latrines, the boiling of drinking water and other innovations to help combat dysentery and cholera. But he met with resistance from both officers and men, some too busy, some too tired, some too ignorant to care about what he was attempting to do. And men continued to die from fever throughout the siege, among them General Barnard, who succumbed to cholera on 5 July.

After the fall of Delhi, the 9th Lancers were made part of Colonel Greathed's mobile column, charged with pursuing the fleeing mutineers, who were regrouping at the town of Muttra, eighty miles to the south; and subduing any towns and villages in its path suspected of disloyalty. It was a march which brought Alfred Jones close to death and ended his fighting days.

On the march, Greathed was inundated with urgent pleas from the garrison at the city of Agra, south of Muttra. The European families there had locked themselves away in the fort for several months in expectation of an attack which had not materialized. They now feared an imminent attack from the mutineers fleeing Delhi, and from those rebels moving north from central India, from Jhansi and Gwalior. Greathed suspected their fears were ill-founded, but nevertheless decided to divert his column to Agra, to show the flag and allay worries. He force-marched his men forty-four miles in twenty-eight hours to reach the city, whose inhabitants, expecting a parade-ground turn out, greeted the dusty, sweating, dishevelled column with little enthusiasm.

The panic which had prompted the urgent pleas had apparently disappeared: the mutineers at Muttra had dispersed and returned to their homes, while the rebels moving north had halted nine miles away and no longer posed a threat. Greathed was greatly put out, as were his men, and he ordered the exhausted column to make camp on the parade ground. The civilian population soon warmed to the soldiers and gathered in numbers to watch and be entertained while the soldiers pitched their tents and settled in; and a carnival-like atmosphere overcame the town as everyone, soldiers included, relaxed and enjoyed themselves for the first time in months.

No pickets were posted that night, no patrols were sent into the surrounding countryside, where fields of high crops obscured vision for miles, and this despite reports from sentries that the sound of tramping feet could be heard from certain sections of the crop. The following morning, Saturday, 10 October, Colonel Greathed rode up to the fort to breakfast, leaving his men to fend for themselves.

All around the crowded parade ground, troops foraged for the basic necessities, clean water, bread, fodder for the animals, and space in which to wash, clean up and eat breakfast. Local vendors pressed their wares on the men, children scampered among the tent lines and the aroma of cooking beef filled the nostrils. A party of Sikhs and 9th Lancers lounged in the centre of the gathering, watching a troupe of jugglers and performers who were wandering through the camp entertaining the throng.

Suddenly, at a pre-arranged signal, the jugglers threw off their costumes, revealing themselves as mutineers. Before anyone could react, they slashed and stabbed the unarmed Sikhs and Lancers with *tulwars*, the heavy Indian sabres, and downed several of them. Simultaneously, a battery of heavy guns opened up on the camp, and out of the fields galloped two troops of rebel cavalrymen, which bore down on the luckless soldiers. At first there was panic and pandemonium as civilians dashed for safety among the troopers, hindering them as they tried to arm themselves and fend off the rebels. The Lancers were first to respond and fell in as best they could: within minutes they were mounted and ready for battle, many of the men still in shirt-sleeves, some in stocking-feet.

Captain French and Lieutenant Jones led 4th Squadron in a counter-charge against the raiding *sowars*, driving through them in a fury and putting them to flight. But Captain French was shot dead in the saddle, and moments later Alfred Jones was struck by a bullet to his bridle arm. He was unhorsed, and crashed to the sod, losing his sabre. Stunned and dazed, he struggled to his feet only to be surrounded by a band of screaming insurgents. The rebels set about him with *tulwars*, hacking and stabbing at him from all sides. Without a weapon, and with one arm useless, Jones used a fist to defend himself and ward off the blows. But his assailants were remorseless, battering and bludgeoning him to the ground until they thought him dead.

The surprise attack was repulsed, the 9th Lancers bravely seeing off the opposing cavalry, and infantry from the fort dashed forward to suppress the jugglers-in-disguise and to capture the heavy guns in the fields. Left for dead in the mêlée, a bleeding bundle of torn flesh, Alfred Jones was made of very stern stuff. He was barely alive, hardly breathing, cut through with twenty-two sword wounds, his left eye ripped from its socket and blinded, his right arm pierced by a musket ball. Miraculously, he survived both his wounds and the medical treatment in the sweltering and festering heat of Agra. For many weeks he lay immobile in bed, swaddled in bandages, while his maimed body healed slowly and battled the infections which threatened his recovery.

For daring initiative and bravery in the face of the enemy, Lieutenant Alfred Stowell Jones was awarded the Victoria Cross. His citation reads:

Alfred Stowell Jones, Lieutenant (now Captain), 9th Lancers. Date of Act of Bravery: 8 June, 1857. The Cavalry charged the rebels and rode through them. Lieutenant Jones, of the 9th Lancers, with his squadron, captured one of their guns, killing the drivers, and with Lieutenant-Colonel Yule's assistance, turned it upon a village occupied by the rebels, who were quickly dislodged. This was a well-conceived act gallantly executed. (Dispatch from Major General Hope Grant, KCB, dated 10 Jan. 1858.)

The citation, based upon Hope Grant's dispatch, conflates the actions at Delhi and Agra, describing them incorrectly as one. 'The cavalry charged the rebels and rode through them' must refer to the counter-charge at Agra in October when Jones was badly wounded, for no such charge took place at Delhi on 8 June, when Jones alone attacked the enemy gun and captured it without assistance. Jones was in fact involved in two bravely fought encounters; the award of the Victoria Cross was all the more merited.

For services to his country in the suppression of the Mutiny, Alfred Jones received the Mutiny Medal with two clasps, and was promoted to captain and later brevet major. He was mentioned three times in dispatches, also. Because of his wounds and the loss of his left eye, he was returned to England; and, brave soldier though he was, he did not participate further in the Mutiny campaign, during which the 9th Lancers went on to greater glory, at Lucknow and Cawnpore, winning a further eleven Victoria Crosses, and earning from their enemy the nickname 'the Delhi Spearmen'.

John Jones, Alfred's father, was the youngest son of a wealthy family, born in Hanover Square, London, in 1792. He took holy orders in the Church of England, and came to Liverpool in 1823 to be vicar of St Andrew's Church in Renshaw Street, a city centre parish created ten years earlier. His wife Hannah, née Pares, was from Leicester, where her father founded the Pares Bank. The couple resided outside the parish, in a church house at 3 Huskisson Street, where their only children were conceived: Agnes was born in 1824, Alfred on 24 January 1832.

Not long after the birth of his son, the Reverend Jones was appointed Waterloo and Rural Dean and for more than thirty years he was the incumbent of Christ Church, situated at the junction of Alexandra and Waterloo Roads, Litherland. The family resided at the manse, 38 Waterloo Road, where Alfred Jones spent his formative years, cossetted by the wealth of both parents. He was very close to his mother, who oversaw his early education at home, and brought him up in the Christian faith, but perhaps not as strictly as his father would have wished. Later, he attended Liverpool College, Shaw Street; and having learnt to ride from an early age, and displaying talent as a horseman, he determined on a military career with the cavalry.

However, just before entering the Royal Military College at Sandhurst in 1851, his mother passed away. He was greatly anguished by her death, and it is believed he lost his faith at this juncture. His career was almost derailed when he appeared reluctant to leave his father and sister. But, encouraged by both, he went off to his military studies. It would be several years before he saw either of them again. Agnes Jones did not marry and remained at home as companion and housekeeper to her father, later Archdeacon of Liverpool, until his death in 1883, aged 90. Agnes retired to live in Birkdale where she passed on in 1915 at the age of 91.

Alfred Jones threw himself into his new life, into the freedom the release from family life had granted him. Adopting the mores and manners of the officer class, he was reborn as a Hoorah Henry and cared not a jot for his Christian upbringing. He studied for a year at Sandhurst, and in 1852 purchased a commission of coronet in the 9th Lancers. Three years later, the dashing young soldier, well supplied with family money, was promoted to lieutenant and set sail for service in India, togged out in the best the Army and Navy Stores could provide. He was slight of build, no more than 5 feet, 6 inches in height, but he packed a good punch. The only surviving photograph of him, taken in later life when the brown hair has thinned and the moustache, once an object of pride, combed and waxed daily, now neglected and of the walrus variety, gives the impression he might have been more readily employed behind the counter of shop rather than astride a charger on the plains of India. But he has the look of a thinker.

His first station was fifty miles north of Delhi, at Umbala, a sprawling, military cantonment established in 1843 as headquarters of the cavalry brigade attached to the northern army. He shared a bungalow with Lieutenant Robert Blair. The men became close friends and were typical, gung-ho members of the regiment. With little outlet for their energies in this, a time of calm in India, the usual sports of hunting, pig-sticking and polo filled their days. But they yearned for real action, for any opportunity to demonstrate their prowess, for battlefield honour and glory. And when news came that a new gallantry award, the Victoria Cross, had been instituted, the pair made a compact to win the honour.

But the Crimean War was the only campaign Britain was fighting at the time, and since Jones and Blair could see no hope of glory in the daily round of minimal garrison duties and sporting pastimes in India, they applied to their commanding officer, Lieutenant Colonel James Hope Grant, to change to one of the cavalry regiments fighting in the Crimea. Hope Grant refused, and was furious, more so with Jones who, following the refusal, went above Grant's head to the officer commanding at Umballa to plead his case. Jones and Blair were firmly put in their places and remained on station in India.

Jones's insubordination, however, did not affect his relationship with his Colonel. Hope Grant recognized the soldier in him and realized that, if weaned from his boastful and elitist ways, he could become a great asset to the regiment and the army. As Grant rose to higher commands, he kept a watchful eye on Jones and attempted to point him in the right direction; and when Jones's eyes were opened by his Delhi experience, he knew he had his man. Hope Grant recommended Jones for the Victoria Cross, and did the same for his friend Blair, who, unfortunately died when winning his. Jones and Hope Grant became close friends, and, upon retirement lived as neighbours in Berkshire.

On his return to England in 1857, Jones was admitted to hospital for further treatment to his wounds and he was fitted with an eye patch. Once fit again and able to ride, he was posted to Leeds Cavalry Barracks in Yorkshire. His recommendation for the Victoria Cross was not made until January 1858 in the dispatch sent from India by Hope Grant, and was not published in the *London Gazette* until 18 June. Jones did not see the announcement, however, nor did any of his fellow officers; and he went about his busy, daily rounds of breaking in horses and training new recruits for the 18th Hussars, which was being raised at Leeds at the time, blithely unaware of the award.

He was to be presented with the honour by Queen Victoria at Southsea Common, Portsmouth, on Sunday, 2 August. It was not until the last day of July, as he took his seat for dinner in the mess, that an order came through he was to attend at Southsea, where, together with eleven other brave men, he would be invested by his sovereign. In a panic, he made a mad dash down to Portsmouth, arriving with only hours to spare to meet the Queen – 'and that was the first intimation I had that I had been recommended for the Cross. A young horse I was riding in the School at Leeds a few days before had thrown up his head and bruised my blind eye-brow, so my appearance was shocking, and made the Queen so nervous that she pricked me in pinning the Cross through my tunic.' But what was a pin-prick to such a man? He delighted in telling the story of the medal presentation from the hands of a nervous sovereign, and it passed into the folklore which has grown up around the Victoria Cross: stabbed by the *sowars*, stabbed by the sovereign.

From Leeds, Major Jones VC entered the Staff College at Camberley, Surrey and graduated in 1860. He served as deputy assistant quartermaster general on the staff of the Cape of Good Hope, when, with the proper authority, he put into practice the tenets of his mentor, Dr Parkes. After his conversion, he became the soldier's soldier, a modern, forward-looking and innovative man who preached that while an army marched on its stomach, the men could march further and faster and give battle at their destination in far greater numbers if they were healthy. To Jones, the loss of men in the field through illness and fever was an avoidable evil which could be remedied by care and attention to the environment in which they had to live. And there is no doubt his pioneering work saved the lives of countless soldiers.

He married Emily Back, the daughter of James Back, of Aldershot Place, Hampshire. The wedding took place at St James's Church in Westminster, on 13 June 1863, and the couple made a home at Peel House, in Groby, Leicestershire. The union was blessed with five sons and a daughter, Harry, Owen, Tertius, Percy, Martin and Marguerita Audrey. After retiring from the army in 1872 with the rank of lieutenant colonel, Alfred Jones brought the family to Wales, to Abenbury Cottage, Abenbury Fecan, Flintshire, where he set up and managed a sewage farm estate of 104 acres, employing seventeen labourers. And, to keep abreast of new developments, he trained as an engineer and became a Member of the Institution of Civil Engineers in 1878.

He was a regular contributor of papers and articles on the treatment of sewage to the professional journals, most notably a competition article on sewage treatment in the journal of the Royal Agricultural Society in 1879, which won first prize; and he penned two books, *Will a Sewage Farm Pay?*, which ran to three editions, and *Natural and Artificial Sewage Treatment*. In 1895, the army called again on his expertise; and for the next seventeen years, until his retirement in 1912, he managed the Sewage Works of the 1st Army Corps at Aldershot.

The remaining years of his life were dark, though the gloom was partially lifted by the arrival of five grandchildren. He was haunted by the memories of his sons. His bravery, his career and fine example had imbued them with the spirit of duty and sacrifice, and they followed his calling: he lived to bury four of them. The eldest, Captain Harry Jones, RN, commanded the battleship HMS *Africa*, and died of acute nephritis, then known as Bright's Disease, in 1914. The youngest, Lieutenant Martin Jones, 11th Hussars, was killed in a polo accident in India in 1895; and the following year, Lieutenant Tertius Jones, RHA, died in Meerut. Percy Jones was an indigo planter in Tirboot, India. When the First World War began, he was commissioned in the 13th Lancers, and was killed in action at Samarhah, Mesopotamia, in November 1917. Captain Owen Jones, RNR, was the only survivor.

Alfred Jones VC saw out his days with Emily at Ridge Cottage, on Ridges Road, in the village of Finchampstead, Berkshire. Close by lived Hope Grant, and his immediate neighbour at North Court was another old comrade-in-arms, General Sir John Watson VC, who had fought at Agra also. His eldest son, Colonel, later Major General, Arthur Watson married Jones's only daughter, Marguerita Audrey, but the couple had no issue.

When Emily Jones passed away in 1918 Alfred was left bereft. In his late eighties and suffering with Alzheimer's disease and bronchitis, he could not cope alone, needing constant attention. A local woman, May Neve, nursed him in his last hours, and was present at his bedside on 29 May 1920, when he died of a heart attack, at the age of 88. He was buried by his son with full military honours in the churchyard of St James's Church, Finchampstead. His medals, including the Victoria Cross, are in private hands.

William Richard Dowling VC
(1824–87)

Adolf Hitler's elder half-brother, Alois, was working as a waiter in the Shelbourne Hotel in Dublin in 1909 when he was introduced to a young lady of the city, Bridget Elizabeth Dowling, at the Royal Dublin Horse Show. They became lovers and planned to marry. But Bridget's father, William, would not countenance the match, and the couple eloped to London and married in June 1910 at Marylebone Register Office. They hid from the irate William in Liverpool, at 102 Upper Stanhope Street, where a son, William Patrick Hitler, was born on 12 March 1911.

In her biography, Bridget Dowling Hitler claimed Adolf Hitler came to Liverpool in 1912 and lived for several months with her and her husband in Upper Stanhope Street, before returning to Vienna in April 1913. She also asserted she was the granddaughter of William Richard Dowling, winner of the Victoria Cross during the Indian Mutiny. Neither story is true. Bridget died in 1969, and her daughter-in-law reported that, before her death, she admitted the story of Hitler's sojourn in Liverpool was a fiction. But, Bridget did not relinquish her claim to being the granddaughter of a Victoria Cross winner.

When William Dowling VC was discharged from the army in 1865, he lived and worked in Dublin for several years; the time frame is such that he could have fathered a son William, who in turn produced a daughter Bridget. However, William Dowling VC left Dublin sometime after 1871, never to return to Ireland, and settled in Liverpool where he died in 1887. He married Maria Colgan, a Roscommon girl, and they had two children only, Joseph Francis, born in December 1863, and Maria, born in April 1865. Neither had a child named Bridget. The direct family relation between Bridget Dowling Hitler and William Richard Dowling VC does not exist.

William Richard Dowling was born in 1824 at Bishop's Lock, in the parish of Tulleherin, a few miles north of the market town of Thomastown, County Kilkenny. The earliest known record of a Dowling in the town is of James Dowling, who in 1752 was living in Market Street with his four sons. One of them, John, fathered Richard Dowling, who in turn was the father of William Richard Dowling VC.

The area around Thomastown was very fertile arable and pasture land, and the region was prosperous, more so with the arrival in Thomastown of Ryan's

Tannery, which still stands today. Richard Dowling did not own any land nor did he farm for others, but served his time as a tanner, and worked at Ryan's until his death. Very little is known of William Dowling's early days, except that after leaving school he was apprenticed as tailor in one of the local drapers. The first record of him is when he enlisted in the 32nd Regiment of Foot at the Curragh Camp in Dublin on 24 January 1845, as 2583 Private William Dowling. Like John Kirk VC, he was to spend most of his army life in India, arriving there, as John Kirk did, in time for the Second Anglo-Sikh War.

He underwent basic training at the Curragh Camp before the regiment was mobilized for service in India in 1846. His first station was at Meerut, sixty miles north-east of Delhi, the town where the Indian Mutiny was to erupt in 1857. He spent a year there acclimatizing to the rigours of the Indian sub-continent, and, no doubt, learning the ways of the men of the British regiments. However, William Dowling was a good soldier and for the first ten years of service, his record was without blemish.

His first taste of battle was during the siege of Multan in 1848. The 10th Regiment of Foot, among whose ranks was John Kirk, would also fight at Multan. In fact, on several occasions, units of the 10th and 32nd fought along-side each other, and both regiments were to the fore in all the major engagements in and around the city. It is possible that John Kirk met William Dowling in the many months they spent in the trenches.

The siege was a prolonged, on-off affair, a blueprint for Sebastopol seven years later. It took several months of skirmishing and small-scale assaults before the two weak points of the defences, the Delhi Gate and the Bloody Bastion, could be isolated and stormed. Both positions fell in January 1849, and the rebels fell back into the city and rallied at the Citadel, a fortified stronghold. On Wednesday, 9 January, during a sortie from the British lines in front of the Citadel, William Dowling was felled by a shell fragment, the shrapnel burying itself in his chest. He was carted from the battlefield to the first aid station where the metal fragment was removed and the wound dressed. The wound took a long time to heal, if heal it ever did, for he was afflicted by the wound for the rest of his army service; and it would be responsible for his leaving the army in 1865.

William Dowling was *hors de combat* for no more than a few weeks. In those days, there was little time allowed for convalescence: if a man could walk, then he could march; and if he could march, then he could fight. Following the fall of Multan, William Dowling, despite his wound, marched 270 miles with his regiment in pursuit of the Sikhs to do battle at Gujarat on 21 February 1849, the final engagement of the conflict. He and the men of the 32nd Regiment were awarded the Punjab Medal with two clasps for their excellent work at Multan and Gujarat.

Following the victory at Gujarat, the Punjab was completely taken under the control of the HEIC. William Dowling and the regiment remained in the

Punjab, stationed at Jelude, policing the peace for the next three years. In 1853, he was promoted to corporal when the regiment moved up to the Afghan frontier, to Peshwar, the northernmost point of British rule and the terminal point of the Great Trunk Road. The following year he was made sergeant, a rank he held for two years, before a misdemeanour resulted in a court martial, followed by five days' imprisonment and reduction in rank to private.

For the next three years, the regiment saw field service along the Afghan border, fighting the rebellious tribes of the region, before being relieved in 1856, when it returned to garrison duty in the city of Lucknow. William Dowling had spent more than six months on one side of a siege at Multan; and he was now to experience a siege from the opposite perspective during the Indian Mutiny, locked up inside Lucknow for 148 days, surrounded by sepoys.

At the time of the Mutiny, Lucknow, 325 miles south-east of Delhi, was the capital city of the state of Oudh, and it had been annexed by the HEIC in 1856. Misgoverned from the beginning, the state was in a rebellious mood; and the appointment of a sensible and practical administrator, Sir Henry Lawrence, as Resident in an attempt to calm the situation, was too little too late to prevent the native garrison from rising in sympathy with the mutineers of Meerut. The only European troops in the city at the time were the 32nd Regiment of Foot, 500 strong, under the command of Lieutenant Colonel William Case, and a detached unit of the 84th Regiment of Foot. On 30 May 1857, the Bengal troops in the city broke into open rebellion. With the assistance of the loyal 13th Native Infantry, and a band of locally recruited civilians, the 32nd Regiment dispersed the mutineers.

The Residency, around which the defence of Lucknow was manned, stood on high ground on the south bank of the River Gumti, overlooking the city, which encompassed an area of twelve square miles. Within that huge spread, the Residency garrison, amounting to 855 British officers and men, 712 loyal sepoys and 153 civilian volunteers, was confined to, and defended, a paltry perimeter of one mile. In addition, 1,280 women and children were also crowded and crammed inside. Facing it were 8,000 mutineers baying for blood.

On 30 June, the 32nd Regiment was reduced in strength to less than 300 men, when, during an ill-prepared reconnaissance of force, it was badly mauled by the mutineers at the battle of Chinhat, five miles outside of Lucknow. The survivors of the encounter, William Dowling included, only just managed to stagger back to the safety of the city, suffering from heat exhaustion, carrying the dead and wounded, and under constant fire from the pursuing rebels. The following day, as the cost of the action was counted, William Dowling regained his stripes and was promoted to corporal.

The siege at Lucknow lasted five months. In the suffocating heat of the summer, the cramped defenders were subjected to artillery bombardments from all quarters, day and night. A constant sniper fire was maintained by the rebels, aimed at anybody, at anything, that moved in and around the Residency. As latrines and cesspits overflowed, cholera and dysentery rose quickly and began to take their toll, particularly among the children; each day ten Europeans died from wounds and disease. And as the siege continued, the dire prospect of famine grew, but the defenders could do nothing but sit and wait for relief, stalked by death in many guises.

Few in numbers, and weakened by the heat exhaustion, short rations, disease and lack of sleep, the men of the 32nd resolved to fight back. It was obvious to all that the enemy artillery was causing the highest casualties among the defenders: Sir Henry Lawrence, the Resident, had died of wounds inflicted by shell fragments at the beginning of July, and his replacement, Major Banks, was killed a week later. The enemy guns became the focus of concerted attacks by the men of the 32nd Regiment.

Under cover of darkness, and sometimes in broad daylight, small parties of armed men silently moved through their own lines and out into no man's land, crawling and slithering forward towards enemy gun emplacements, carrying iron nails and hammers. If the guns were unmanned, the men would quickly spike the guns, driving the nails into the small vent holes in the breeches, thereby rendering them inoperative; sometimes the rebel gunners would have to be disposed of first, which would involve bitter, hand-to-hand struggles; and on some occasions, the men were detected by the sepoys and ambushed. Many men of the 32nd perished during these forays into enemy territory. But some survived, and would continue to go out many times into the inky darkness to spike guns.

Corporal William Dowling, together with another Irishman of the 32nd, Private Cuney, deservedly won acclaim during the siege for their coolness and bravery and total disregard for their own safety in taking the fight to the enemy. For fighting men such as Dowling and Cuney, confined by the siege to defensive duties, and having to watch helplessly as enemy sniper fire and artillery bombardments killed their friends and reduced the defences piecemeal, any opportunity to confront the enemy was welcomed. Many of the sorties they led against the enemy guns were not sanctioned officially by their officers – very often they went out without orders when they themselves thought conditions were ideal for an attack. But so successful were they in rendering enemy guns inoperative, that a blind eye was always turned to their unofficial expeditions.

On several spiking forays Dowling was discovered but he always managed to fight his way out of trouble; on one occasion, confronted in front of a gun by a *subadar*, a lieutenant, he killed the man in a hand-to-hand encounter. But Cuney was not so lucky: wounded on more than one occasion in close-quarter combat, he was killed in August while attempting to spike a gun.

For outstanding bravery during the siege of Lucknow, often under intense enemy fire, in spiking the enemy guns, and thereby giving some relief to the defenders from the constant rebel bombardment, William Dowling was awarded the Victoria Cross. His citation reads:

> William Dowling, Private 32nd Regiment. Dates of Acts of Bravery: 4th and 9th July and 27th September 1857. For distinguished gallantry on 4th July, 1857, in going out with two other men, since dead, and spiking two of the enemy's guns. He killed a *subadar* of the enemy by one of the guns. Also for distinguished gallantry on the 9th of the same month, on going out again with three men, since dead, to spike one of the enemy's guns. He had to retire, the spike being too small, but was exposed to the same danger. Also for distinguished bravery on 27th Sept. 1857, in spiking an 18-pounder gun during a sortie, he being at the same time under a most heavy fire from the enemy.

Only William Dowling's officially recorded forays against the guns were recognized in the citation; no account of the many unsanctioned attacks he undertook of his own volition. He is also mistakenly referred to as a private, but he had in fact been promoted to corporal on 1 July 1857.

But William Dowling was not concerned solely with fighting the enemy on the ground: he fought the enemy underground, too. During the siege, the mutineers became highly proficient in undermining the British defences: they dug shafts and galleries towards the British lines with the intention of placing explosives charges therein, which, when detonated, would breach the ramparts and open the way for an all-out assault on the city. Towards the end of July, the sepoys exploded a mine, which caused a breach, but they were thrown back when they tried to exploit it. On 10 August, a second mine was detonated; and a week later a third blew a hole in a wall. But every time the sepoys followed up they were thrown back by the men of the 32nd Regiment.

Counter-measures were adopted by the British, particularly by the 32nd Regiment, with its history of recruitment from Cornish tin miners. William Dowling and his men dug at least twenty shafts, some of them more than 200 feet deep, and from them cut more than 4,000 feet of galleries. Armed soldiers would accompany the diggers, listening for sounds of the enemy tunnelling; and whenever and wherever the opposing galleries crossed and were intercepted, underground skirmishes would ensue; some of the fiercest encounters of the siege were fought underground with pistols, knives, fists, shovels and pickaxes. Enemy tunnels were blown, and even though the rebels continued their mining throughout the siege, they were able only to detonate three mines, so effective were the British miners and their escorts in disrupting their work.

For his outstanding work underground, William Dowling was mentioned in a dispatch of 31 October 1857 from Captain Crommelin, the Chief Engineer at Lucknow, to the Governor General: 'I cannot close this report, without noticing, in the most favourable manner, the important services performed by the under-mentioned soldiers, as superintendent of miners – A/Sergeants

Cullimore, Banetta, and Farrer; and Corporal Dowling, all of the 32nd Regiment. ... Their duties have been of a very dangerous and arduous character, and have invariably been performed to my complete satisfaction.' Over the ground and under the ground, there was fighting to be done during the siege, dangerous work, which required nerves of steel and high levels of courage. Whenever men were needed for such duties, William Dowling was always there.

On 23 September, Major General Sir Henry Havelock in command of a relief force defeated a large rebel force four miles to the south of the Lucknow Residency. Two days later, supported by a second force under Lieutenant General Sir James Outram, he marched into Lucknow. But the ordeal for the emaciated defenders was not over: Outram decided against evacuating the Residency to Cawnpore because of the high numbers of casualties his men had sustained during the advance. Starving and ravaged by disease, William Dowling and the bedraggled defenders of Lucknow were forced to hold their positions.

Outram pushed back the rebels and expanded the perimeter around the Residency; and ordered an increase in the number of night attacks against the enemy guns by the men of the 32nd Regiment, despite the objections of their new commanding officer, Lieutenant Colonel John Inglis, who felt his men had done and suffered enough. William Dowling, as his citation states, continued his spiking forays against the enemy guns.

Lucknow was relieved for the second time on 17 November, when Lieutenant General Sir Colin Campbell dispersed the besieging rebels during a murderous assault on the city. Two days later, Campbell ordered the Residency evacuated and abandoned it to the rebels. The distraught and sickly civilian population of the Residency were loaded into all available wheeled transport, and, under escort, was eventually carried to safety in Allahabad and Calcutta. Corporal William Dowling and the remnants of the 32nd Regiment, having done their duty, proudly marched out of Lucknow, their heads held high.

Despite the privations they had suffered, the men were given no rest, and did not ask for any. They joined Campbell on the march to Cawnpore, which was controlled by the rebels under the command of Tatya Tope, an implacable foe of the HEIC. This was a fight the 32nd would not miss: a contingent of seventy-four men from the regiment had been stationed in the city at the outbreak of the Mutiny; and they had been massacred under a white flag on 27 June 1857 after the city had fallen. Among the dead was 2833 Private Thomas Dowling. In all probability, he was a close relative, and William Dowling was on a mission to exact retribution. On 6 December, a vengeful British army of 5,000 bloodthirsty men, the 'Devil's Wind', stormed through the city and routed 25,000 rebels in a terrible slaughter.

From Cawnpore, William Dowling and his comrades tramped for eight months all over Oudh, weeding out pockets of resistance until the Mutiny was suppressed in June 1858. Half-starved, fatigued, footsore and licking their wounds, the men of the 32nd were retired from the field and assumed garrison duty at Bareilly and Allahabad. But it would appear the constraints of garrison duty did not suit William Dowling after being on active service for so long, operating for most of the time on his own initiative. In March 1859, Corporal Dowling was again demoted to private after being confined to the cells for three days for taking a glass too many of 'billy-stink'.

Notification of William Dowling's award of the Victoria Cross was not made in the *London Gazette* until 21 November 1859, almost two years to the day when he had marched out of Lucknow. By that time, he was back in England. He sailed for England from Fort William, Calcutta, on 28 March 1859, never to return to India, his years as a fighting man over. The regiment disembarked at Portsmouth. On 26 August, at Dover Castle, the 32nd was inspected and paraded before Queen Victoria, and presented with the India Mutiny Medal with the Defence of Lucknow clasp. When news of his Victoria Cross award came through, Private William Dowling was in barracks at Aldershot: he was promoted immediately to sergeant.

On 4 January 1860, in the quadrangle at Windsor Castle, William Dowling and twenty-three other brave men were presented with their Victoria Crosses by Queen Victoria, while Prince Albert, the Duke of Cambridge, Commander-in-Chief, and Sir Sidney Herbert, Secretary of State for War, looked on in admiration. And for its sterling work during the defence of Lucknow, Queen Victoria granted the regiment the much-coveted distinction of redesignation as a Light Infantry Regiment, renamed the 32nd (Cornwall) Light Infantry.

However, three months after receiving his Victoria Cross, and while garrisoned at Plymouth Citadel, William Dowling VC was reduced again in rank to private after a court martial, offence unknown. He served twenty days' imprisonment in the cells. But it was not all bad news: he was in love and courting Maria Colgan, who lived at 2 Cecil Street, Plymouth. She was an Irishwoman, the daughter of Philip Colgan, a Land Steward of Roscommon, and it was not too long before the banns were being read in church.

On 23 March 1862, and with his commanding officer's permission, Corporal William Richard Dowling VC, aged 35, married Maria Colgan, aged 32, at the Roman Catholic Cathedral Church of St Mary and St Boniface in Plymouth. He had gained promotion back to the rank of corporal the day before the wedding. The following year, after a short stint at Devonport, the regiment was posted to the Curragh Camp, Dublin, and William Dowling VC brought his bride back to Ireland and started a family. In Dublin he was restored, for the final time, to the rank of sergeant.

On 15 April 1865, Sergeant William Dowling VC was brought before a regimental medical board. For some time he had been suffering from chronic fatigue and loss of strength, together with pain in the chest, in the area wounded by the shell fragment at Multan. The doctors diagnosed asthenia, loss of strength, and chronic bronchitis, and suggested that the old chest wound had both contributed to and exacerbated these conditions. William Dowling VC was declared unfit for further military service. On 2 May, he was discharged from the service. As a soldier who had participated in the siege of Lucknow, he was allowed to reckon one year of additional service to the twenty years and seventy-one days he had served with the colours, to bring his time served, for pension calculation, to more than twenty-one years. For his gallant conduct, he received a disability pension of one shilling and sixpence a day, which was increased to two shillings a day in 1867; and this, together with his Victoria Cross pension of £10 per annum, was to be paid to him in Dublin, where he made a home with Maria and the children, Joseph Francis and Maria.

William Dowling VC struggled to earn a living in civilian life. Trading as a tailor whenever work was available, and drawing two pensions, he was unable, nevertheless, to support his family: twenty years on from the Great Famine and the death and migration of 3 million souls, Ireland remained in social and economic decline. But across the Irish Sea, Liverpool was booming, and there was plenty of work. Dowling moved to the city with his family and took up residence at 2 Rokeby Street, off Everton Brow. The children were placed in St Francis Xavier's School, and Dowling found work as a uniformed customs officer on the Liverpool Docks.

Every week, hundreds of ships docked in Liverpool. Thousands of passengers, carrying thousands of pieces of luggage, crowded the landing stage and customs hall, where the ODOs of HM Customs and Excise searched them for contraband, alcohol, tobacco, coffee and tea. William Dowling VC, Joseph Prosser VC and, much later, George Nurse VC, worked as customs officers in Liverpool. It may have been the policy of HM Customs to employ ex-soldiers – the uniform, the *esprit de corps*, the chain of command, were all part of a soldier's life, and could be carried over into civilian life in the uniformed branch of HM Customs. However, Dowling and Prosser were Irish, and Nurse had been born in Ireland: perhaps there was an Irish connection, an Irish mafia which looked after its own kind. Such a connection certainly existed in those days within the city's dock labour force, which the Irish dominated.

Despite full-time employment and two pensions, Dowling lived close to the poverty line. His chest condition gradually worsened, and an incapacitating fatigue left him unfit for work for weeks on end, especially through the winter; and his medical bills took away most of his salary. The family moved to Kirkdale, to 19 Rickman Street, in the parish of St John the Evangelist in Fountains Road. Joseph Francis found work as a clerk after leaving school, and remained at home to help provide for, and look after, his ailing father.

At the beginning of a very cold February in 1887, William Dowling VC was admitted to Stanley Hospital, close to his home, suffering with bronchitis and asthenia, barely able to breathe, and unable to walk. There was nothing the medical staff could do for him except make him comfortable in his final days. On Thursday, 17 February, fortified in the rites of the Church, William Dowling VC passed away in the arms of his wife at the age of 63.

Like John Kirk VC, William Dowling VC was a forgotten man. 'The Land' ignored him and did not give him 'honour for all of his days'. This brave soldier was buried unknown and unnoticed, without ceremony, on 20 February in Ford Cemetery, watched over by his wife and children only. His final resting place was an unmarked pauper's grave, which was to be disturbed several times in the years to come when other poor unfortunates were interred with him.

After his father's death, Joseph Frances Dowling worked as an insurance agent in Liverpool, living at 29 Newcombe Street with his mother and sister. In the early summer of 1896, he married Elesia Agnes Smout, from Shrewsbury. Their first child, Josephine Maria Elesia, born on 31 August, died the following month. A second daughter, Wilhelmina Maria, born in September 1900, died a month before her first birthday. Joseph and Elesia lived at 33 Bartlett Street, off Smithdown Road for a number of years with Joseph's mother until she passed away in 1904 at the age of 68. She was buried at Ford Cemetery.

The couple separated soon after her death, and there were no other children from the union. Joseph lived alone at 8 Birch Street, near Stanley Dock, where he died in September 1936. He was buried at Ford Cemetery; and his wife, Elesia, who died in Belmont Road Hospital in November 1948, was buried with him. Of William Dowling's daughter Maria only rumour survives; and this says she died a spinster in Liverpool during the Second World War.

Some years after William Dowling VC enlisted in the army, and more than likely in the wake of the famine, the majority of the Dowlings left Thomastown, many of them emigrating to England and America – that is, except for one branch of the family: William Dowling, brother of John Dowling, grandfather to William Dowling VC, remained in Thomastown, and his descendents continue to live there today. However, in 1867, the birth and christening of John Dowling, great-nephew of William Dowling VC, was registered mistakenly by the priest in the name of John Doolan. And despite attempts to have the error rectified, the Dowling family in Thomastown are known to this day by the name of Doolan.

John James Doolan, the nephew over six generations of William Dowling VC, lives in Legan, Thomastown, with his daughter, Bernadette. His father, also John, served with the machine-gun section of the Royal Dublin Fusiliers, the 'old toughs', on the Western Front, and his younger brother was with the Merchant Navy in the Second World War. John James himself maintained the family tradition and did duty with the Royal Engineers.

No known likeness of William Dowling VC exists. In his army file he is described as 5 feet, 7½ inches tall, having brown hair, green or grey eyes and a pale complexion. His army record shows he was clearly well liked and thought of within the regiment, and it appears he had a very good relationship with his officers. However, a story has grown up around him that he 'did not take kindly to army life' and that 'he was one of the worst characters in his regiment and this reputation was such that it is one of the few things that anybody can remember about him'. Nothing could be further from the truth; it is a mystery how this piece of character assassination ever arose, unsupported as it is by any factual evidence.

For his first ten years with the colours, William Dowling's record was unblemished; he was recognized as a leader of men and promoted to corporal and sergeant, the only bad mark a confinement to the cells for five days in 1855. Several other minor lapses of insobriety followed, but the longest term of imprisonment he served was twenty days in 1860. By the known behaviour of the rank and file of that era, Sergeant William Dowling's conduct was very good, and on and under the battlefield he was a brave and dedicated soldier, a man who could be relied upon in any circumstances.

In Liverpool, he passed his days quietly as a sober, family man and a regular worshipper at the local Catholic church, where parishioners remembered him as an unassuming, former soldier who worked as a customs officer and kept himself to himself. No one in the area knew that this modest man was the gallant holder of the nation's highest honour, the Victoria Cross. And this is how he should be rightly remembered.

In January 1990, the Duke of Cornwall's Light Infantry, the old 32nd Regiment of Foot, in conjunction with Liverpool City Council and HM Customs, London, erected a memorial tablet to William Dowling VC at Ford Cemetery. However, because of the problems of vandalism at the cemetery, and on the promptings of Denis Rose, the tablet was removed and installed at the Church of St John the Evangelist, Fountains Road, where William Dowling VC worshipped in the latter years of his life. The regiment acquired William Dowling's Victoria Cross, and it is on display at the Regimental Museum, Bodmin, Cornwall.

William Connolly VC
(1817–91)

Horse artillery brigades were fast-moving artillery units which gave highly mobile and rapid-fire support to an army. The guns were drawn on sturdy limbers by teams of horses, and the gunners rode into battle astride the horses or on the carriages, usually ahead of the infantry. Trained to perfection, they could dismount, unlimber, position and lay the guns in rapid fire within two minutes, and could equally as quickly reverse the procedures to move on to another position or to retreat. Used mainly in conjunction with the cavalry, the horse artillery concentrated quick-fire barrages of canister shot on tight infantry formations, such as the square, to open up the way for the cavalry to charge.

Essentially a hybrid between cavalry and artillery, much of the élan and ethos of the elite cavalry regiments, with their dashing young men in flamboyant uniforms, was transferred to, and adopted by, the horse artillery battalions. The men stood aloof from their counterparts in the field artillery and acted accordingly, proud of their horsemanship, boastful of their training, timing, precision and speed of manoeuvre, and their role of preceding the infantry into battle.

William Connolly fought with the horse artillery. He was an inch or two under 6 feet in height, a tall man for his times, black-haired, dark-eyed, and with a swarthy complexion. 'Black Irish' is the term usually applied to men of his physical appearance, mistakenly thought to be descendants of survivors of the Spanish Armada, washed ashore in Ireland, but who are more likely to have had their origins in prehistoric migrations to the country from the Iberian Peninsula. It is thought he was a man who stood out, commanding respect not only from his comrades but also from his officers, a gunner who upheld the ethos of his unit, a proud member of the artillery elite. A quiet man all his life, his manner and his deeds did his talking for him.

When William Connolly paraded on a field day in the winter, he wore a dark blue jacket with brass buttons, trimmed with red cuffs, the collar laced in yellow, and white overall trousers and polished black boots, topped by a brass, Roman helmet sporting a red plume. In the summer, a short, white shell jacket with painted cuffs replaced the blue jacket, and the headdress was changed to a white, tropical pith helmet or peaked forage cap and neck cover. In the sticky heat and swirling dust of the Indian summer, in the rains and running mud of the monsoon season, no more inappropriate uniforms could be found. But dress had to be maintained fresh, clean and polished at all times, for the uniform was a statement of his membership in an elite band. And no one was prouder of his uniform and what it stood for than William Connolly.

The Bengal Army of the HEIC fielded three battalions or brigades of horse artillery. Each battalion comprised six troops, each troop deploying six guns, each gun manned by six men. Gunner William Connolly was with the 1st Troop, 3rd Battalion, Bengal Horse Artillery, at the onset of the Indian Mutiny, on station at Rawalpindi, in the North West Frontier Province.

Discipline was firm in the horse artillery, and long, daily drills were the norm, in contrast to the easy life many infantry units were allowed to enjoy. Rapid fire for William Connolly and his team with a six-pound, muzzle-loading cannon was three rounds per minute. Training was intense, and only through constant drilling could a gun team attain and maintain the high level of expertise demanded of them. The cleaning, loading and firing of the gun was a well defined step-by-step procedure, involving close coordination and timing between members of a gun crew: an error could result in a misfire, or premature ignition of the powder charge, threatening the loader; or cause the gun to explode, killing the crew.

The first step in firing a cannon was to search the barrel with a worm, a double corkscrew on a pole, to remove any debris from the previous firing. The barrel was then swabbed by the spongeman, the sponge being a damp sheepskin ball which fitted snugly inside the barrel and which extinguished any burning embers. The powder charge, sewn into a fabric bag, was brought forward from the powder box to the muzzle by the powder-handler, the wormer loading it into the barrel; and the spongeman, reversing his sponge pole, rammed it home. The shot, canister, or ball, was then loaded and rammed into position.

The most experienced in the team was the vent-tender. While the gun was being loaded he would keep his thumb, wrapped in a leather thumbstall, over the vent or touch hole to prevent any air from escaping. He pricked open the fabric bag with a priming wire through the vent, and filled the vent with powder through a powder horn or hollow quill, thereby priming the piece. The firer stepped forward with the linstock, a slow-burning match on a rod, and on the order to give fire, touched the match to the vent hole filled with powder, which carried the ignition to the primary charge, firing the gun. The powder-box handler was responsible for the safe storage of the powder, and in battle ensured it was secure from burning debris.

But the efficiency of the gunners could only be tested on the battlefield. Galloping their guns into the fray, the gunners dismounted and went into action: 300 yards' range was good, 200 very good, and 100 even better. Under fire from the moment their feet touched the ground, the brave gunners never wavered: the discipline, the speed and efficiency remained intact; and when men were shot down, the other team members doubled up their tasks, and continued to rattle out the required rate of fire.

The history of William Connolly's troop records that he fought in 'the age of panache on the battlefield, when men fought and died in their gilded accoutrements. It was the age of rigid discipline in close order drill and . . . lines of battle drawn . . . a hundred yards apart. It was one in which battlefields were shrouded in drifting powder smoke and the balance hung on the ability of soldiers to endure a sudden and daunting number of casualties and still retaliate with parade ground precision.' No better description can be found of the action in which William Connolly fought during the Indian Mutiny and won his Victoria Cross.

Before his death in the Lucknow Residency, Sir Henry Lawrence sent orders to the garrison at Rawalpindi to disarm two regiments of native infantry. The Mutiny had yet to spread to that part of the Punjab, but rumours of disaffection were growing and Lawrence sought to quell the problem before it erupted. He emphasized utmost secrecy so that the sepoys could be taken by surprise: the 58th Native Infantry at Rawalpindi and the 14th Native Infantry on station at Jhelum, seventy-five miles to the south-east, were to be disarmed simultaneously.

Colonel Charles Ellice was ordered to move on Jhelum rapidly, without being told why. He was given sealed orders, to be opened one day's march away from Jhelum, and he put together a compact force of 300 men of the 1st Battalion, 24th Regiment of Foot, and a squadron of Lind's Multani Horse, an irregular cavalry unit. For artillery support, he took half a troop of three guns from the 1st Troop, 3rd Battalion, Bengal Horse Artillery, under Lieutenant Henry Cookes, and which included Gunner William Connolly.

On the morning of 6 July, Colonel Ellice and his compact force reached the village of Deenah and he opened his orders. Having digested their content, he sent a messenger to the garrison commander at Jhelum: he would arrive at the town before daybreak of the following day and surround the parade ground. The commander was to parade the 14th Native Infantry at dawn, and before the sleepy sepoys could realize what was happening, they would be under his guns. Ellice allowed his men a brief rest, knowing they were exhausted from the forced march of two and half days in the high heat of summer, but knowing also that he had to be in Jhelum on 7 July, the date set for the simultaneous disarming.

Mirza Dildar Baig, a lieutenant in the 14th Native Infantry, was the man who led the conspiracy among the sepoys at Jhelum. He had heard of the rising at Meerut and the siege of Delhi, and though his men were initially reluctant to disobey their British officers, he kept up such an onslaught of agitation that by the time of the morning parade his regiment was ready to revolt.

The commander of the Jhelum garrison misinterpreted the orders he had received from Colonel Ellice: he paraded the sepoys before dawn, before Ellice was in position. The misunderstanding sparked a revolt. As the sleep-befuddled sepoys paraded, they became aware of Ellice leading his troops through the outskirts of the town. Mirza Baig, realizing what was to come, screamed betrayal and ordered his men to break ranks and defend themselves.

Unfortunately, Sir Charles Napier, conqueror and former Governor of Sind Province, had built a very sturdy quarter-guard adjacent to the military cantonment in Jhelum. The quarter-guard was a fortified building and the standard focal point of security within garrisons in India. The regimental colours, the armoury and treasury were kept within its confines, as were unruly troopers, in the small lock-up. Mirza Baig and his mutinous sepoys took up positions in and around the quarter-guard, and opened fire on their officers and the approaching column.

As dawn broke over the wakening town, Colonel Ellice ordered forward his horse artillery. Lieutenant Cookes galloped the three guns to the front of the infantry, and William Connolly and the other gunners dismounted and positioned the guns less than a hundred yards from the quarter-guard. Within two minutes, they were laying down round after round of canister-shot into the massed ranks of the sepoys in the disciplined manner in which they had been so precisely trained. The sepoys were also well trained and equally disciplined, and they returned fire with continuous fusillades of musketry.

The battle was fought at close quarters within the narrow confines of the town, and once the 300 men of the 24th Regiment of Foot had joined the fray, the field was quickly enveloped in dark clouds of powder smoke, which hung on the early-morning air, obscuring the rising sun, and masking targets. Both sides fired blindly, and a ferocious battle raged for almost half an hour, with neither side giving way.

It is not known for certain what role the 40-year-old William Connolly played in his team, but it is thought he acted as wormer and loader, and when the spongeman and rammer of the team was felled with a musket round while advancing to position the gun, he doubled up as spongeman. Wearing regulation thick leather gloves, he searched the barrel, swabbed it, loaded and rammed the charge home, loaded and rammed down the shot, before handing over to the vent-tender. However, no sooner had he fired two rounds when he was brought down, wounded through the left thigh by a musket ball. Losing blood and in great pain, he staggered back to his feet to resume his post.

Then Lieutenant Cookes ordered a retirement. The gunners had done their job: the quarter-guard was in danger of collapse and the sepoy lines were crumbling under the devastating firepower of Ellice's command. The mutineers began a fighting retreat to the adjacent village of Samli, pursued by the infantry and horse artillery, and picked off by Lind's charging cavalry. Badly wounded though he was, William Connolly was determined to stay with his team, and he was helped to mount a horse, galloping off with his gun towards Samli.

When the guns were positioned in front of the village, William Connolly refused medical treatment and insisted upon remaining at his post. Bravely, he ignored the pain in his thigh and set to again, worming, sponging and loading the gun, maintaining rapid fire. By mid-morning, the rebels were deeply entrenched in the village and were fighting courageously to keep the British at bay.

Just before noon, he was hit again, in the hip; collapsing to the ground, he lost consciousness for a time, a continuous stream of blood pumping from the deep wound. Seeing him fall, Lieutenant Cookes went to his aid and ordered him removed to the rear for immediate treatment. But William Connolly was made of very stern stuff. Regaining his senses, he pulled himself to his feet and told his lieutenant he would stand fast and continue to work. He took up his sponge pole and was quickly into his rhythm again, working with his fellow gunners as they pounded the village and the enemy within.

As the day wore on, the three guns were advanced to within 100 yards of Samli. The insurgents responded by targeting the artillery, blazing away at the gunners who were causing the most damage to the defences and the most casualties among the defenders. A storm of fire broke over William Connolly and his team. But they held their ranks and discipline. Exhausted, mouths parched, eyes blinded with acrid smoke and running sweat, broiled by the sun beneath their tight-fitting tunics and scorched by the heat of the guns, they poured round after round into the village.

William Connolly became lightheaded through loss of blood and, in great pain, he was often close to collapse. Nevertheless, he fought on, and, above the furious roar of the battle, it was his voice that could be heard. He rallied the men, urging them on to greater efforts, encouraging the wounded and bellowing out for quicker supplies of ammunition and powder. And then, while sponging the barrel of the gun, he was struck for a third time: a ball tore through the calf muscle of his wounded left leg, and he collapsed to the ground in agony.

Before anyone could come to his aid, however, he was back on his feet, loading the gun, ready with his worm to clear the barrel, armed with the rod to swab again. Six rounds he helped to fire before the inevitable occurred: his body finally gave way and he lost consciousness, falling into the arms of Lieutenant Cookes. In a dead faint, he was carried away in a cart from the battle to receive medical treatment.

For undaunting courage when manning his gun, Gunner William Connolly was awarded the Victoria Cross. In one of the longest and most detailed citations ever published in the *London Gazette*, Lieutenant Cookes insisted on recording every instance of William Connolly's bravery. His citation reads:

William Connolly, Gunner, Bengal Horse Artillery. Date of Act of Bravery: 7 July, 1857. This soldier is recommended for the Victoria Cross for his gallantry in action with the enemy at Jhelum on 7 July, 1857. Lieutenant Cookes, Bengal Horse Artillery, reports that, 'About daybreak on that day I advanced my half-troop at a gallop, and engaged the enemy within easy musket-range. The sponge-man of one of my guns having been shot during the advance, Gunner Connolly assumed the duties of second sponge-man, and he had barely assisted in two discharges of his gun when a musket-ball through his left thigh felled him to the ground; nothing daunted by pain and loss of blood, he was endeavouring to resume his post, when I ordered a movement in retirement, and, though severely wounded, he was mounted on his horse in the gun-team, and rode to the next position which the guns took up, and manfully declined to go to the rear when the necessity of his doing so was represented to him. About 11 o'clock a.m., when the guns were still in action, the same gunner, whilst sponging, was again knocked down by a musket-ball striking him on the hip, thereby causing great faintness and partial unconsciousness, for the pain appeared excessive and the blood flowing out fast. On seeing this, I gave directions for his removal out of action, but this brave man, hearing me, staggered to his feet, and said, "No, sir, I'll not go there whilst I can work here," and shortly afterwards he resumed his post as sponge-man. Late in the afternoon of the same day my three guns were engaged at one hundred yards from the walls of a village with the defenders, viz, the 14th Native Infantry, mutineers, amidst a storm of bullets which did great execution. Gunner Connolly, though suffering severely from his two previous wounds, was wielding his sponge with an energy and courage which attracted the admiration of his comrades, and while cheerfully encouraging a wounded man to hasten in bringing up ammunition, a musket-ball tore through the muscles of his left leg; but with the most undaunted bravery he struggled on, and not till he had loaded six times did this man give way, when through loss of blood, he fell in my arms, and I placed him on a wagon, which shortly afterwards bore him in a state of unconsciousness from the fight.'

The battle for the village of Samli petered out and Colonel Ellice withdrew his column to Jhelum. Because of the urgency of the situation and the need to be in the town by 7 July, and not expecting or anticipating a full-scale engagement, Ellice had not been fully supplied with ammunition. It was evening, just after William Connolly had received his third wound, that supplies of munitions became dangerously low; and with little prospect of taking Samli in the face of the determined resistance put up by the sepoys, prudence demanded a withdrawal. Ellice carried away thirty-five dead men from his column. During the night, the rebels abandoned their position and made good their escape, joining up with other mutineers further south.

How William Connolly survived his wounds, and the medical treatment of the day, on the fly-infested, squalid hospital ward in the summer heat, is nothing short of a miracle. He was wounded in the leg and the hip through his clothing; and in each wound was embedded shreds of fabric from his uniform, carrying bacteria with the potential to infect the wound. Infection would lead to pus formation and the blocking of the blood supply, which would have greatly decreased oxygen levels in the wound. If the pus was not drained, necrosis of the surrounding tissue followed: wet gangrene would develop and eat away at healthy tissue, spreading through the limb, poisoning the system, and causing death inevitably. In William Connolly's day, treatment for gangrene was by amputation.

The hip wound may have included a chipped pelvic bone, and while the soft tissues of the leg healed without gangrene setting in, it was this wound that would always cause him problems and left him with a limp. William Connolly would never fight again; after a year in hospital, he was pensioned off by the HEIC on 10 October 1858, and was packed off home to Liverpool. He was a cripple, incapable of work, and would live out his days supported by his Victoria Cross and HEIC pensions.

He was gazetted for the award of the Victoria Cross on 3 September 1858, fourteen months after his brave stand. The chaos and confusion created by the Mutiny and the travel time for dispatches to reach England both contributed to the delay in the announcement. When he received his award, where and from whom, are unknown. But there was an error in the inscription on the reverse of the suspension bar: the engraver, possibly due to lack of space, misspelled his surname as Conolly.

William Connolly was born in Liverpool in May 1817. He was the only son of James and Rebecca Connolly, both natives of Ireland. James Connolly was an agricultural labourer, one of the many landless Irishmen who, unable to find work at home, became seasonal workers in England, descending on the rich soil of Lancashire to sew and later to reap, and earn a few shillings to send home to feed their families. One year, he brought his wife with him and they decided to make their home in Liverpool. James and Rebecca lived in Oakes Street, off London Road, and in addition to William, they were blessed with four daughters, Rebecca, Catherine, Barbara and Charlotte.

After leaving school, William Connolly found work as a stableman and groom in the city. But at the age of 20, he decided to join the army. At the time, 'John Company' administered India through three presidencies, Bengal, Madras and Bombay, each of which had its own armed force. On 2 May 1837, William Connolly enlisted at Liverpool in the Bengal Army of the HEIC, as a Gunner, 1st Troop, 3rd Bengal Horse Artillery. Later that year, he sailed for India aboard the troopship *Exmouth*. His first station was Barrackpore, fifteen miles north of Calcutta, Bengal.

William Connolly's first ten years in the country were peaceful. It was not until trouble flared again inside the Sikh Kingdom of the Punjab following the conclusion of the First Anglo–Sikh War of 1845–6, threatening to spill over into the neighbouring domains of the HEIC, that he saw any fighting. The Second Anglo–Sikh War of 1848–9 afforded the opportunity for William Connolly and his comrades of the Bengal Horse Artillery to put into practice what they had been trained to do.

The centre of the Sikh rebellion was Multan, where John Kirk and William Dowling fought. But a Sikh ally of the HEIC, Sher Singh Attariwalla, defected to the rebels, and rampaged through the Punjab. William Connolly and the Bengal Horse Artillery were made part of the Army of the Punjab under the command of General Sir Hugh Gough, with orders to contain the marauding rebel force of Sher Singh. Gough was delayed in taking to the field by the monsoon season, and he did not make contact with the insurgents until November, when his army was checked by the Sikhs at the River Chenab. Gough forced the river early in the new year, and made contact with an outpost of the Sher Singh's command near the village of Chillianwala, on the left bank of the River Jhelum, eighty-five miles north-west of Lahore.

On 13 January, Gough's army attacked Sher Singh's force without artillery support, suffering heavy casualties. It was a desperately fought, yet indecisive, battle, which dented and undermined British prestige and force of arms, paving the way to the Indian Mutiny. Some of Gough's infantry units lost their colours amid the fiery chaos and confusion, and part of a cavalry unit fled in panic. At one point in the battle, the Sikhs were in a position to completely annihilate Gough's army. William Connolly and his comrades saved the day. 'In this crisis when everything seemed to frown on the Bengal Army, the behaviour of the Bengal Horse Artillery was superb. ... Never did it render more valuable, more efficacious service to its country ... than on that memorable 13 January.'

William Connolly and his comrades fought as they had been drilled and trained to do. They beat back the charging Sikhs with rapid fire of canister and grape, and their steadfast example rallied the wavering ranks of the infantry and the dispersed cavalry. They would show the same courage and determination in the final, decisive battle of the war at Gujarat on 21 February, when 'the heavy artillery continued to advance ... whilst the rapid advance and beautiful fire of the [Bengal] Horse Artillery ... broke the ranks of the enemy at all points.'

For his doughty services during the Second Anglo–Sikh War, Gunner William Connolly received the Punjab Medal with two clasps, Chillianwala and Gujarat. The war proved very costly to the Sikhs: their kingdom in the Punjab was annexed by the HEIC and became the North-West Frontier Province. However, during the Mutiny, the Sikhs remained loyal to their new rulers, and would assist the British in restoring law and order in India.

The next eight years for William Connolly were spent in peace and quietude. He remained in the new province, stationed on garrison duty at Rawalpindi, until the sub-continent was set alight by the Mutiny. At the time of the revolt, he had completed twenty years' service with HEIC, and he must have been hoping for one more year of inactivity to be followed by retirement on a good pension, and returning to his family in Liverpool.

During his absence, his sister, Charlotte, married George Edwin Jones, a lithograph printer, and they lived at Phythian Street, West Derby. She took in her mother and sister, Rebecca, when William's father died. Rebecca remained a spinster. Barbara married Henry Hurst, with whom she lived at 8 Park Place, off Warwick Street. Henry was the sacristan at the local Catholic Church of St Patrick. Catherine Connolly married Thomas Burrows of St Helens in 1848, and the couple were living at 124 Mann Street, off Stanhope Street, when William Connolly VC returned home a cripple from India in the spring of 1859.

He lived with his sister Catherine and brother-in-law Thomas for several years in Mann Street. Thomas died in 1869, Catherine in 1876, and it is believed that Barbara, Rebecca and Charlotte passed away before the turn of the decade. And from that time, the crippled William Connolly VC was alone and had to fend for himself. The hip wound was painful and walking an ordeal. But he did not lie down, and the courage he had shown in front of Jhelum and Samli drove him on: he was a survivor, and he would live to the ripe old age of 74.

He took lodgings at 40 Seacombe, off Netherfield Road, with the Dodd family for some years, but by 1886 he was in dire straits: in debt and living on handouts and charity, he declined into beggary. His memories and his pride would not put food in his stomach or a roof over his head; and he was forced to give up his only treasure, that symbol of the land which had forsaken him. On 9 February 1886, his Victoria Cross came up for auction at Sotheby's and was knocked down to Spink of London, dealers in orders, decorations and medals, for the sum of £10. With this money and his pension, he scraped along for a few more years until he was reduced finally to paupery. Suffering with bronchitis, he was admitted as an inmate to the Walton Institution, the workhouse on Rice Lane, Walton, run by the West Derby Union, which administered relief to the poor of thirty parishes in Liverpool. He was expected to end his days in that institution.

Elizabeth Johnson was a widow who owned a herbalist shop at 14 Westminster Road, Kirkdale. Living with her were three of her daughters, a son-in-law, and several grandchildren. Next door but one, at No. 10, lived another daughter, Emma, the wife of John Catterall. The Johnson girls had grown up above John Catterall's baker's shop in Heyworth Street, Everton, and Emma and John had married in 1870. They made their home in Westminster Road, and were soon followed by Elizabeth Johnson and the rest of the brood. Emma Catterall provided a valuable service to the families of the area, as many women of her ilk did in the poorer districts of the city: she would wash, dress and lay out the dead in preparation for confinement in the coffin.

In the summer of 1891, Elizabeth Johnson took William Connolly VC from the workhouse and gave him lodgings in her home. Perhaps there was a family connection, or she had known him in the past; perhaps she was simply a caring, charitable woman. No one knows. He had nothing, but she gave him a home. And his last few months on earth were lived in comfort, surrounded by people he knew. Suffering with bronchitis, he struggled on until the end of the year.

William Connolly died at 14 Westminster Road on 31 December 1891. The physician certified bronchitis as the cause of death, and Emma Catterall, on hand to do her duty, appended her mark to the death certificate before tending the body. At one o'clock on 4 January, a cold, dreary afternoon swept by rain, William Connolly was laid to rest in a pauper's grave at Kirkdale Cemetery. Only the Johnson family mourned his passing. The location of the burial plot was lost over the years, but a headstone commemorating this brave man was erected near the entrance to the cemetery in 1994.

The whereabouts of William Connolly's Victoria Cross are a mystery. Spink sold the medal on to a Mr M.H. Bobart. In November 1894, it came up for auction again at Sotheby's, when Bobart's collection was sold following his death. The medal's provenance was indisputable. However, the reserve price was not reached, and the auctioneer passed it as not sold. William Connolly's Victoria Cross was retained by Adolphus Grimwood-Taylor, an executor of the will of Mr Bobart, and it has remained in his family ever since.

In 1998, his great-grandson, James, took the medal to Hancock's for verification, and it was declared a reproduction, not the original. However, this medal is unlike any other copy, reproduction or forgery of the Victoria Cross which exists today. The only explanation is that William Connolly VC lost his original medal – perhaps it was stolen – and replaced it with the copy which he sold in 1886. The British in India Museum, in Colne, Lancashire, at one time believed it held William Connolly's original Victoria Cross in its collection, but it has recently been assayed a forgery. The location of his Punjab Medal and clasps is also unknown.

Frederick Whirlpool VC
(1829–99)

The chronicles of the Victoria Cross relate that James Conker was a complex character, a man at war with himself, an awkward loner adrift on the ocean of life unfettered by the anchors of love and friendship. Janus-like, he presented two opposing personalities to the world: at once cantankerous, sullen and tiresome, he was also placid, cheery and charming. In manhood, he cast off his birth name and assumed another, Frederick Whirlpool, and as such was the first man honoured with the Victoria Cross under a *nom de guerre*. He later adopted a second, Frederick Humphrey James, to conceal the duality, before withdrawing from society to live as a recluse. Until recently, historians have been unable to account for the man's unusual behaviour, but the latest research has now uncovered the facts through which the full story of this part-time curmudgeon and Liverpool hero can be told for the first time.

Throughout their lives, James Conker, Frederick Whirlpool VC and Frederick Humphrey James suffered with migraine. Beset by a migraine attack, which could last for up to three days, they were rendered prostrate with pain, becoming irritable and withdrawn. Their symptoms of pulsating, throbbing headaches, nausea and abdominal discomfort were very often preceeded by wild mood swings, blurred vision and a creeping numbness, which spread from the arms to encompass the mouth, lips and tongue, and interfered with speech. When the bout subsided, they rose from their sick beds without infirmity.

The illness struck James Conker in his youth. He is believed to have been an only child, and doubtless his parents sought to remedy the complaint and bring him comfort. Willow bark infusions and opium, in the form of laudanum, were the prescribed analgesics of the day to offset the painful effects of the illness, but its cause was thought to be stagnation of the blood in the head and neck, which reduced supply to the brain. A recognized cure was to stimulate the congested areas employing the ancient Chinese technique of cupping: small glass cups are heated and applied to the neck; and as the air inside them cools, a suction effect is produced, drawing the covered skin up inside the cups, thereby restoring the idling fluid to full flow.

Cupping marks the skin temporarily with purple blotches, but excessive and careless procedures can lead to permanent disfigurement. This was the case with James Conker: his service record notes he was scarred by cupping on the neck and shoulders. Despite the overzealous application of the cups the migraine attacks persisted into manhood, and they became the focus of discord within the Conker family. His father was a military man, and this alone may account for the fact he lost patience with his son's predicament. Believing James should have outgrown what he considered to be a childhood ailment, he argued that the headaches, the pain and associated moodiness and irritability were mental, claiming his son's mind was a 'whirlpool' which was responsible for, and conjured up, the complaints. The boy should set his mind right and act like a man: a spell in the army was the only remedy.

The relationship between father and son became fraught, and deteriorated from bickering to mutual antagonism and hostility. After one particularly bitter exchange, James Conker packed his bags and travelled to Glasgow. Mindful of his father's harsh words, he took the name Whirlpool and signed on for a ten-year enlistment in the army of the HEIC on 23 October 1854. Describing himself as a clerk by profession, he stated Liverpool was his place of birth and his age 23, which gives a birth year of 1831. The inducting officer noted he was 5 feet, 7 inches tall, with brown hair, grey eyes, a fresh complexion, and marked by cupping. However, migraine was not a bar to service with the HEIC, and Frederick Whirlpool was sent to its depot at Warley in Essex for kitting out and introductory training.

Nothing is known of his mother; and all that can be ascertained of his father, besides his lack of sympathy for his son's plight, is that he was a major in the regular British army. In the third decade of the nineteenth century, he is thought to have been on station in Liverpool before being appointed post-master in Dundalk, Ireland, where his son was brought up. And it is reasonable to suppose that James Conker benefited from everything his father's station in life could provide, including a good education. The position of postmaster was one of great responsibility and within the remit of the army because a great deal of the mail was of military nature: mail coaches collected and distributed letters, and mail ships, the packet boats, ferried the post between Dublin and Liverpool.

Frederick Whirlpool arrived in Bombay on 26 March 1855, on board the troop-ship *Salamanca*, and was posted as 2987 Private Whirlpool to the 3rd Bombay (European) Regiment at Poona, a hundred miles to the east. There, he completed his training and took on the additional task of bugler for the regiment; and he stayed on station at Poona until the Mutiny erupted two years later. Very few records of the time are extant, but it is believed he was unable to make lasting friendships among his comrades, most of whom were from the slums of the industrialized cities and towns of Britain: they were wary of him. His background and education made him stand out and should have put him in line for promotion. But he did not advance and remained a private for the duration of his service: the migraines continued and he was troubled and troublesome, one day all bustle and go, the next languid and dismissive, barely able to rise from his bunk, reluctant to, sometimes incapable of, attending to his duties.

The 3rd Bombays was a new regiment, raised in November 1853, and though made up mainly of new recruits who had never been in action, distinguished itself as a formidable fighting force in the suppression of the Mutiny. Most of the fighting took place in the north of the sub-continent in 1857. But two rebellions arose in Central India, at Jhansi and Gwalior, which were not suppressed until the spring and summer of the following year, when Major General Sir Hugh Rose advanced the two brigades of the Central India Field Force (CIFF) from Sehore and captured both towns. Private Frederick Whirlpool of the 3rd Bombay (European) Regiment won the Victoria Cross fighting with the CIFF.

Today, Jhansi lies in the state of Uttar Pradesh. But in the nineteenth century the town and the surrounding country was an independent state, an hereditary principality within British Bundelkhand, which was overseen by the HEIC. In 1838, Gangadhar Rao was installed as rajah, but when he died childless fifteen years later, his kingdom was annexed by the Governor General of India, Lord Dalhousie, under the Doctrine of Lapse. This law allowed the annexation of any principality or vassal state whose ruler had died without a direct heir, and supplanted the long-established right of an Indian ruler without an heir to appoint a successor. Jhansi fell under the hegemony of British Bundelkhand and the HEIC in February 1854, against the fervent pleas and arguments of the rajah's wife, Rani Lakshmi Bai, her court and her people. The seed for the rebellion at Jhansi was sown.

On 5 June 1857, the Star Fort, which stood on Bangra Hill overlooking the town, and which held the armoury and treasury, was overrun by mutinous sepoys of the 12th Bengal Native Infantry and *sowars* of the 14th Irregular Cavalry. They looted the fort, released its prisoners and went on the rampage through the European cantonment. The following day, Captain Alexander Skene, 68th Bengal Native Infantry, Superintendent at Jhansi and Jaloun, and Captain Michael Gordon, 10th Madras Native Infantry, Deputy Commissioner of Jhansi, gathered the men, women and children into the town fort, an extended quarter-guard, with its own water supply. A salvo from the heavy guns was fired on the rebels in the hope of frightening them away, but they stood their ground and replied in kind, causing several casualties to the garrison. They invested the fort and dug in for a long siege. With little food and ammunition, the Europeans faced a grim future, and Skene and Gordon knew they could not hold out for long.

Skene surrendered to the mutineers on 7 June on condition of safe passage for all; and next day led his people out of Jhansi. But, south of the town, in an area of gardens and temples, the rebels turned on the evacuees in the garden known as Jokhan Bagh; and using their *tulwars* slaughtered the forty-seven men and women and twenty children of the garrison.

A scene of utter devastation greeted the men of the 3rd Bombay (European) Regiment when Sir Hugh Rose brought them before Jhansi on 21 March 1858: to the south of city, the cantonment and the homes of the English residents had been burned to the ground, and all outbuildings had been demolished to open up a field of fire. In the Jokhan Bagh, the dried, white bones of the murdered innocents poked through the thinly scattered earth of their graves, and were a plaintive reminder of horrors past, and a goad to Sir Hugh Rose and his men.

As he stood before Jhansi, Frederick Whirlpool was battle-weary and foot-sore, little more than skin and bones, his face, blackened by the sun, encased in a straggly beard, his khaki uniform ripped to shreds and matted with mud and gore. But he was breathing fire, impatient to take on the insurgents. The 3rd Bombays, under Lieutenant Colonel Liddell, was part of the 2nd Brigade commanded by Sir Hugh Rose himself. He had taken the field in the first week of January 1858, amid continuing news and rumour of massacre of European civilians. The mood of his men was grim, the usual chafing and joking absent, replaced by the rasping sound of bayonets being honed to razor sharpness.

Covering 300 miles in a little over two months, Frederick Whirlpool and his comrades cut through steamy jungles, forded rivers, scaled mountain passes and stumbled across arid, stony plains, suffering from heat exhaustion, hunger and thirst. They engaged and defeated the rebels in several bloody encounters: at the fortress town of Rathghur, sixty miles to the north-east of Bhopal, they put to flight 500 rebels, and in hot pursuit overtook and annihilated the fleeing insurgents at the River Beena, giving no quarter to those who surrendered. The men were then given their heads: they marched quickly on to the fortress at Barodia, six miles up river, and stormed and carried the garrison at bayonet point. Sir Hugh Rose, in his first dispatch of the campaign, singled out the men of the 3rd Bombays for their excellent fighting qualities.

Taking advantage of this gritty fighting spirit, Rose forced marched the 3rd Bombays through the jungle to attack Garrakota, twenty-five miles east of Sagar. The men emerged seemingly exhausted from the sweltering heat of the jungle passage; and the rebels, confident of victory over what appeared to them to be a dishevelled force, sallied forth from the fortress to give battle. Frederick Whirlpool drew breath and sounded his bugle. The 3rd Bombays fell on the sepoys, and, in a brutal, close-quarter fight, chastised them for their self-assurance, driving them back into the fortress with heavy casualties. Garrakota was bombarded for several days by the siege guns while Rose's force gathered its strength. On 13 February, the 3rd Bombays led the way into the fortress, only to find that the rebels had slipped away during the night.

Leaving behind a small force to garrison the town, Rose brought his brigade to Sagar for resupply and recuperation. Other regiments of the CIFF were now referring to the men of the 3rd Bombays as the 'brassheads', in recognition of their ability to withstand and ignore the gruelling effects of the very high regional temperatures, and their refusal to allow the heat to deflect them from their purpose. And they caused further comment when they were kitted out in a new uniform of lightweight, stone-coloured cotton shirts and trousers, to replace the close-fitting heavy, red tunics and blue trousers, the wearing of which contributed to the high incidence of heat exhaustion in the ranks. A forage cap took the place of the traditional shako. This was the first occasion in which a British army unit was kitted out in khaki.

Towards the end of February, the 2nd Brigade was on the move again, heading north-east towards Jhansi. Three rebel strongholds at Narut, Dhamoni and the mountain pass at Mundipur barred its advance, but when they fell, the road was open to Jhansi and Gwalior. On 17 March, Rose encamped his force along the banks of the River Betwa. And after resting for four days, they crossed the river and stood before Jhansi.

The walls of the town were 10 feet thick and rose up to 30 feet high in places, running for four and a half miles to enclose the town, except in the west where Bangra Hill ascended from the plain and upon which stood the formidable Star Fort, with walls of granite 15 feet thick. In the south, close to the Jokhan Bagh and the ruined cantonment, the wall was interrupted by a mound, a cliff face, which the rebels had fortified with a strong circular bastion to hold six guns, and around part of which was drawn a ditch, 12 feet deep and 15 feet wide. The walls adjacent to the mound, behind which stood the Rani's palace, and which Rose christened the 'mamelon', for he had been at Sebastopol, were the weakest point of the defences and would bear the brunt of his attack.

When the 1st Brigade, CIFF, under Brigadier General Stewart, arrived at Jhansi on 25 March, Sir Hugh Rose ordered his men to dig in south of the town, out of range of the enemy muskets, and sent in the engineers to throw out saps towards the mamelon, while the artillery positioned its guns and ranged targets on the weakest points. For eight days the heavy British siege guns battered the mamelon with ball while the infantry kept up an incessant and remorseless fire upon the sepoys and *sowars* manning the walls, and against the women who could be seen carrying supplies to the rebel batteries in the bastion. The insurgents, 11,000 strong, fought back and their artillery was the equal of the British. The 'Old McCormac' beat down on besieged and besiegers alike, causing almost as many casualties through heatstroke as the flying lead and cannon shot; and a swirling, scorching wind swept the smoke and dust of battle into a blinding screen, through which scampered and crawled the water-carriers, responding to the croaking demands of thirsty men.

On the last day of March, a breach was opened between the mamelon and the walls of the town, close to the Orcha Gate, but the rebels improvised a stockade across the yawning gap. All guns were turned on the stockade, which was quickly destroyed. But before Sir Hugh Rose could chose the forlorn hope to storm and exploit the breach, a rebel force of 20,000 men arrived at the River Betwa. They were commanded by Tatya Tope, intent upon breaking the siege and keeping alive the rebellion in Central India. Rose was forced to delay the assault on Jhansi and divert part of his force to deal with the threat.

He marched 1,500 men, among them 226 men of the 3rd Bombays, against Tatya Tope, and with artillery and cavalry support, engaged the enemy in a fiercely contested battle, which lasted most of the day. The vastly superior army of Tatya Tope was decisively beaten and fled the field, leaving behind more than 1,000 casualties. Rose was now able to return to his main business.

On 3 April, the assault on Jhansi began. At three o'clock on a bright, moonlit night, the storming parties collected their scaling-ladders and formed up into four columns. The 3rd Bombays, which Rose rightly considered his strong right arm, crossed the Jokhan Bagh from the right and stormed the breach near the mamelon, while the 86th Regiment of Foot, of Stewart's 1st Brigade, came in from the left. As they advanced, they were met with a savage fire of round-shot, rockets, musket balls and stinkpots. The 3rd Bombays were directed along the wrong path, and some of the men fell beneath the fire pouring down from the walls. After finding the right path, the men were further afflicted at the mamelon, when they discovered that the poorly and hastily constructed ladders were short by several feet; and many of them gave way and collapsed under the weight of the men as they climbed towards the breach.

Chaos and confusion ensued: men of the 3rd Bombays plummeted to their deaths and disrupted the second and third waves of the attack, which came under relentless fire from the sepoys. They were forced to withdraw from the wall, leaving many wounded out in the open. Frederick Whirlpool volunteered to return to the wall to carry to safety some of his fallen comrades. Showing remarkable courage in the face of the enemy fusillades, he dived back into the site of the earlier mêlée and began to extract the dead and wounded, dragging them out of range to the rear. Several times he risked his life going back under fire to rescue his helpless comrades before he was forced to take cover. A small party of the 3rd Bombays joined the attack of the 86th on the left, and helped to force the breach in their sector. Lieutenant Colonel Liddell rallied and re-grouped his men and renewed the attack on the breach. During the fighting, it was noted again that Frederick Whirlpool dashed forward to assist the wounded and bring them under cover.

The 3rd Bombays beat back the enemy from the breach in fierce hand-to-hand fighting, forcing them to take up positions in the streets of the town, with their backs to the Rani's palace. Jhansi was ablaze, but the majority of the sepoys now stood their ground among the houses, fighting to the death as the British fanned out, intent only on death and destruction. Ordered to spare no one above the age of sixteen, except women, the rampaging troops vengefully exceeded this command, and a horrifying massacre was perpetrated against the rebels and their sympathizers throughout the rest of the day and into the next. The Rani Lakshmi made her escape with her adopted son, but 1,500 Afghans of her bodyguard made a spirited defence of the palace, and they were overcome only when Rose sent in the ever-reliable 3rd Bombays. Towards evening, the regiment entered the Star Fort, which had been abandoned by the rebels. But, it was not until 5 April that Sir Hugh Rose was able to rein in his troops, and an uneasy peace settled over the shattered town. It was estimated that 5,000 defenders died in the slaughter. Frederick Whirlpool lost twelve of his comrades dead and forty-two wounded.

Rose rested his men for three weeks at Jhansi, waiting for fresh supplies of food and ammunition. Then he set off north-east, towards the city of Kunch, another centre of rebellion, which had granted asylum to the fleeing Rani. Patrols of the 1st and 4th Hyderabad Cavalry scouted the Kunch road ahead of Rose's Brigade, and when one of them encountered resistance at a stockade in the village of Lohari, he sent out a small punitive force under Major Richard Gall, 14th Light Dragoons, to suppress the mutineers.

Major Gall marched on the village with the left wing of the 3rd Bombays. Private Frederick Whirlpool was in the ranks. Ninety rebels had taken up positions inside the mud and wicker fort; and when called upon to surrender, they refused. On 2 May, the 3rd Bombays stormed Lohari. One account states that Bugler Frederick Whirlpool was the first man through the gate of the stockade, followed by two officers, one of whom was Lieutenant Doune.

The three men were instantly mobbed by a gang of sepoys armed with *tulwars*, and all three sustained wounds in the initial charge. Lieutenant Doune was the first to go down, beaten to the ground with swords and sticks. Without a thought for his own safety, Frederick Whirlpool went to his assistance, crashing through a knot of rebels, who now turned their attention to him. They slashed and stabbed at him with their heavy sabres, inflicting several horrific wounds as he stood over the injured Doune, parrying their thrusts with his musket.

Despite his injuries, despite the fury of the assault, Whirlpool managed to keep his feet, until help arrived. Both men were rescued when the 3rd Bombays overwhelmed the sepoys who fought and died to the last man. When the bloody fight was over, Private Whirlpool collapsed to the ground. He received seventeen wounds to his person; and one slashing blow from a sabre almost severed his head. Still conscious as he was carted away for medical treatment, he allegedly cajoled the stretcher-bearers to 'take care, lads, and don't shake my head off.' Perhaps he also saw the humour in the loss of his head as a cure for his migraines.

For bravery under fire in front of Jhansi, for the defence of a wounded officer at Lohari, Private Frederick Whirlpool was awarded the Victoria Cross. His citation reads:

Frederick Whirlpool, Private, 3rd Bombay European Regiment. Dates of Acts of Bravery: 3 April and 2 May, 1858. For gallantly volunteering on 3 April, 1858, in the attack on Jhansi, to return and carry away several killed and wounded, which he did twice under a very heavy fire from the wall; also for devoted bravery at the Assault of Lohari on 2 May 1858, in rushing to the rescue of Lieutenant Doune, of the regiment, who was dangerously wounded. In this service Private Whirlpool received seventeen desperate wounds, one of which nearly severed his head from his body. The gallant example shown by this man is considered to have greatly contributed to the success of the day.

Whirlpool was confined to hospital in Indore, and later Poona, for five months, where he learnt that Sir Hugh Rose had recommended him for the Victoria Cross. And, like Alfred Stowell Jones and William Connolly, he miraculously survived the ministrations of the doctors on the diseased wards. In time he made a full recovery, but he would always carry the scars from the encounter, most noticeably the thick, raised mark which disfigured his neck, to remind him of the only time he was wounded in four months of tireless campaigning in India.

He was released from his contract with the HEIC in February 1859, passed as unfit for further military service, and was pensioned off at a weekly rate, equivalent to eight pence in today's money. He refused the opportunity to be repatriated to England, the abode of so much early heartache, and instead chose to be domiciled in Australia. Eight months later, as he settled in to his new home in Melbourne, and still incapacitated by his wounds, the *London Gazette* of 21 October announced the grant of the Victoria Cross to Private Frederick Whirlpool, formerly of the 3rd Bombay (European) Regiment.

Rumour has it that he applied to join the Victoria Police Force, but was refused entry because of his physical condition. He did find a billet, however, with the Hawthorn and Kew Rifle Company Volunteers, one of several militia units in the colony of Victoria which had grown up in response to the depredations of bushranger gangs. The unit had its headquarters three miles to the east of Melbourne, not far from where he lived. But he was not active as a militiaman and the enlistment was allowed simply to provide him with a military uniform to wear when he received his Victoria Cross.

He was due to be decorated on 24 May 1861, when the great and the good of Victoria, in common with all other colonies of the British Empire, paraded in honour of Queen Victoria's birthday. Frederick Whirlpool was elated at the prospect, the first time the award would be made on Australian soil, and anticipated the event with enthusiasm and great excitement. However, in March, the Queen's mother, HRH Duchess of Kent, passed away, and the mourning period delayed the annual birthday ceremonies until Thursday, 20 June.

On that day in Melbourne, amid great fanfare and publicity, 10,000 spectators pushed and shoved and craned their necks to watch 2,000 members of various volunteer militia units march past the dais upon which stood the

Governor of Victoria and his lady wife, Lord and Lady Barkly, and other civic dignitaries. But the public had not come to see them: the onlookers were watching for their hero. The militiamen formed up into three sides of a square and Private Frederick Whirlpool was called from the ranks to thunderous applause and cheers. The Deputy Adjutant Lieutenant Colonel Carey then read the citation before Lady Barkly stepped forward and pinned the honour on Whirlpool's breast.

He revelled in the ceremony, the hullabaloo, the acclaim, the publicity. When all the fuss died down and he was no longer the focus of attention, however, he drifted into the doldrums; and within weeks of the investiture, he changed his name by deed poll to Frederick Humphrey James and decamped to New South Wales, wandering through the colony for four years, taking odd jobs here and there to support himself. Beneath this new guise, he was the same man, still the victim to the migraine affliction, and, more than likely, beginning to exhibit symptoms of depression. It has been suggested he could not cope with the recognition and publicity, and sought escape into privacy through a new identity in another location. But, events were to prove he was not averse to having his names in print. They unfolded in 1865, when Frederick James finally put down roots and was hired to teach at the new National School near Wiseman's Ferry on the Hawkesbury River, forty-six miles north of Sydney.

Frederick James found a home and was a success in the role: the teaching staff admired him and enjoyed his company, and pupils and parents alike appreciated his commitment and effort. His future appeared assured. But while his first year at the school was a triumph, the second was a disaster. It opened with discord: he fell out with the school secretary, they argued, and quickly became bitter enemies. Allegations of impropriety, of what kind is unknown, were then levelled against him by the secretary, and he was suspended from his post. Sides were taken, the community was divided and the case became a well-publicized cause célèbre. However, although supported by the parents, the secretary's charges were accepted by the Education Board, and Frederick James was dismissed from his post in 1867.

He would not truckle to the Board's decision, believing himself innocent and that an injustice had been done, and he pressed for reinstatement: his appeal was rejected. Out of work, and his names and face blazoned in the press, Frederick James, however, did not move on to a new beginning under another assumed name: there was sympathy for him in the town, and he decided to brazen it out and applied for other teaching posts. But, when the letters of rejection began to pile up, he came to the conclusion he was blacklisted and would not be allowed to teach again. In turn, tediously and angrily rehearsing his misfortune on a daily basis to his supporters quickly lost him that backing. People avoided him and he was marginalized as an object of pity; and it was hoped he would move on because his presence had become an embarrassment. Frederick James was made an outcast.

If he had to live as such, then he would do so in a place and in a manner of his own choosing. Moving ten miles downriver, to the settlement of McGrath's Hill, close to the town of Windsor, he took possession of an abandoned slab hut. These huts, which dotted the Australian outback, were of a very primitive design, simply built from lengths of rough timber held together with whatever came to hand. Such quarters provided the barest comfort and minimal protection from the elements. In this decrepit and dilapidated abode, Frederick James became a recluse, and lived a mean, solitary existence for the remaining twenty-one years of his life. He shunned society, which had turned its back on him, and his only contacts were through his quarterly calls to Windsor to collect his pensions, the weekly grocery delivery and, in the twilight of his life, an itinerant Scotsman, a swagman, who befriended him and who would call at the hut from time to time.

James Conker was rejected by his father because of his illness and was forced to leave home. Frederick Whirlpool found a refuge and a niche in the armed forces. But the army cast him off, too, and for similar reasons, discarding him because of his wounds. Frederick James's attempt to be accepted ended in ignominy in Wiseman's Ferry, and he was made an outcast. Bedevilled by migraine, perhaps clinically depressed and also showing signs of paranoia in later life, all three had been greatly disappointed by others. Solitude was perhaps the only way in which they could cope.

Frederick Humphrey James was found dead in his hermitage on 25 June 1899 by the grocer delivering the weekly supplies. Three days later, a coroner's jury, sitting at McGrath's Hill, pronounced that Frederick Whirlpool VC had died of heart failure 'on or about the 24th June'.

On 29 June, Frederick Whirlpool VC was buried in a pauper's grave in the Presbyterian Cemetery, Windsor. He was a forgotten man, albeit of his own choosing, and at the graveside there was no military presence, recognition or remembrance of his gallant service in India. His Victoria Cross came into the possession of Denys Cross, who made a study of his life; and on his death, his widow Emily presented it to the Australian War Memorial, Canberra, where it can be seen today.

George Hinckley VC
(1819–1904)

The only surviving likeness of George Hinckley VC was made in 1869, probably on the occasion of his fiftieth birthday. In the style of the day, he is looking away from the camera, staring off into the middle distance, his features registered in a resolute cast. The print gives the impression of a comfortable, middle-aged gent of the mid-Victorian era, a teacher, a preacher, a small businessman, perhaps, and there is an avuncular hint to the grizzled beard and receding hairline. But beneath the glossy surface was a man of little education or finesse, a rugged warrior, a rough and ready tar whose second home was the brig. For almost a quarter of a century, he served before the mast with the Royal Navy, from Africa to the Antipodes, scorched and weather-beaten by the harsh sun and driving winds and rain. He enjoyed more than his fair share of rum and fun on shore, cocked a snook at authority and defied the odds to win the Victoria Cross.

The camera never lies, however. And it is in the eyes that the soul of this rip-roaring old seadog can be glimpsed. They are the windows to another, gentler side to the man, one only recently brought to light. At the age of 50, and still robust, raucous and raring to go, George Hinckley took voluntary retirement from the navy; and for the next twenty years, his sole concern was his three children, two of whom were handicapped.

He was 46 when he married. His bride was Jane Oliver, a farmer's daughter from the Lizard, Cornwall. They made their vows in Devonport in the summer of 1865. But, one or both of them carried a hereditary disorder. Their first home was in Garden Street, Morice Town, where a daughter, Jane Frances, was born in September the following year. She was not disadvantaged; but her sister, Rosina Frances, born in December 1867, and her brother George Richard, born in March 1869, were. In the terminology of the day, they were 'deaf and dumb' from birth.

George Hinckley quit the navy on 1 June 1869. Moving his family to a larger home in St John Street, he set a new course for himself. He did not seek employment, supporting himself with his naval and Victoria Cross pensions, and devoted all his time and energies to the welfare and happiness of his children. The family was necessarily close-knit, insular even: the term 'dumb' had pejorative connotations, then as now, of idiocy and stupidity, and the

Hinckleys would not permit Rosina and George Richard to suffer the imprudence of ignorance by scorn, ridicule or pity. The children were taught at home in their early years and a rudimentary signing for communication, and later lip-reading, evolved within the family.

For George Hinckley, now confined as a landlubber to home and the care of three young children, a greater contrast to his former life, spent solely in the company of men at sea, could not be found. But, supported and encouraged by his wife, he persisted in his endeavour to ensure his offspring would lead the best lives possible. Together, they succeeded, with a little outside help.

In 1826, the good burghers of Exeter had founded a local school for the deaf, which soon grew in both size and reputation to accommodate children from a much wider catchment area, including Devonport, fifty miles away. By 1860, it had relocated to premises in a large villa close to St Leonard's Church, under the stewardship of John Hobbah. Rosina and George Richard were given places at the institution in 1877; and boarded there for several years, coming home during the school holidays.

At St Leonard's, they learnt a standard signing language, which in turn they taught to their parents and sister, and received a good education and training in a variety of trades, though the development of vocal skills was not considered a priority. When their school days were over, Rosina and George Richard lived with their parents again, and their father guided them both into apprenticeships. Rosina was indentured as a milliner, and George Richard as a tailor, trades they plied successfully in Morice Town.

George Richard worked all his life in the town, living with his parents, and supporting them in their old age. He did not marry, and survived his father by ten years, passing away in September 1914 at the age of 45. Both girls married and brought up families. Jane Frances's husband was John Little, a sailor; they resided in St Sevan Road, Devonport, where they had one child, a son Arthur. Rosina worked for several years as milliner before marrying John Samuel Lethbridge, in October 1892. John was deaf and had been educated at St Leonard's also, and he was a boot riveter and finisher by trade. The couple lived in Holdsworth Street, Devonport, and had four children, George, Percy, William and Rosina. Only George escaped the family affliction.

George Hinckley VC lived to the ripe old age of 85 and died at his home in Plymouth, on 31 December 1904, a credit to his family as they were to him. He was born in Liverpool on 22 June 1819. It is thought his father was a butcher in the city, but nothing for definite is known of George until he emerged into the spotlight at the age of 23. There are no records of the name Hinckley, or variations of it, such as Hinkly, Hinkley, Henckley, Inckley, in the first National Census of the city, or Merseyside, for that matter. The family may have been absent temporarily from the city during the census; or, more than likely, had moved away permanently before it was taken, since the name Hinckley is not recorded in subsequent censuses. Another possibility is that

Hinckley's parents were not from the area, but were passing through or living temporarily in Liverpool when George was born, and returned later to their home town.

The first official record of George Hinckley was documented on 22 February 1842 when he joined the Royal Navy. Giving his age as 21, he was in fact almost 23 years of age, and he was assigned a berth aboard HMS *Tortoise* with the rating of able seaman. The vessel had been working as a store ship since 1840 at Chatham in Kent. It was a fifth rate frigate, an ex-East Indiaman, the *Sir Edward Hughes*, of approximately 1,000 tons with thirty-eight guns, commissioned into the navy in 1807. The vessel was seaworthy and in 1842 it was manifested to carry supplies to the naval station at Hobart, Tasmania. But its main task was to carry back Kauri timber from the forests of North Island, New Zealand, to the naval shipyards of Britain: the Kauri conifer grows tall and straight and was highly valued for masts and spars.

Prior to 1853, sailors could transfer between the Royal and Merchant Navy and take their rating with them. Since George Hinckley's initial Royal Navy rating was able seaman, he must have been an experienced sailor able to hand, reef and steer – that is, he had been taught and trained to handle sails and rope, reef sails and steer a vessel by compass. Born in Liverpool, George Hinckley first put to sea with the Merchant Navy, probably as a cabin boy as young as 10 years old. He swapped the more relaxed life of the merchant marine for the rigid discipline aboard a Royal Navy vessel, where pay was four times less for an able seaman. But he was guaranteed his pay, the berth was all found with good rations and there was always the added bonus of prize money.

In the wake of the Spithead mutiny of 1797, wages in the Royal Navy were fixed and paid regularly, food rations were dictated by decree and shore leave was permitted. On the round trip to the Antipodes, which took eighteen months, George Hinckley's daily fare was four ounces of salt pork or beef, eight ounces of fresh vegetables, a gallon of beer, a few ounces each of tea, sugar and cocoa, and sixteen ounces of bread in the form of ship's biscuit, hard tack, which had to be soaked in water to make it edible. The beer in those days did not travel well, and its supply was usually exhausted quickly: a daily pint of wine or half a pint of rum was substituted. And he would have had shore leave with his shipmates in Rio and Cape Town and dabbled in the easy delights on offer. Passing with flying colours the lengthy and gruelling introduction to the Royal Navy, being noted as an industrious and diligent sailor, George Hinckley was rewarded in the autumn of 1848, chosen from a long list of volunteers to man a new type of warship, HMS *Penelope*.

The first steam-powered warship commissioned by the Royal Navy was HMS *Rattler*, launched in the spring of 1843. HMS *Penelope*, a fifth rate frigate of 1,100 tons, with forty-two guns, was the first British naval vessel converted from sail to steam power. With the addition of boilers and giant paddles, she became a paddle sloop of 1,600 tons with twelve guns; and, following trials in the summer of 1843, she took to sea in December with able seaman George Hinckley on board. Reefing and unfurling sails above decks was now supplemented by hot laborious work below, in the scalding, dusty and sweaty environment of the fire and engine rooms, feeding the hungry boilers, monitoring pressure gauges and cleaning and oiling shafts.

The work was hard but George Hinckley was not a man to duck a challenge. He served two years on HMS *Penelope* learning new skills, and spent the next seven years applying them on other steam-powered sloops and frigates, HMS *Vixen*, HMS *Spartan* and HMS *Growler*, on station with the Channel fleet, and in the Mediterranean and the Atlantic. But, depite his experience, he never rose in rating above able seaman. Several confinements to the brig notwithstanding, he could not be considered for promotion because the navy was in the doldrums.

Britain ruled the waves after the Battle of Trafalgar in 1805; but for more than sixty years, between 1850 and 1914, no ship-to-ship actions were fought by the Royal Navy. Naval operations were confined to police duties, to supporting the army, as in the Crimea, and to improving diplomatic relations through the judicious bombardments of land-based targets. Recruitment was curtailed and serving tars had to wait for dead men's shoes to gain a promotion. The men grumbled, and the lack of prize money only added to the discord. But, when George Hinckley took berth on the sailing sloop, HMS *Linnet*, under Commander Henry Need, in October 1852, his prospects both for promotion and prize money were suddenly improved. And, perhaps without realizing as such, he would follow, albeit very lightly, in the footsteps of a great Liverpudlian, the poet and reformer William Roscoe.

The growth and wealth of Liverpool during the eighteenth century was founded on the lucrative African slave trade. Vessels from the port sailed to West Africa, laden with manufactured goods and textiles, which were exchanged and bartered for men and women kidnapped from the interior of the continent. The abductées were shipped across the Atlantic to the New World in the most inhuman conditions imaginable and sold into slavery for hard cash. The money purchased molasses, rum, tobacco and cotton, which the same vessels hauled back to Liverpool. The triangular trade produced fat gains for the owners, investors and seamen alike, and created two of London's great banking houses, Barclays and Lloyds. William Wilberforce is rightly reknowned for leading the abolitionist movement in Parliament, but it was Roscoe who faced the wrath of the greedy purveyors of human flesh, bearding them in their offices, clubs and coffee houses to demand an end to the trade.

Britain abolished slavery in 1807, but the evil trade continued to flourish; and the colony of Sierra Leone became the centre of the illicit traffic. To police and enforce the slavery ban, the West African Squadron of the Royal Navy patrolled the coast of Sierra Leone and hunted down the slave ships, the 'blackbirds'. A vessel intercepted on the high seas and found carrying a human cargo was seized as a prize by the Royal Navy and taken in to the colony's capital, Freetown. There, the victims were released and their erstwhile captors imprisoned. The 'blackbird' was auctioned to the highest bidder, and the proceeds were divided between the government and the British crew. HMS *Linnet* joined the squadron in 1852, with a complement of eighty, consisting of fifty-six officers and men, eleven Royal Marines, ship-based soldiers, and thirteen boys.

Even though he was continuing the work of William Roscoe, and opportunities for promotion and prize money were dangled before his eyes, George Hinckley, like many a sailor, would have greeted duty off Africa with dread. Sierre Leone was an unforgiving and poisonous posting: food and water rapidly spoilt in the tropical heat, and their supply was always problematic. Dysentery, cholera and yellow fever were rampant; and contact with the locals and shore leave were forbidden. On station for four years, HMS *Linnet* lost eleven of her crew to disease.

On 30 April 1854, off Kabenda on the northern coast of Sierre Leone, the lookout on HMS *Linnet* spied the slaver *Mellidon* breaking out into the Atlantic with a human cargo. The *Linnet*'s crew were quickly to action stations to give chase, and the 'blackbird' was overhauled and arrested by a shot across her bow. The boarding party and prize crew from the *Linnet* brought the slaver to Freetown. It was George Hinckley's first capture, and what should have been his first share of prize money. Unfortunately, the arbitration court sitting at Freetown the following month ruled the seizure illegal, and the *Mellidon* was returned to its owners. George Hinckley's purse remained empty.

The arrest of the *Mellidon* was the one and only highlight of George Hinckley's years on station in Africa. However, there was a consolation prize: on his return to England in January 1856, he was transferred to HMS *Partridge*, and at the age of 37 was given his first promotion in the Royal Navy, to the rank of quartermaster. Previously, his conduct had been described as 'fair, good, very good' and, ominously, as 'not given', naval shorthand for disreputable behaviour; and he had seen the inside of the brig several times. Now a man of some authority on and below deck, he was expected to set a good example to those in his charge and curb his wayward tendencies. But he fell from grace after only six months aboard HMS *Partridge*.

It is alleged on this occasion he transgressed against the civil rather than the naval authorities, which would not agree to time in the brig as punishment; and he was sentenced to three years in a civilian gaol for assault and affray. There is some documentary evidence to support this tale: from July 1856 until October 1859 his naval record is a blank, with no explanation other than that for the period in question he was not a member of Her Majesty's Royal Navy, and the lost years did not contribute towards total time served for pension calculations. Other explanations for the absence have been mooted, but the allegation may be true: he did in fact go to prison, but the affray was an affair of honour, naval honour.

In October 1859, he was reinstated in the Royal Navy on full pay with his old rank of quartermaster. This is highly suggestive, particularly at a time when the Admiralty had reduced naval recruitment to a minimum while Pax Britannica prevailed. It lends weight to the notion that his absence was not frowned upon by his superiors, perhaps had even been approved of, since he was welcomed back as a long lost son. His new berth was with the gunboat HMS *Snap*, commanded by Lieutenant Commander William Butler.

HMS *Snap*, together with HMS *Bouncer*, was escorted to China by the corvette HMS *Encounter*, and took up station in the South China Sea. On arrival on 28 May 1860 Hinckley was immediately transferred to HMS *Sphinx*, under the command of Commander George Fiott Day. He was about to embark, despite one or two minor hiccups, on the greatest adventure of his life: it was as a member of the naval brigade from this vessel that George Hinckley won his Victoria Cross.

The naval brigades were fighting detachments from British warships, naval officers and ratings, and Royal Marines, which were landed ashore to undertake naval duties or to support the army in a wide variety of campaigns. The blue-jackets received regular training in all the techniques of sea and land warfare at the gunnery school in Portsmouth, HMS *Excellent*. The brigades were first deployed in 1824 at the beginning of the Burma Wars, and they fought in all the major wars and campaigns throughout the Victorian era, and in the First World War as part of the Royal Naval Division, until they were disbanded finally in 1920. Their contribution on land to the defence of the British Empire is not as well documented as the exploits of the fighting men at sea, but the brigades rendered great service on land during their ninety-six years of existence.

HMS *Sphinx* was a first class paddle sloop of 1,000 tons and six guns, launched at Woolwich on 17 February 1846. She served with the Indian Squadron for a number of years and saw action during the Second Burmese War in 1852; and two years later she was in the Black Sea taking part in the naval bombardments of Sebastopol. From the Crimea she was posted to the Chinese Squadron, tasked with maintaining British trade routes to and from China and suppressing smuggling and piracy on the high seas.

George Hinckley took time to settle in on board HMS *Sphinx*: within five months of taking his berth he had been reduced in rank to able seaman; and eight months later in Hong Kong, having allowed his fists to do the talking, he was obliged to spend 335 days in the brig. But this was his final confinement; and his return to active duty under Commander Day in May 1862 coincided with the resurgence in the activities of the Taiping rebels.

The Taiping Rebellion, the bloodiest civil war in history, erupted in 1851, when the messianic Hong Xiuquan, claiming to be the younger brother of Jesus

Christ, rose up against the Qing Government of China. Within a very short time, with sword and sermon, Hong gained control of the greater part of southern and central China. The tide was turned when the ruling powers employed a mercenary force led by the American soldier of fortune Frederick Townsend Ward. The 'Ever Victorious Army', as it was known, which one day would be led by Charles 'Chinese' Gordon of Khartoum fame, routed the rebels; and by 1860, the revolt petered out. But, the following year, Hong returned to the battlefield.

From the fortified town of Fung-wha, the rebels began to threaten the city of Shanghai, eighty-five miles to the north, one of the main centres of European power and authority in the country. At the beginning of October 1862, the Ever Victorious Army, approximately 3,000-strong, moved on Fung-wha, supported by 500 men of a French-Chinese naval force. In addition, on the night of Saturday, 8 October, HMS *Encounter*, *Flamer*, *Hardy* and *Sphinx* landed a naval brigade of 300 men on the coast, thirty miles west of Fung-wha. At the age of 43, George Hinckley was to receive his baptism of fire.

On a moonless night and amid a torrential downpour, the naval brigade marched the thirty miles to Fung-wha over terrain like a moonscape, along roads no better than animal trails and churned to a squelching mud in the heavy rain. Just before dawn, sodden and exhausted, the men reached the town and took up position in front of the east gate. After checking their powder, the seamen ate a quick breakfast of hard tack and salt pork while the artillery of the Ever Victorious Army bombarded the walls of the town. Then, just before eight o'clock, every man was issued a tot of rum and then came into line for the assault on the east gate.

The rebels were hardened fighters. They had been at war for more than ten years and were well armed and disciplined. Their weaponry equalled that of their opponents and they knew how to utilize it to the best advantage. Among their arsenal were the gingall and the stinkpot. The gingall was a large musket of Asian origin which was fired either from a fixed rest or from a mount on a mobile carriage. It could deliver a fearsome and devastating blast of shot at close quarters. The stinkpot or stinkball, which had been used by European navies in ship-to-ship encounters for many years, was a combustible jar of resin, gunpowder and sulphur, ignited by fuse, which was hurled among the enemy to produce a stinking, suffocating and choking sulphurous smoke, which blinded and disorientated men, and caused confusion and panic when breathing became impaired.

A shrill blast from a whistle sent the naval brigade on its way. Screeching at the tops of their lungs, the tars charged the gate. A heavy grey cloud billowed from the walls of the town, presaging a deadly hail, and rapidly broke over their heads: a veritable tornado of musketry and grapeshot erupted and whirled through the ranks, slicing and scything down the men in groups. The seamen came on bravely and gained the lee of the gate from where they returned fire as best they could. But the enemy's firepower was overwhelming: musket fire rained down from above, while on the ground, the dense clouds of smoke from the stinkpots brought men choking to their knees, rendering them incapable of further fight; and as the ranks were thinned with no gain of a foothold or breach in the gate and adjacent walls, the order came through to fall back out of range. Gasping and choking for breath, George Hinckley and his mates picked up their wounded and staggered back to a joss-house, approximately 150 yards from the gate. There, under cover, they took stock.

The head count revealed that Lieutenant Croker, second in command to Commander Day, was missing. It was not until a freshening breeze began to disperse the smog that he was located, lying wounded in front of the east gate. George Hinckley, certainly not the youngest or the fittest among the survivors, stepped forward immediately and volunteered to rescue him. He was un-scathed from the assault but suffering, like his comrades, from the after-effects of the sulphurous stinkpot smoke. He went out alone to bring in Lieutenant Croker.

The remaining wisps of the dreadful smoke, which hung like giant cobwebs in front of the gate, now came to his aid, partially masking his movements from the enemy. He crawled and scrambled across the open terrain, utilizing what little cover there was, and paused briefly to gather his strength for the final, perilous dash to the gate through the hell of musket and gingall fire. Reaching the wounded officer, he lifted him onto his back, and nimbly beat a hasty retreat, dodging and weaving his way to the safety of the joss-house.

George Hinckley must have felt very lucky on that Sunday morning, that nothing could harm him and God was on his side. He ran the gauntlet again. After handing over Lieutenant Croker to the medical officer, he reported seeing a second, wounded man lying close to where he had found Croker. With barely a pause, he set off once more into the jaws of death, dashing along the hazardous pathway to bring in the injured man. Within minutes he was back, exhausted, gasping for breath and close to collapse. But, he carried on his shoulders the wounded body of Captain Bremen of the Ever Victorious Army.

For gallantry in the face of the enemy, able seaman George Hinckley was awarded the Victoria Cross. His citation reads:

George Hinckley, Able Seaman, of her Majesty's Ship *Sphinx*. For volun-teering while under the east gate of the city of Fung-wha, to carry to a Joss-house one hundred and fifty yards distant under a heavy and continuous fire of musketry, gingalls and stink-pots, Mr Coker, Master's Assistant of the *Sphinx*, who had been wounded in the advance to the gate, in which object Hinckley succeeded. On his return to the gate under a similar fire he again volunteered, and succeeded in carrying to the Joss-house Mr Bremen, an officer of Ward's forces, who had also been wounded in the advance on the gate, and he again returned to his post under the gate.

Both Croker and Bremen survived their wounds and had the unselfish courage of George Hinckley to thank. It took a further two days of desperate fighting before Fung-wha fell; and with the town's capitulation and the capture of its garrison, the rebellion in that part of China was over; and the inhabitants of Shanghai could sleep soundly in their beds.

George Hinckley's award was gazetted on 6 February 1863; and when news reached his squadron in the China Seas, he was immediately promoted again to quartermaster. It is not known from whose hand he received the honour, or where the investiture took place. He was the only man to win the Victoria Cross between August 1860 and September 1863, and it is doubtful whether a special ceremony was arranged for this single award. More than likely, as in the case of Joseph Prosser VC, the medal and a copy of the citation were sent to the commanding officer of his squadron in Hong Kong, where the award was made.

George Hinckley VC did not see active service again. He returned to England in July 1863, to a shore posting of four months with HMS *Indus*, a guard ship at Devonport. A second shore posting at Devonport with HMS *Royalist* followed. Misfortune struck, however, while he attended the funeral of a shipmate in November 1863: during the rites, his Victoria Cross, which he was wearing probably for the first time, disappeared from his breast, lost or stolen. He received a replacement medal, for which he was charged twenty-four shillings, but he was bereft by the loss. The original medal never came to light and its location today is unknown.

The following year, he was posted to the West Indies for fifteen months on board HMS *Aboukir* and HMS *Shannon*, not the ideal station for a man with a predeliction for the grog. However, since his award, he was a reformed character and avoided trouble, at least to the extent that he became a stranger to the inside of a brig. He came home in April 1865 to prepare for his nuptials with Jane Oliver, and they married not long after he took berth on HMS *Scorpion*, a vessel from his home port of Liverpool.

He was several months on sea trials with HMS *Scorpion*, a ship unlike any in which he had served, the vessel being an iron-hulled turret ship of 2,750 tons which the British had seized from the Confederate Navy in 1863 at the height of the American Civil War. The keel had been laid in Birkenhead at the John Laird, later Cammell Laird, shipyard, the previous year, behind the fiction that she was the Egyptian warship *El Tousson*. The men responsible for the deception were the Confederate agents James Dunwoody Bulloch and John Low, close friends of the Liverpool merchant Henry Lafone, whose son would one day win the Victoria Cross. The iron ship was destined to become CSS *North Carolina*, but the Union government caught wind of the project and diplomatically forced the British authorities to intervene and confiscate the vessel.

From the *Scorpion*, he was returned to land-based duties in January 1866 with HMS *Britannia*, a cadet training ship at Dartmouth. Its master, Captain Jack Corbett, described Hinckley's character as 'very good', and reported that, like his cadets, he was honoured to serve with him. It was not Hinckley's intention to see out his days training cadets at Dartmouth, though by all accounts he enjoyed the experience, because he continued to look for placements that would take him back to sea.

But the birth of his disabled daughter Rosina Frances in 1867 prompted his immediate return home to his wife and family. There was little he could do at the time, except stay close; and the naval authorities, made aware of the problem, alleviated his situation and allowed him to live at home while he worked a berth on board HMS *Indus* again. The move meant demotion to able seaman because the vessel already had its full complement of quartermasters. And, following the birth of George Richard he applied for retirement and took his pension.

So it was as an able seaman, the rank he held on his first joining, that George Hinckley VC retired from the Royal Navy at the age of 50. He had given twenty-three years to the navy, twenty-six years if that unexplained absence of three years is included. He settled down in his small, rented house in St John Street with his wife and three children and his memories. He husbanded his pension and educated his family, and, after the girls left home to marry, he took his wife and son to 44 North Street, Plymouth, where he died on Saturday, 31 December 1904.

George Hinckley VC is buried in Ford Park Cemetery in Plymouth. Lying with him are his son and his wife, Jane, who passed away on 13 July 1917 at the age of 88. His replica Victoria Cross is in private hands.

Paul Aloysius Kenna VC
(1862–1915)

A unique sporting record was set in 1912 when equestrian sport was first introduced to the Olympic Games at Stockholm: two members of Great Britain's squad were holders of the Victoria Cross. Colonel Paul Aloysius Kenna VC captained the team of Lieutenant Brian Lawrence VC, Lieutenant E. Radcliffe-Nash and Lieutenant H.S. Scott. The team performed well without winning any medals, but Paul Kenna VC further enhanced his worldwide reputation as the finest horseman of the era.

The first event of the equestrian programme was a combined team and individual contest, subdivided into five trials, the first of which was a long-distance ride of thirty-three miles, to be completed within a time limit of four hours. This gruelling marathon took place on a blistering hot day, and many riders withdrew, suffering from heat exhaustion. It speaks highly of Paul Kenna VC, of his grit and tenacity, of his mental and physical toughness, of his great skill with a horse and its training, that at the age of 50, in the sweltering cauldron that knocked out younger competitors, he completed the course within the time limit; and that after the second and third trials, the cross-country ride of three miles and the steeplechase, he was in sixth place in the individual competition. Had the sport been introduced, as enthusiasts had hoped, in 1908, to the London Olympics, Paul Kenna, four years younger, undoubtedly would have won an Olympic gold medal to complement his Victoria Cross.

With a fine eye, good hands and a natural seat, Paul Kenna was the consummate horseman. Described as a 'dark-haired, dark-eyed, slightly-built Irishman', a fraction under 5 feet 6 inches tall, he sported a bushy, handle-bar moustache and a monocle; and, with a wiry frame and ramrod-straight back filling his military uniform, he was the very epitome of the dashing cavalryman. Between 1905 and the beginning of the First World War, he captained Great Britain many times on the equestrian field and in the show ring, in England, Europe and the United States. Individually, he won the King's Cup at the International Horse Show at Olympia in 1913, and rode several winners on the flat and 'over the sticks' at Punchestown and Sandown Park racecourses. 'It was a sheer delight to watch him ... in competition with the best horsemen. ... He was certainly first, but also easily first.'

His skills were honed during seven years' service in India as a young lieutenant with the 21st Hussars, on the polo field, in gymkhanas and hunting and chasing across the countryside; and for three consecutive seasons he was the leading rider on the sub-continent, a feat never achieved before or since. But it was in County Durham, riding through lush, green fields soaked in dew and leaping over hedgerows of hawthorn, ash and elder, that his talents as a rider were first manifest; and assiduously he schooled them there for four years at the expense of the military career he had set his heart on after leaving school.

Paul Aloysius Kenna, third son of James 'Jas' Kenna and Julia Kearney, was born on 16 August 1862 at 87 Everton Road, Liverpool. Jas was a native of Enfield, in the south of County Meath, and it is believed he crossed to Liverpool in the 1850s when, like the Cullen brothers of Dublin, he saw the enormous potential of importing Irish dairy produce for the burgeoning market of immigrants who had settled in the city in the wake of the great famine. With his friend Thomas Maher he traded in cattle as Maher and Kenna, and dabbled also in land speculation.

Julia Kearney hailed from Moynalty, north-west Meath, not far from the ancient town and monastery of Kells. Her two elder brothers, Matthew and Francis, established themselves in the north-east of England with their uncle the Reverend Phillip Kearney, who was parish priest of St Mary's Church, in Bridge Street, Sunderland. Matthew prospered as a wine merchant and landowner in Lanchester, County Durham, and became Deputy Lieutenant of the county in 1867 and High Sheriff twelve years later. After the death of her parents, Julia, a very pious woman, lived with Francis, who was parish priest of St Cuthbert's, Lanchester, until she married Jas Kenna in 1854.

Jas and Julia Kenna were blessed with five sons, James, Patrick, Paul, Thomas and Joseph, and two daughters, Ann and Margaret. The Kennas were a devout, church-going family, very much involved in charitable works for the poor and destitute of the city; and Paul, from an early age, was noted for his charity and piety. Jas's land speculation took him to Anfield, and he invested in the prestigious housing development of Oakfield, in Breckfield Road, acquiring one of the larger properties, the Oaks, where young Paul grew up among a swarm of relatives and servants.

Like his brothers James and Patrick, he attended St Francis Xavier's School in Salisbury Street, but Patrick died in 1871 at the age of 11. The death deeply affected the family, Jas in particular, and he never came to terms with the loss. The Oaks must have carried too many painful reminders for him: he uprooted to a new residence, 22 Richmond Terrace, Everton, the following year. He died not long afterwards, some say of a broken heart, during a business trip to France in December 1873.

After the death of her husband, Julia Kenna sold up his interests in Maher and Kenna and removed the children to Ramsgate, Kent, where the Kenna boys were boarded and educated at the very select, private school attached to St Augustine's Abbey. When their school days were over, Julia set up home with her two daughters in Holland Road, London, where she died in 1888.

At the age of 17, Paul Kenna entered Stonyhurst College, the independent Roman Catholic School in the Ribble Valley. He spent two years at the school under the tutelage of the Reverend William Eyre, and was regarded as a 'cheery and vigorous boy, abounding with energy, and a strenuous player of all games'. The passion of commitment he took from his father; his mother's legacy was a piety that underlined all aspects of his life. It was at Stonyhurst that he opted for a military career; and in anticipation, he grew a bushy, drooping moustache, which no self-respecting soldier would have been without. Leaving school in the summer of 1881, he went to live temporarily with his uncle Matthew at Ford Hall, Lanchester, to mull over his choice of regiment.

His equine passion intervened, however, and overrode his military ambition, which he satisfied with a commission in the part-time, local militia of the 4th Durham Light Infantry, which met for training two or three times a year. But, pressed by his uncle, he picked up the military thread, and in September 1885 entered the Royal Military College, Sandhurst, as a Gentleman Cadet. The following year, he was commissioned as a Second Lieutenant in 2nd Battalion, West Indian Regiment, and was posted to Jamaica and later Sierra Leone. In 1888, he was gazetted as a lieutenant in a cavalry regiment, 21st Hussars, where he knew his horsemanship would find a proper home. Joining the regiment in India the following year, he served in Bangalore, Hyderabad and Secunderabad, and set the sub-continent alight with his wonderful horsemanship. His days there, he was later to report, were some of the happiest of his life; and his future in uniform seemed secured. In 1895, he was promoted to captain.

But in the summer of 1896, a depressed and disconsolate Paul Kenna sailed from Calcutta, bound for Africa, where he would represent his country for the first time on the battlefield. His close friends even feared his suicide. On the long voyage across the Indian Ocean, he nursed a broken heart and the memory of a loving wife, Lady Cecilia Josephine Bertie. The couple had met in Hyderabad, and after a courtship of eighteen months married on 18 July 1895 at St Mary's Church in Ootacamund, the queen of Indian hill stations nestled in the Nilgri Hills.

Cecilia's death from typhoid fever three months later in October pushed Paul Kenna into a suicidal depression which was to persist for two years. Suicide was not an option open to him: his strong religious upbringing and his faith, which sustained him throughout his life, barred that path, though fellow officers would say later the complete indifference to his own safety he showed on the battlefield was driven by the fervent desire, the unspoken wish, to be reunited in death with his wife.

In Egypt, a miserable and detached Paul Kenna barely went through the motions in preparation for war. The regiment was re-equipped as a lancer formation and redesignated 21st (Empress of India) Lancers, and was attached as the only regular British cavalry unit to Major General Sir Horatio Kitchener's Nile Expeditionary Force of 26,000 British, Egyptian and Sudanese troops. Kitchener was under orders to punish and mete out revenge to the Ansar, the followers of the Mahdi, the chosen one, responsible for the death in Khartoum of General Charles 'Chinese' Gordon in 1885. The Mahdi had died of typhus fever several months after Gordon's demise, and his successor Khalifa Abdalli had established the capital of the Mahdiyya, the Mahdist state, at Omdurman, a mud-brick town four miles north of the ruined city of Khartoum.

From the oasis of Wadi Halfa in the north of Sudan, through the fastness of the Nubian Desert, to the plain of Omdurman in the south, Kitchener's men trekked and trundled and gave battle to the Ansar, driving them back. In his first taste of battle, which occurred at Dunqula, birthplace of the Mahdi, Kenna was reckless and foolhardy during the rout of the Khalifa's men; and was more so at Abu Hamed, and later in the encounter at the River Atbarah, where Donald Farmer stood in the ranks. But, during the final, climactic march of the campaign, his friends perceived a change in him: no longer distracted, he was planning ahead, asking advice; and he appeared to anticipate the showdown with relish.

Faced by the relentless advance of Kitchener's juggernaut, the Khalifa ordered his men to fall back on Omdurman, to them a sacred place, for it held the tomb of the Mahdi. Here, the Ansar would stand and fight to the death. In the last week of August 1898, the avenging army invested the outskirts of Omdurman and readied to oblige. The infantry dug in on the banks of the Nile, behind a *zaribah*, a fortified fence and trench system, facing the town across an open plain, which was bordered by the Kerreri Hills on the right flank and Surgham Hill on the left. Across the rocky scrubland of the plain and over the bare hills, Paul Kenna led his troop on patrol, watching and waiting for the enemy; and on the night of 1 September, the army slept fully armed and accoutred, knowing the battle was nigh. Before the sun rose the next day, cavalry patrols from 21st Lancers scouted the ridge at Surgham Hill and observed the Ansar massing.

At dawn on Friday 2 September 1898, the infantry stood ready with fixed bayonets, supported by Colonel Charles Long's guns and the cavalry mustered on the left flank. Opposing were 40,000 warriors, armed with swords, flintlocks, clubs and spears, who shuffled and stamped their feet to the beat of war drums, and waved the black and green banners and flags of the Khalifa. And when the huge, white dome of the Mahdi's tomb appeared through the desert haze, the zealous Ansar charged.

Fire was opened with Long's cannons, which inflicted appalling casualties, and as the Ansar came on, they fell within range of the Maxim machine guns, which quickly added to the carnage. The battlefield was enveloped in a dense cloud of choking dust and smoke, and amid the roars and clatter of men and machines, the Ansar assailed the *zaribah*, frantically clambering over the bodies of the dead to join with the infantry. But they were remorselessly driven back, and after two hours of fighting, they broke and fell back on Omdurman.

Rather than oblige the enemy in hand-to-hand combat in the narrow streets and alleyways of the town, Kitchener ordered his cavalry to cut off the fleeing Ansar and drive them into the desert. The 21st scrambled to their horses. Colonel Martin led his regiment forward at a trot to the ridge in front of Surgham Hill and sent out several small patrols to reconnoitre ahead. The 21st came on slowly, 'a great square block of ungainly brown figures and little horses, hung on over with water-bottles, saddle-bags, picketing-gear, tins of bully-beef, all jolting and jangling together, the polish of peace gone, soldiers without glitter, horsemen without grace.'

From the ridge, Colonel Martin observed scores of Ansar directly ahead, but, in the distance, the bulk of the enemy was falling back to the city. Patrols reported that beyond Surgham Hill, between the 21st and the main body of the enemy, a *khor*, a dried-up river bed, was infested with approximately 700 stragglers. Colonel Martin sent a heliograph message to Kitchener asking for further orders. But while the Lancers idled on the ridge waiting for a reply, unnoticed the *khor* was reinforced with fresh blood from the reserve. And by the time Kitchener's reply, 'advance against the main body', was flashed across the desert, the Ansar had crowded twelve deep into the winding ditch and lay ready to ambush the cavalry.

The Lancers descended the ridge and advanced at a walk across the plain in the face of desultory musket fire from the retreating enemy. Colonel Martin ordered the bugler to sound 'right wheel into line'; and to its shrill blasts, the sixteen troops of the four squadrons swung round and locked up into a long, galloping line, sights firmly fixed on the bulk of the Ansar beyond the *khor*. The last regimental charge of the British Army against a standing enemy was about to begin.

The gallop broke into a charge. The troopers buried their chins in their chests, leading with their helmets, as the tempo of the enemy musketry increased. But as they neared the crease in the ground where ran the *khor*, they were met by a baying roar; and 3,000 Ansar rose to their feet to meet the 400 men of the Lancers. No thought was given to checking the charge as the trap was sprung: each rider urged on his mount, hoping to gain sufficient momentum to drive through the solid press of men and gain the safety of the far bank.

With a mighty roar the Lancers plunged into the *khor*, crashing into their foe at full tilt. The shock of the impact was stunning: 'for perhaps ten wonderful seconds no man heeded his enemy. Terrified horses wedged into the crowd;

bruised and shaken men, sprawling in heaps, struggled, dazed and stupid, to their feet, panted, and looked about them.' Captain Kenna's B Squadron collided with the enemy where they were most densely packed.

The impetus of the charge carried the Lancers across the *khor*, but on the steep incline of the opposite bank it slowed and was brought to a standstill by the press of bodies. Now the killing began. As the troopers desperately spurred on their scrambling mounts, the frantic Ansar lunged at them from all sides: swords and knives flashed in the sun and slashed and hacked at men and horses, at reins and leathers; muskets and pistols were discharged at point-blank range; spears jabbed wildly against lances and into yielding flesh; and clubs and musket butts smashed limbs and cracked skulls.

Major Crole-Wyndham, second-in-command of the regiment, had his horse shot from beneath him, killed by a musket shot. He crashed to the ground, but managed to roll clear, only to be immediately surrounded by the enemy. Captain Paul Kenna, coming up behind, barged through the massing warriors to his side, and, fending them off with his pistol, took up the major behind the saddle and battled his way out of the *khor*. But, Kenna's mount plunged and reared under the unaccustomed weight and threw both men. Undeterred, Kenna captured his mount and was quickly back in the saddle, but he had lost sight of the major and went in search of him.

Meanwhile, Lieutenant Raymond de Montmorency, having safely crossed the *khor*, now returned in search of his troop sergeant who had been unhorsed in the charge. He could not find him immediately and pushed on deeper into the river bed, skirting bands of Ansar looting the dead. Among a pile of bodies, he recognized that of Second Lieutenant Grenfell. Unsure of whether Grenfell was alive or dead, he dismounted, and, seeing Captain Kenna and Corporal Swarbrick, both of whom had returned to bring out the wounded, he called on them to help. The three men tried to lift up Grenfell on to de Montmorency's saddle, but the horse shied and galloped off. Kenna and Swarbrick went in pursuit of the animal while de Montmorency stood guard over Grenfell. But he had been spotted by the prowling enemy.

When the two men returned with the mount, a group of Ansar launched an attack, firing off muskets and throwing spears. Despite being under fire, the three Lancers again attempted to lift the body, but it was too heavy. Grenfell, who was dead, was abandoned, and the men had to fight their way back through the clutches of the raging foe to their own mounts and out of the *khor* before dashing off to safety.

For bravery in the face of the enemy, Captain Paul Aloysius Kenna was awarded the Victoria Cross. His citation reads:

Paul Aloysius Kenna, Captain, 21st Lancers. At the battle of Omdurman, on the 2nd September 1898, Captain P.A. Kenna assisted Major Crole-Wyndham, of the same regiment, by taking him on his horse, behind the saddle (Major Wyndham's horse having been killed in the charge), thus enabling him to reach a place of safety; and after the charge of the 21st Lancers, Captain Kenna returned to assist Lieutenant de Montmorency, who was endeavouring to recover the body of Lieutenant R.G. Grenfell.

Total casualties among Kitchener's men at Omdurman numbered forty-eight dead and approximately 308 wounded. But the 21st Lancers alone lost twenty-one men killed and fifty wounded. The figures are a very good indicator of the ferocity of the action in the *khor*, which lasted only minutes, and of the steady determination and courage of Captain Paul Kenna. Three hours after the charge, Omdurman fell, and the death of 'Chinese' Gordon was avenged.

For services in Sudan, Paul Kenna received the Khedive's Medal with Khartoum clasp. His award of the Victoria Cross was gazetted on 15 November 1898. Two months later, on 6 January, he was summoned to Osborne House on the Isle of Wight and invested by Queen Victoria. He was further honoured when invited to dine in private with Her Majesty, a memorable occasion for Paul Kenna, and one which was to blossom into duty and service with the monarchy.

He had come home to England a changed man. The arduous campaign proved cathartic. The emotional baggage had been jettisoned slowly and the depression dispelled: men looked to him for assistance, for advice, for leadership. A new *raison d'être* was born: he had proved himself a good, fighting soldier, of worth to the army, with more to offer than just his sporting prowess. And he attended the celebratory round of parties thrown in his honour with a renewed vigour for life and began to take an interest in the opposite sex again. At a house-party given by Lord Clifford at Ugbrooke Park, Devon, he fell in love with Angela Mary Hibbert, youngest daughter of Hubert Hibbert. But, before he could press his suit, war intervened.

It was the Boer War that set the seal on Paul Kenna's army career. He proved an intelligent and astute commander, building on his experience in Sudan; and, as the first of the Kennas to join the army, with no family or military ties to exploit to his advantage, his advancement was gained purely on merit. Arriving in South Africa in November 1899 as Assistant Provost Marshal, Cavalry Division, on General Sir John French's Staff, he saw action at Colesburg, near the Orange River, and was mentioned in the dispatches of Lord Roberts. He took part in the relief of Kimberley and was promoted to brigade major with the 4th Cavalry Brigade in the Orange Free State. In 1901, he took command of one of the ten mobile columns tasked with hunting down and confining the Boer Commandos, and fought in the Transvaal and into Natal along the Zululand frontier. He was mentioned again in dispatches and was awarded the Queen's Medal with six clasps, and the King's Medal with two clasps. His contribution to the war effort was described by Lord Kitchener as 'invariably excellent'.

At the end of hostilities in 1902, he was made a Companion of the Distinguished Service Order and was promoted substantive major. However, he remained in Africa and did not come home with the victorious troops. In November of that year, he was posted to the British Protectorate of Somaliland, where another Mahdi had risen in rebellion; and for eighteen months, with the local rank of lieutenant colonel, he pursued and hunted down the rebels, distinguishing himself at Badwein and later Jidballi, where the Mahdi's forces were soundly defeated. He was mentioned three times in dispatches and was awarded the Africa General Service Medal and two clasps, Somaliland and Jidballi, for his services.

He was back in England by the summer of 1904, where he rejoined the 21st Lancers, reverting to the rank of major. With little time off between campaigns, he had been on the battlefield for eight years; meanwhile, in the background, and unheard by him, were mutterings that he had not been fully acknowledged for his honourable service. The first to intervene on his behalf was King Edward VII, who, on 7 September, personally recommended his promotion to brevet lieutenant colonel. More recognition followed quickly. He was appointed Secretary to the War Office, Cavalry Committee, and promoted to brigade major, 1st Cavalry Brigade, Aldershot, a post he held until gazetted to command 21st Lancers in September 1906. Three months later, he was promoted brevet colonel and appointed aide-de-camp to the king. He performed that duty also for his successor, King George V, who referred to him affectionately, if not condescendingly, as 'our dear little man'.

In the saddle, he became the star and darling of the equestrian circuit and the racecourse. And life was made sweeter still after he resumed his courtship of Angela Hibbert and she accepted his proposal. They married in great style at London's Brompton Oratory on 2 March 1905 and honeymooned in Europe. Two daughters were born to the couple at the Hibbert family home in Beaumont Gardens, Kathleen Mary Pauline and Cecilia Mary Ethel. The girls were his delight; and for the few remaining years of his life, he was passionately devoted to them and their mother.

In 1910, he relinquished command of the 21st Lancers, and moved his family to a small estate he had purchased in Leicestershire, North Kilworth Hall, near Rugby. There, he prepared himself and his mounts for the Olympic Games, the crowning achievement to his great sporting career. Weeks before he sailed for Stockholm, he took command of the Notts and Derby Mounted Brigade with the rank of brigadier general on 1 April. Had he been superstitious, he might have attached some significance to the date. The brigade was a yeomanry unit of the Territorial Force of Cavalry, and was destined to fight in the First World War. For Paul Kenna VC, it was his final command.

A month after war was declared, the brigade joined the 2nd Mounted Division, the Mounteds, and mustered at Churn, in Wiltshire, under the command of Major General William Eliot Peyton, who, as a captain in the 21st

Hussars, had also fought at Omdurman with Paul Kenna. Also joining the division was Major Alexander Lafone of the London Mounted Brigade. The Mounteds were blooded in the last battle of the disastrous Gallipoli campaign. Landing at Suvla Bay without their mounts on 18 August 1915, they were sacrificed as infantrymen three days later on the smouldering pyre of Scimitar Hill.

From Suvla Bay and the tiny village of Lala Baba stretched the dried-up bed of the Salt Lake, a rocky desert which sprawled eastwards into an open plain overlooked by a series of rises and hills. Two of the hills, Green Hill and Chocolate Hill, were in Allied hands, but due east of the latter, rose Scimitar Hill, the key to the Turkish defences. On 21 August, Scimitar Hill was assaulted. The opening naval barrage ignited the mountain shrub and raised a choking, grey smoke, which mingled with a heavy mist descending over the battlefield in the late morning. Visibility was reduced to zero, and when the men rose from the trenches at three o'clock in the afternoon, they disappeared into an opaque smog from which few of the first wave of attackers were to emerge alive.

The Mounteds moved forward towards evening, crossing the Salt Lake in extended formation under a murderous Turkish fire. Reaching the lines at the base of Chocolate Hill, they were thrown into battle immediately. The smoggy haze was so dense now the yeomen could not see the summit of Scimitar Hill. Nevertheless, on they came, marching blindly up the hill under intense fire, all to no avail. By nightfall the decision to withdraw was made, and Paul Kenna VC pulled back his men to Lala Baba. The following afternoon, he was ordered back to reserve lines on Chocolate Hill.

The positions on the rocky face of the hill were no more than scratch lines, hardly trenches at all, and offered minimal protection to the soldiers from the Turkish artillery and sniper fire coming from Scimitar Hill. One of the lines, however, meandered off a straight line and bulged out into a salient. Kenna ordered his men to dig a new line and to continue work on the communication trench.

On the morning of Sunday, 29 August, he heard Mass and received Holy Communion. In the afternoon, the guns fell silent: the campaign had ended, and the Allies would begin withdrawing from Gallipoli in December. But there was still work to oversee. And, in the evening, like all good commanders in the field, Paul Kenna VC went forward on a tour of inspection to check on the digging. The communication trench remained a work in progress, and he had to cross 30 yards of open ground to reach the front. At half past nine, as he covered the last 5 yards, the quiet of the night was broken by the sharp crack of a single rifle shot. General Paul Kenna VC stumbled and fell, mortally wounded. The bullet penetrated his arm, smashing the elbow, and passed on through into his chest. Still conscious, but in great pain, he was carried down by stretcher to the field ambulance station in Suvla Bay.

He knew he was dying and asked for a chaplain. Father Farrel administered the last rites as he drifted into unconsciousness. Brigadier General Paul Aloysius Kenna VC died at two o'clock in the morning of Monday, 30 August 1915. 'On this dark battlefield of fog and flame,' wrote Winston Churchill, 'Brigadier-General Lord Longford, Brigadier General Kenna VC, Colonel Sir John Milbanke VC, and other paladins fell.' It is both tragic and incongruous that a soldier who had fought his enemy face to face and stared death in the eye on many occasions, should fall victim, at a distance, to a faceless foe after the battle, after the war in that part of the world, was over.

General Paul Aloysius Kenna VC, DSO, warrior and sportsman, was buried on the plain overlooking Suvla Bay. 'Every officer and man in the Brigade deplored the General's loss. Both as a soldier and a man he had won everyone's esteem and ... his courage and personal disregard of danger had been an example to all.' His body was subsequently re-interred at Lala Baba Military Cemetery. His final resting place is marked with a tablet which holds a sculptured replica of his Victoria Cross, and the inscription: 'On whose soul sweet Jesus have mercy. May he rest in peace.'

His widow, Angela, would receive his final honours: the 1914–15 Star, the British War Medal and Victory Medal. After the war, she married Lieutenant Colonel Allen Johnson, DSO, Royal Fusiliers, son of General Sir Charles Johnson, GCB. Kathleen Kenna married Lieutenant Commander Lionel Tyrwhitt on 11 September 1936, at St Mary's Cathedral in Sydney, Australia. He gave distinguished service during the Second World War, winning the DSO and DSC, and was mentioned in dispatches on three occasions. He went down with his ship, HMS *Jaguar*, torpedoed off the coast of North Africa, near Tobruk, in March 1942. The couple had no issue. Cecilia Kenna did not marry, and passed away aged 97, in October 2006.

A memorial plaque to Paul Kenna VC was erected at Stonyhurst College, one of seven at that famous school honouring alumni who won the Victoria Cross. His name is also remembered on the War Memorials at the College and at North Kilworth, his last home. The 21st Lancers were disbanded in 1921, but were reconstituted the following year and later became part of a new formation, the Queen's Royal Lancers Regiment. Paul Kenna's Victoria Cross and his other medals and decorations were donated by his daughters to the Regimental Museum and are on display at Belvoir Castle, Leicestershire.

George Edward Nurse VC
(1873–1945)

Corporal George Nurse won his Victoria Cross at the Battle of Colenso in the opening months of the Boer War, when British forces attempted to cross the River Tugela during the advance to relieve the town of Ladysmith. His citation, however, in which his name is appended almost as an afterthought, gives him no credit for the gallantry he displayed, and is the most inaccurate, confused and niggardly ever published in the *London Gazette*. Probably this accounts for the fact that he is better remembered for his encounters on another battle front, that of married life, in which he made a name for himself as party to one, possibly two, bigamous marriages.

George Edward Nurse was born in Enniskillen, Fermanagh, Northern Ireland on 14 April 1873. He was the second son of Charles Nurse, a serving soldier from London, whose regiment had recently returned to Ireland for home duty from Bermuda, where his first son Alfred had been born in 1867. His mother is thought to have been Jane Selina Coles, also a native of London, who died shortly after giving birth to George. Charles Nurse managed to bring up his two sons within the regiment, but in the spring of 1878, when he returned to civilian life, he married Jessie Benson in London. Two daughters, Emily and Edith, came from this union.

The following year, Charles purchased the Cobo Hotel in Castel, on the Isle of Guernsey, where George Nurse grew up. He had a good childhood, according to his family, and he attended the Chamberlain Academy, and later the Boys Intermediate School, receiving a better education than most young boys of his own age on the island. A bright boy, quick to learn and good with his hands, he had an above average academic record. Outside school, his main interest was horses; and, when not helping out in his father's hotel, he was running and riding wild with his pals all over the island. As he grew older, the ladies came to his attention, and one in particular, Kathleen Meagher, was to dominate his life. Photographs taken when in his late twenties show a dapper, well-groomed man, who clearly cared about his appearance: the brown hair is styled and neatly trimmed, the moustache is full but not extravagant, and, at 5 feet, 8 inches, with blue eyes and a lean, sturdy frame, he must have cut a dash and caused many a heart to flutter.

On leaving school, he was indentured as a farrier with a local blacksmith, H.R. Hansford, and he also joined the local Gunnery Militia; and it was probably this experience that decided him on a life in the army. After completing his apprenticeship, he enlisted as 88315 Private George Nurse in the Royal Artillery at St George's Barracks in London on 6 January 1892, and was posted five days later to the depot at Woolwich, where he joined the 67th Battery, Royal Field Artillery (RFA), on a short service enlistment of seven years and an additional five years on the reserve list.

His first five years of service were spent on home duty in England and Ireland. He was a popular man in his unit, and his intelligence and diligence was soon apparent to his superiors, leading to his promotion through the ranks to corporal. During his time with the colours, his conduct was exemplary and no black marks ever appeared against his name. However, the same could not be said of his private life. In 1895, while on station in Limerick, he met Kathleen Meagher. This was the woman he would court and pursue through several turbulent years and three marriages.

George Nurse and Kathleen Meagher married in Plymouth on 26 April 1896, and they quickly started a family: a daughter Christina was born the following January. At the time, an enlisted man could not marry without the authorization of his commanding officer. George Nurse wed without permission and so the marriage, and the birth of his daughter, had to be kept a secret. Because he was not entered on the Regimental Marriage Rolls and was not in receipt of the usual allowances and preferments, Kathleen had to live apart from her husband. However, the couple's first attempt at married life was short-lived: George had to kiss his wife and his baby daughter goodbye on 14 April 1897 when 67th Battery was posted to South Africa to take up garrison duties in Ladysmith, Natal.

His time in South Africa passed uneventfully, and by January 1899 he had completed his full enlistment term of seven years without firing a shot in anger. He was placed on the reserve list and should have been sent home immediately, but he was kept on in Natal for a further five months. In his absence, Kathleen had found a house in London and lived with Christina at 36 Adair Street, Kensington, earning a living as a dressmaker. By the time George Nurse returned to the bosom of his secret family, it was June, and the worsening situation in South Africa meant his stay was very short. He was recalled to the colours on 9 October, two days before the outbreak of the Boer War, and was restored to the rank of corporal. But he was unable to return to his old unit, and was posted to 66th Battery, RFA, which formed part of 1st Division, RFA, alongside the 7th and 14th Batteries. On 23 October, he waved Kathleen and Christina goodbye at Tilbury Docks and sailed for South Africa on board the overcrowded troop-ship SS *Armenian*.

The vessel made port at Cape Town on 13 November, and then sailed on to Durban, where the division disembarked and used the rail link to travel up-country to Frere, a small stop on the line approximately twelve miles south of the River Tugela. Here, General Sir Redvers Buller VC, the newly appointed commander-in-chief, was mustering his force to relieve Ladysmith, ten miles to the north of the river.

The Tugela was a formidable obstacle, meandering eastwards across the midlands of Natal to Durban; and its northern bank, which Buller planned to attack at the hamlet of Colenso, was heavily invested and defended by General Loius Botha and his Boer commando. The river transcribed a quarter-circle to the north and west of Colenso, and a ford, Wagon Drift, and a wooden bridge, Wagon Bridge, gave access to the north bank. Major General Hildyard's 2nd Brigade, supported by artillery, would launch the main assault and secure the two crossing points and establish the lodgement on the north bank. The attack would commence at dawn on Friday, 15 December.

Colonel Charles Long was given command of the field guns in support of Hildyard's attack, six naval 12-pounders and the twelve 15-pounders of the 66th and 14th Batteries. Buller's instructions to Long on the night before the attack were precise: he was to remain well out of rifle range from the river, bringing his field guns to within two and a half miles of the quarter-circle the river made around Colenso. Buller had misgivings about Colonel Long, which were to prove justified: he had rebuked Long severely on 15 November when his lax command had been responsible for the derailment of an armoured train by the Boers south of the river. Several men had been killed and many captured, among them the correspondent of the *Morning Post*, Winston Churchill. Long, who had been Kitchener's artillery man at Omdurman, was determined to redeem himself and his reputation by a spectacular feat of arms. In front of Colenso, Long would be reckless: he would be chastised for his folly in a fierce firefight from a well-entrenched enemy armed with long-range, magazine-fed Mauser rifles and supported by modern artillery pieces; and he would be responsible for the needless deaths of many of the men under his command.

The night before the battle was cool and windless, the merest whisper of a breeze bringing some comfort to the sun-baked soldiers. In good humour at the prospect of some 'fun' with the Boers, they teased and chaffed one another while they made final preparations. Corporal George Nurse tended his horses: he fed them fodder and water, checked their shoes and harnessed them. He saw the gun carriages, the limbers, hooked in to their teams, the guns limbered and finally the wagon trains stocked with munitions. And, as the black sky of night paled and was pierced by streaks of blue and red, heralds of the dawn, the last dawn for many of the laughing soldiers, George Nurse and the 66th Battery moved forward.

From his vantage point on Naval Gun Hill, which overlooked the battlefield, General Buller VC ordered his long-range guns to open the preliminary barrage on the north bank of the river at five-thirty in the morning. An hour later, as the bombardment continued, Major General Hildyard's Brigade advanced on Colenso. But, as the rising sun dispersed the haze on the veld, and to everyone's amazement on both sides of the river, it was not the infantry that was leading Hildyard's column: riding out at least a mile in front of the infantry was Colonel Long and an orderly procession of guns and wagon trains, galloping as if on a field day on Salisbury Plain, and giving the impression that the prospect of battle was as remote as the stars which had fled before the dawn.

Long galloped his procession past a *donga*, a shallow, dried-up river bed, and on for another 500 yards before calling a halt. The guns were unhooked from the limbers, which the drivers took off to the rear, and ammunition was brought down from the wagons. Orders were barked and the gunners methodically set about positioning the guns and registering targets with ranging shots, then laying the guns ready for action. Major Foster, commanding the 66th Battery, gave the order to fire.

The position Long took up was on the flat, open plain, 1,000 yards from the river, well beyond the limits set the previous night by his commander, and well within rifle range of the 800-strong Krugersdorp Commando. The Boers were hidden in trenches on the banks of the river ready to surprise Hildyard's infantry when they came for the crossings. But Botha realized his men would be blown to pieces in their shallow trenches if Long could bring accurate fire to bear at such short range, so he had no option but to forgo the element of surprise and attack the guns. At seven o'clock, as the first twelve rounds from Long's batteries struck the north bank of the river, Botha gave the order to return fire. Long and his guns were caught in the open with no place to hide.

The air around George Nurse and his battery suddenly came alive with the crackling, whistling rush of flying lead and steel as the Boers opened up with their Mausers and field guns. Colonel Long was one of the first men to fall, shot and critically wounded in the liver. His second-in-command, Lieutenant Colonel Hunt, was knocked over also, as was Major Foster. The gunners suffered too, dropping like flies as the high velocity bullets found their marks. It was not that the Boers were great marksmen: it was the sheer volume of fire they unleashed and concentrated on a small area as 800 Mauser magazines were rapidly exhausted and replaced, and just as quickly emptied again, which produced the devastation among the men, giving the impression machine guns were in action against them. 'The bullets were pattering around us like hail,' reminisced George Nurse. 'One went through my haversack, piercing a handglass and a piece of bread I had in it, hit my revolver pouch and splintered one of the fingers of my right hand in two places.'

Orderly and methodically the men of the 66th and 14th Batteries returned fire as they had been trained to do. But they had no defined targets upon which to concentrate their fire: the entrenched Boers were using the newly invented smokeless cordite, and their positions were not betrayed by the smoke of their fusillades and salvoes. Firing blindly, the British gunners fought back and were remorselessly slaughtered. Nevertheless, they maintained their drill, and the second line of ammunition wagons was brought forward and the depleted first line was calmly removed to the rear under the murderous volleys.

The groans and cries of the wounded and dying were lost beneath the roar of guns and crashing explosions. Colonel Long called out to his men to stand fast and remember their training. The sun rose steadily as the fight continued, and the 'Old McCormac' seemed to favour the Boers, beating down mercilessly on the gunners whose throats were parched and constricted while they sweated to exhaustion behind the booming, smoking guns. Brave men were the British gunners, brave men indeed. But they were human, too. When a third of them had either been killed or wounded, when flesh and blood could face no more, the acting commander ordered the men to take shelter. 'Abandon the guns?' cried out a delirious Colonel Long. 'We will not abandon the guns.' But the dying colonel was ignored.

Gathering up their wounded and dead, and abandoning the guns of both batteries, the surviving gunners scrambled, staggered and crawled to the safety of the *donga*, 500 yards to the rear, their only cover on the open veld. The Boers poured a continuous fire into their backs, a fire so intense that one of the dead was later found to have been struck by sixty-four bullets. How any of the men survived the dash to safety was nothing short of a miracle. But survive they did; and among them was George Nurse, cradling a broken hand.

In the *donga* the wounded were rested in the lowest recesses and ministered to with whatever came to hand. There was no water, no shade, not a breath of cooling wind to ease their plight; and all around the air hummed, and the ground drummed, to the relentless rhythm of flying lead, while on the plain, the twelve guns stood forlorn and silent. A courageous surgeon, Major William Babtie, made the perilous dash to the *donga* with medical supplies and some water. He attended the wounded, including Colonel Long, who, in his delirium, still cried out for the guns to fire.

This was the scene which greeted General Buller VC when he rode into the firing line to investigate why Long's guns had fallen silent. Contemptuous of the bullets flying around him, he trotted his mount along the length of the *donga*, calling out to the gunners to save the guns. To lose the guns was to lose the battle; and the cry of 'save the guns' had echoed through the chronicles of war ever since the days of Marlborough. Corporal George Nurse was the first to his feet to volunteer; and he was quickly followed by six of his men. But more men were needed to make up at least two teams to extricate the guns. The general now turned to his staff and asked them to help. Captains Schofield and Congreve and Lieutenant Roberts came forward.

Under heavy fire, George Nurse climbed out of the *donga* and set to work. 'I got hold of some loose horses and hooked them into the limbers, Lieutenant Roberts holding my horse meanwhile.' Captain Congreve helped to set up the second team. When the Boers across the river realized the British were preparing to rescue their guns, they redoubled their fire. Together, the two teams galloped off across 500 yards of empty veld towards the guns and into the teeth of a gale of lead. Captain Congreve, in the rear, was wounded and unhorsed; Lieutenant Roberts, riding alongside Captain Schofield, was shot and tumbled from his mount. But the two teams came on, urging on their frightened mounts towards the silent guns. 'Then we got to the guns, through a tornado of rifle bullet and shell. One gun had the spade clamping gear jammed. I ran to another gun and with Captain Schofield's help limbered it up, then ran back to the former gun, found the pin, and managed to limber it up myself.'

The clamping or axle spade was connected to a spring in the trail of the gun and reduced rearward movement of the gun when fired. A jammed axle spade could have been the death of Corporal George Nurse as he struggled to release it amid the fury of the Boer attack. But, steadily, he stood his ground, and worked at his task. Alone he hooked up the trail of the second gun to the limber. He was almost knocked over when struck by pieces of flying shrapnel in the chest and ribs, but he managed to keep his feet, mounted his horse and organized the retreat. The two guns were pulled clear and hauled back to the rear.

For bravery under fire, Corporal George Edward Nurse was awarded the Victoria Cross. His niggardly citation reads:

> George Edward Nurse, Corporal, 66th Battery Royal Field Artillery. At Colenso, on the 15th December 1899, the detachments serving the guns of the 14th and 66th Batteries, Royal Field Artillery, had either been killed, wounded, or driven from their guns by infantry fire at close range, and the guns were deserted. About 500 yards behind the guns was a *donga*, in which some of the few horses and drivers left alive were sheltered. The intervening space was swept with shell and rifle fire. Captain Congreve, Rifle Brigade, who was in the *donga*, assisted to limber up a gun. Being wounded he took shelter, but seeing Lieutenant Roberts fall badly wounded, he went out again and brought him in. Captain Congreve was shot through the leg, through the toe of his boot, grazed on the elbow and the shoulder, and his horse shot in three places. Lieutenant Roberts, King's Royal Rifle Corps, assisted Captain Congreve. He was wounded in three places. Corporal Nurse also assisted.

Several more attempts were made to rescue the remaining ten guns as the day wore on, but all ended in bloody failure; and rather than risk further lives, at eleven o'clock General Buller VC gave the order to retire, abandoning the remaining guns and the field to the Boers. The Battle of Colenso was over before it had really begun. The intrepid but reckless Colonel Long died on the battlefield. George Nurse was one of the walking wounded and stood in line at the field hospital awaiting treatment to his hand. His chest and ribs, though battered by shards of shrapnel, were only bruised and required no medical treatment. And he would be immediately promoted to sergeant and awarded the Victoria Cross, which was gazetted on 2 February 1900.

His wounded hand did not merit a ticket home, but it impaired and pained him throughout the rest of the campaign. He was mentioned in dispatches on 26 January 1900, just before his battery was in action again during the relief of Ladysmith in February, and he was present at the relief of Mafeking in May, when he was wounded by a gunshot to the right leg. Hospitalized for several months, upon release from hospital in December, he was placed on light duties and posted to the battery's depot in charge of supplies. However, on 1 January 1901, still troubled by his hand, and further inconvenienced by the wound to his leg, he was returned to England.

It is believed he received his Victoria Cross at Buckingham Palace at the beginning of February, but it is not known whether the king made the presentation. For his services during the Boer War, George Nurse was awarded the Queen's South Africa Medal with clasps, Cape Colony, Tugela Heights, Relief of Ladysmith, Orange Free State and Transvaal.

Having been granted leave after receiving the honour, George Nurse VC collected his wife and child, and, on 6 February 1901, he sailed with them from Weymouth to Guernsey on the SS *Gazelle*. They landed the next day at the White Rock, the northern arm of St Peter Port Harbour, to a less than rapturous welcome and the indignity of an official snub. Only his former employer, H.R. Hansford, and William Sharp, headmaster of his old school, together with a group of excited pupils, were on hand to greet him. The schoolboys unhitched the horses of the carriage awaiting the family, and with Nurse on board, pulled it along St Julian's Pier, before the horses were put back in the shafts to drive Guernsey's hero to Castel and a reception at his father's hotel.

That evening, through the columns of the *Guernsey Evening Press*, local dignitaries pleaded they had received insufficient warning of the hero's return in which to organize an official welcome and civic reception and had not snubbed him deliberately. However, Nurse remained on Guernsey until the end of February and no attempt was made to rectify the situation and reward him with a civic reception. It was hinted in the *Evening Press* that social prejudice towards his lowly status as the son of a public house landlord, coupled with the less than enthusiastic Victoria Cross citation, accounted for the rebuff. However, two years later, and only after George Nurse's marital attachments were unravelled in public, it was suggested that, in line with the prevailing moral code, he was rebuked by the island's hierarchy simply for his morals: he was not married to Kathleen, and his daughter was illegitimate. But, all that was to come in 1903.

In March, George Nurse was transferred to 131st Battery, RFA, stationed at Southill Barracks, Kent. Here, he was counted in the 1901 national census, and declared himself to be a single man. Not long afterwards, he owned up to being married. He was entered on the Marriage Rolls on 1 April, and details of his marriage to Kathleen Meagher and the birth of Christina were recorded in his service record. But, the following year, while stationed at Kildare Artillery Barracks outside Dublin, he was publicly confronted with the fact that his marriage to Kathleen Meagher was bigamous: Kathleen had a legal husband when she contracted her marriage to him in 1896. His marriage was declared null and void, and Kathleen was arrested for bigamy.

In all probability, Nurse knew the marriage was bigamous: the fact that he kept it a secret for six years is suggestive. But his love for the woman overrode all considerations, and would continue to do so in the future. However, under the Offences against the Person Act of 1861, bigamy was a felony punishable by up to seven years' imprisonment. It is not known whether Kathleen Meagher's polyandrous and bigamous relationship with George Nurse ended in a gaol sentence. All that can be said is that she disappeared from George Nurse's life for three years.

Despite the public scandal, his position within his unit was unaffected; and, recognized as the injured party, he was not censured in any way. He was seen as a great asset to the regiment, and remained as popular and respected as ever, so much so that at Kildare in December 1903, as he neared the end of twelve years of service, he was re-engaged for a second time, for a further nine years with the colours. He may well have been heartbroken by the loss of Kathleen, but it appears he soldiered on manfully. In the months following her departure, he was comforted by another lady named Kathleen; and so effective were her ministrations that he allowed her to lead him down the aisle.

George Nurse VC, bachelor, married Kathleen Sweeney, spinster, at the Church of Our Lady of the Souls, Kensington, on 24 October 1904. Still with the colours, Nurse nevertheless gave his occupation as farrier, and his address as 45 Ladbrooke Road, the implications being that he was a civilian and not a soldier. All that is known of Kathleen Sweeney was that she was the daughter of Edward Sweeney and lived at 86 Malvern Road, Leytonstone. Needless to say, George Nurse VC had married again without the permission of his commanding officer; and this marriage, like his first, was kept a secret.

On 4 April 1908, George Nurse was transferred to 31st Battery, RFA and promoted to battery sergeant major, on station in Kilkenny, where his marital adventures took another turn. Kathleen Sweeney Nurse did not accompany him to Ireland. He may have divorced her, she may have died, or he may have simply abandoned her in England and conveniently forgotten their marriage. There was no room for her in his life: Kathleen Meagher had returned.

In Waterford, on 25 October 1908, Battery Sergeant Major George Nurse VC married Kathleen Meagher. She must have been free of her first husband to marry George Nurse VC, but it is not certain whether he was free of his lawful wife Kathleen Sweeney. In all probability, the newlyweds could chalk up at least one bigamous marriage each. On the occasion of this, his third marriage, however, he had the blessing and permission of his commanding officer; and details of the marriage were duly entered in his service record. A son was born to the couple on 26 June 1909, and in Kilkenny the following month, he was christened Charles Patrick Colenso Nurse. However, the birth was tinged with sadness: it is believed that Christina died some weeks after her brother's arrival.

The couple went into married quarters in Kilkenny and lived contentedly together for the next three years. In the year their son was born, Nurse received the Long Service and Good Conduct Medal; and in December 1911, he packed up his family and returned to England for what he believed was to be his final posting with the Royal Artillery. He joined 5th Battery, 4th South Midland Howitzer Brigade, RFA, stationed near Coventry, and was expected to be discharged in 1913. However, like Donald Farmer VC, he was allowed to extend his service with the colours beyond twenty-one years for pension entitlement, and he was not discharged until 5 January 1914.

As far as it has been ascertained, George and Kathleen Nurse had no connections with Liverpool. However, they decided to make their home there in 1914. They moved to the city in February, and lived at 5 Westmoreland Street, near Edge Lane. But George had hardly had time in which to settle before he found himself back with the colours. When the First World War began, he enlisted immediately, and, at the age of 41, he was commissioned as a second lieutenant in the Royal Artillery on 15 September 1915.

He did not see active service on any of the fronts, but acted as a recruiter and goodwill ambassador for the armed forces throughout Britain. It is known he visited America and that he was an artillery instructor at various barracks there as he toured the country. On 1 July 1917, he was promoted to lieutenant, and his final discharge from the colours was ordered in 1919. In total, he served his country for twenty-seven years. For his service during the First World War, he received the 1914–15 Star, the British War Medal, the Victory Medal; and in 1937, he was honoured with his final award, the King's Coronation Medal.

After the war, George Nurse VC, like Joseph Prosser VC and William Dowling VC, worked as a customs officer on the Liverpool Docks. He had his army and Victoria Cross pensions to supplement his wages, and with just a wife and son to provide for, he must have had a decent standard of living. However, his marriage to Kathleen, after all the trouble and fuss it had taken for it to become a reality, broke down. In 1929, the couple parted. George took lodgings at the home of a friend, Edward Meakin, at 15 Crosfield Street. Kathleen lived nearby at 125 Botanic Road, and nothing more was heard of her.

At the time of the separation, Charles Patrick Colenso, known within the family as Colenso, was courting a Liverpool girl, Elizabeth Price: the couple married in 1932. Their only child, Charles George Colenso, was born two years later. The family eventually moved to the south of England, and Colenso Nurse died in Chippenham, Wiltshire, in 1996. His son, Charles, married

Elizabeth Evans in 1954, and their son, Kirk, became a junior gunner with the Junior Leaders Regiment of the Royal Artillery. He died at the age of 20, in 1978.

In his late fifties, George Nurse began to suffer with kidney problems; and it is believed he had one of them removed just before his sixtieth birthday. He took early retirement from HM Customs, and continued to live in digs with Edward Meakin, sitting out the Second World War partially incapacitated. On 25 November 1945, he was rushed into Broadgreen Emergency Hospital suffering from acute uraemia, or kidney failure. He died shortly after admittance. Edward Meakin collected the body and oversaw its burial in a private family ceremony in Allerton Cemetery three days later. George Nurse VC died a forgotten man: there were no military honours at the graveside, no last trumpet calls, nothing at all to inform a casual observer of the brave man being laid to rest in the cold earth. A headstone was erected in 1989 to mark the grave.

The medals of George Edward Nurse VC, including his Victoria Cross, are held by the 159th (Colenso) Battery, RA, at the Royal Regiment of Artillery Museum, Woolwich.

Arthur Herbert Lindsay Richardson VC
(1872–1932)

When Arthur Richardson enlisted in the Gordon Highlanders at Aberdeen, Scotland, at the outbreak of the First World War, he submitted to the authority a typewritten declaration which stated that he had won the Victoria Cross during the Boer War. The regiment welcomed the hero into its ranks and exploited his kudos in recruitment campaigns. He served bravely in France and was promoted to corporal, and in 1917 was wounded in action.

After the war, he returned to Aberdeen and was feted a hero. On 26 June 1920, he attended the Garden Party hosted by the king to honour Victoria Cross holders, and was introduced to members of the Royal Family and Earl Haig. He worked as a commissionaire at a cinema in Aberdeen, and wore the crimson ribbon of the honour on his uniform coat. But he fell on hard times, lost his job and his health failed. In March 1924, he collapsed and died in the street. He was buried with full military honours, as befits a holder of the Victoria Cross, and his passing was widely reported in the British media.

Mrs Caroline Richardson of Mannering Road, Liverpool, was stunned when she read in the *Liverpool Echo* of the death of Arthur Richardson VC. There was only one holder of that name, her son, and he had died ten years earlier, in 1914: a nurse had written from Canada, where he had been living since 1891, to say he had passed away under her care in a Montreal hospital. In a state of puzzlement, she contacted the local press.

Nationwide investigation quickly uncovered a Captain Butler, second cousin to Caroline, who said her son had in fact died in 1904; Mrs Todd, another relative, stated he had passed away in London in 1913; and a Canadian living in Kent claimed he had died in 1923, in the bed next to him at the Euclid Hall Hospital, Toronto. Within days, however, it was established that the former Gordon Highlander, Arthur Henry Leonard Richardson, was an imposter; and that Arthur Herbert Lindsay Richardson, Caroline's son and the real holder of the Victoria Cross, was dead and was buried either in England or Canada.

After reading this reportage in his home at 144 St Domingo Vale, Everton, Arthur Richardson VC, prompted by his daughter, rose reluctantly from his self-imposed obscurity to set the record straight. He contacted the *Liverpool Echo* and handed over for inspection his 'ring papers', official documents that showed he was Arthur Herbert Lindsay Richardson, son of Caroline, holder of the Victoria Cross, and that he had been drawing his pension of £10 per annum from his home address in Liverpool since 1908.

Following on from this report of a modern-day Lazarus, Mrs Richardson informed the media she was delighted her heroic son was alive. But, when asked how she had believed him dead when, in fact, he had been living for the past sixteen years not two miles from her palatial home, she refused to comment. Arthur Richardson VC, likewise, had nothing to say. The media smelt a story, a family scandal: the Richardsons were besieged and the family background probed. But all that was uncovered was what has always been in the public domain; and no hint has ever been forthcoming of what was a deep and painful estrangement between mother and son.

Arthur's father, William Duke Richardson, was the son of a small landowner, Robert Richardson, from County Tyrone, and was born there in the townland of Annagh in 1837. As a young man he came to England and took up residence in London, working as a commission agent in the City. It is not known when or where he met his future wife, Caroline, but it is possible they were collaterally related: Caroline's surname was Richardson also. She was the second daughter and third child of William and Mary Richardson, and was born in St John's Street, Peterborough, Northamptonshire, in 1846. Her father was a successful veterinary surgeon and wine and spirits merchant; and Caroline grew up in a well-to-do, middle-class home with a nanny-cum-nurse, Rhoda Warren, in constant attendance.

William Duke Richardson married Caroline Richardson on 13 December 1865 at St John the Baptist's Church in Peterborough. They began a family immediately, in the town of Eccles, near Manchester. In quick succession, Robert, Edith and Mabel arrived, before the family moved across Lancashire to Southport, where Ernest, Arthur Herbert, born on 23 September 1872, Douglas, Walter, Stewart and Maud, joined the family; and to help with her growing brood, Caroline brought her old nanny, Rhoda Warren, from Peterborough to live in the family home in Rectory Roe Lane.

In 1880, the Richardsons moved into Liverpool, taking up residence at 41 Rodney Street, the Harley Street of Liverpool, where William Duke died eight years later. Caroline Richardson, Carrie, as she was known within the family, had received a substantial legacy from her father's estate, and was left well provided for by her husband. She appears to have been a formidable, resourceful and highly practical woman who was set on increasing the family fortune: she let the lower part of the family home as a doctor's surgery and took in lodgers. At one time, her house accommodated six of her children, a doctor and his nurse, nine boarders and five servants. She also insisted on a good education for her sons, and saw them all into good occupations: Robert and Ernest became medical representatives, and Douglas qualified as an electrical engineer.

Arthur Richardson, Bertie to his family, was educated at the Liverpool Institute and School of Arts in Mount Street, a fifteen-minute walk from his home; and after graduation, he was apprenticed as a dentist to the firm of Royston, Matthews and Bates of 60 Rodney Street, under the supervision of Reginald Bates, dental surgeon. He was a tall, gangling youth, an inch short of 6 feet, having his father's dark good looks, brown hair and sparkling blue eyes. All appeared to be on course for the young man until just before his nineteenth birthday when his relationship with his mother broke down.

He quit his apprenticeship in 1891, packed his bags, and left home, taking passage on one of the many liners which sailed from Liverpool to Canada. Upon arrival, he immediately headed out west, bypassing the growing cities of the east, and landed in Stoney Mountain, near Winnipeg, Manitoba, where he found work on a horse ranch. Three years later, he moved on to Regina in southern Saskatchewan, and made application to the North West Mounted Police, the 'Mounties'. He carried a letter of recommendation from the Stoney Mountain rancher who described him as being of 'excellent character . . . sober, industrious'. On 7 May 1894, he joined the Mounties at the Depot Division in Regina on a five-year enlistment as Constable 3058. By now he had grown to full manhood, tall, wiry, muscular, and he sported a heavy handlebar moustache.

> I got 50 cents a day extra for four years for breaking-in horses. . . . At the time of the great Yukon gold rush . . . I went up to bring down the first pack of huskie dogs that carried the mails . . . I and others went 160 miles from Battleford to the Indian reservation, where the dogs, a pack of sixty of them, were waiting. . . . We brought them back along the trail used by the people who struggled to the goldfield. . . . These dogs were used by the North West Mounted Police for carrying mails between Dawson City and Skagway Pass.

He thrived in the great outdoors, and lived the life many young men in Liverpool could only read and dream of, roughing it in the rugged, Canadian wilderness, smartly turned out in the red tunic and blue trousers, scouring the horizon in search of the bad guys, the renegade Indians and the damsel in distress.

His days in the wilds, he would later state, were the best of his life, and if he regretted the break with his mother and his siblings, he never said so. He had made a new life for himself in Canada. And when his first term of enlistment was over, he gladly re-engaged for a further three years, stationed 120 miles further north in the town of Prince Albert, where he was promoted to corporal. He was well thought of by his superiors for his intelligence and leadership skills, so much so that there were hints of a commission when he was posted to the Depot Division in Regina to assist in the training of new recruits. Here, just prior to the outbreak of war, he began courting Florence Elizabeth Hughes, a Welsh girl, who had come to Canada as a child.

When the Boer War opened, Lord Strathcona, a Scottish-born entrepreneur, offered to raise and equip at his own expense a mounted regiment of Canadians to serve in South Africa. He put up a small fortune of £150,000 for twenty-eight officers, 518 men and 599 horses, for what was to become Lord Strathcona's Horse. Arthur Richardson was one of the first men to enlist. On 6 February 1900, he passed a medical examination with flying colours; and eight days later he attested to Lord Stracona's Horse at Chapleau, Ontario. He carried his Mountie rank of corporal with him into A Squadron, and his regimental number was 46. The term of enlistment was for six months, with liability of extension to one year.

Strathcona's Horse sailed from Halifax, Nova Scotia, on SS *Monterey* on 17 March 1900, and arrived at Cape Town, South Africa, on 11 April. It was a journey full of incident. The weather was atrocious: storms and rough seas caused the deaths of 120 horses on board, and when the regiment disembarked, Corporal Arthur Richardson was carried ashore on a stretcher, his left leg in a wooden splint – in heavy seas, he had fallen into the hold and broken it.

He spent six weeks in hospital. But in June, fully recovered, he rejoined the regiment on the trek by sea and land into the Transvaal. Strathcona's Horse reinforced General Sir Redvers Buller's cavalry, the 3rd Mounted Brigade, as he began the push to drive General Botha's army from the Transvaal following the fall of Johannesburg and Pretoria. The mounted troops mustered at Standerton, on the River Vaal.

Towards the end of June, units of Strathcona's Horse scouted the terrain ahead of Buller's advance. Corporal Arthur Richardson rode out on patrol with Captain Cartwright and his troop of thirty-eight men. In the early hours of Thursday, 5 July, fifteen miles west of Standerton, having completed a sweep of the immediate area, the troop approached the hamlet of Wolve Spruit. There were signs of enemy activity around the settlement, and Captain Cartwright brought his men on cautiously. Picking their way through the outskirts, the Canadians suddenly came under a heavy crossfire from a Boer Commando of eighty men, dug in along a *spruit*, a dried-up watercourse.

Fire was returned. But the sheer volume of rapid fire from the Boers was overwhelming, and Captain Cartwright ordered his men to fall back. As they reined in and turned, Privates McDougal and Sparks were wounded, but managed to stay in the saddle, and were led to safety. Private Alex McArthur was struck also, shot in the arm and the leg, and his horse was wounded, too. Horse and rider crashed to the rocky ground, and McArthur was pinned beneath the dying beast. As he struggled to free himself, he became a target of the Boer marksmen, some of whom advanced to try to take him prisoner. Corporal Richardson was the first to react.

He turned and spurred his pony. Lying along the neck of his mount, he charged the Boers through a withering crossfire, galloping towards his fallen comrade. Dismounting amid a hail of whistling lead, Richardson dragged the dazed McArthur from beneath the dead animal, lifted him to his feet and threw him across the saddle. The Boers kept up a relentless fire, concentrating their attack on Richardson and McArthur, the only men still within range, determined on a body count from the encounter. Scornful of the Boer marksmanship, Richardson climbed up behind his wounded comrade, and dashed to his own lines.

For bravery in the face of the enemy, Arthur Herbert Lindsay Richardson was awarded the Victoria Cross. His citation reads:

> Arthur Herbert Lindsay Richardson, Sergeant, Lord Strathcona's Horse. On 5th July, 1900, at Wolve Spruit, about fifteen miles north of Standerton, a party of Lord Strathcona's Corps, only thirty-eight in number, came into contact and was engaged at close quarters with a force of eighty of the enemy. When the order to retire had been given, Sergeant Richardson rode back under a very heavy crossfire and picked up a trooper whose horse had been shot and who was wounded in two places, and rode with him out of fire. At the time when this act of gallantry was performed Sergeant Richardson was within 300 yards of the enemy and was himself riding a wounded horse.

It was found later that several bullets had pierced Richardson's uniform tunic during the rescue, but miraculously he himself was unscathed. His horse was hit twice and died shortly afterwards from its wounds and through exhaustion. McArthur survived his wounds. That night, under cover of darkness, the Boer Commando slipped away, taking their wounded with them. Richardson and the troop returned to Standerton.

Notice of Richardson's award was given in the *London Gazette* of 14 September 1900. The writer inadvertently promoted Richardson to sergeant, a rank he had not held. But on 10 October, when news of the award reached South Africa, Lieutenant Colonel Sam Steele, the regiment's commander, promoted Arthur Richardson VC to sergeant.

The Canadians continued to skirmish with the Boers and fought several sharp encounters in the Transvaal, south into the Orange Free State and north, up towards the border of Mozambique. Their battle honours read like a roll call of the small towns, villages and hamlets of the veld: Wolve Spruit, Devil's Knuckles, Amesfoot, Machadodorp, Helvetia, Watervaal, Badfontein, Vlakfontein. Sergeant Arthur Richardson VC fought his last engagement on 23 December at Clocolan in the Orange Free State before the regiment was retired from the field. For his services, he was awarded the Queen's South Africa Medal and clasps, Belfast and Natal.

Strathcona's men returned to Canada at the end of February 1901 without Sergeant Richardson VC, who travelled home to Liverpool to stay with his sister, Mabel, at 4 Livingston Avenue, off Aigburth Drive. Mabel, and her sister Maud, were the only two members of the family who had sided with their brother in the family dispute. Mabel had married Edward Gregory in 1898, and had started a family. Her first child, Dorothy, was Arthur's favourite, and he named his one and only child Dorothy, also.

His arrival in Liverpool was the occasion of great celebration. He was carried shoulder high from the landing stage through cheering crowds of well-wishers, and was feted and wined and dined at various unofficial celebrations in his honour. But there was no official parade or a civic reception for the hero, and his homecoming was reported only briefly in the local press. His mother was to say later she only heard of his visit and kept photographs of him taken at the time. She was living not far from Mabel, in a mansion at 11 Albert Park Road, Sefton Park, together with three of her brood, Robert, Edith and Ernest Richardson, but she did not open her home to Arthur.

Back in Canada, he was re-engaged as a sergeant for a further three years with the Mounties, and was posted to his old hunting grounds with C Division at Battleford. Here, he married Florence Elizabeth in 1901, and Dorothy was born the following year. And so at the age of 30, Sergeant Arthur Richardson VC settled down to family life, and by all accounts he intended to see out his days in his adopted country.

However, in June 1902, he returned unexpectedly to England. The coronation of Edward VII was to take place at Westminster Abbey on 26 June 1902. The Canadian government was asked to nominate a Victoria Cross holder to act as one of a mounted guard of honour of four Victoria Cross holders, the others coming from England, New Zealand and South Africa. The guard was to accompany the state coach which would carry the king and his queen, Alexandra of Denmark, to and from Westminster Abbey. Sergeant Arthur Richardson VC was chosen as the Canadian representative and was sent to London.

He arrived in England to the news that the enthronement was delayed because the king had undergone an emergency appendectomy; and it was not until 9 August that the ceremony took place. According to Richardson, he lived with his spinster sister Maud in Peterborough, and she accompanied him to Buckingham Palace when he finally received his honour from the king on 2 August. But, it would be the last time he spoke to Maud: he sundered his relationship with her, and Mabel also, during his prolonged visit.

The coronation was captured on an early Pathé newsreel, which was later made part of the early documentary film *Through Three Reigns*, showing scenes from the reigns of Queen Victoria, Edward VII and George V. In March 1924, Arthur Richardson paid a visit to the cinema in Liverpool to see it. 'The film showed scenes at the Coronation of King Edward, and, bless me if I didn't see myself. It was splendid ... and I nearly dropped in surprise. ... It was an extraordinary sensation to see myself doing something I had done so many years before.'

After the coronation and the break with his sisters, Richardson returned to Canada, where more problems awaited him, troubles which would dictate and shape the rest of his life. Sickly following the birth of Dorothy, Florence had been diagnosed with tuberculosis in his absence. The wasting illness spread to her spine; and over the next five years she suffered greatly, constantly in need of medical attention and treatment, crippled and unable to care for Dorothy. Arthur stood by his wife with the same fortitude he had shown at Wolve Spruit: bullets had not stopped him then, and now he would allow nothing, job, friendships, family to deflect him from his purpose, the care and welfare of Florence and Dorothy.

He was promoted to sergeant major on 23 May 1903, and the extra pay helped alleviate the financial burden of his wife's medical bills. But, he began to press the Police Commissioner, and even wrote to his Member of Parliament, demanding the commission mooted in Regina before the Boer War began. Never a coy man, he stood up for himself in the belief that his time served, his experience and his leadership abilities merited proper recognition, and he would not endure what he considered to be an injustice. His request was denied, but he would not let the matter drop.

Physically and psychologically, he began to suffer, and when not absent from duty caring for Florence and Dorothy, he was on sick leave himself. He had monetary difficulties also, borrowing, and not repaying, cash to finance his wife's treatments; and he was forced to pawn his Victoria Cross. His superiors were aware of his situation but chose not to intervene or assist, and their patience finally ran out when, on 9 January 1907, he was declared unfit for his duties as a sergeant major. Then, surprisingly, he was thrown a lifeline and was recommended for the post of quartermaster. However, wearied and dis-illusioned, he decided to quit, and on 12 November 1907, after thirteen years of dedicated service, he purchased his discharge from the Mounties at a cost of $50.

Leaving Battleford, he took up the position of town constable in Indian Head, a small town fifty miles east of Regina. There his problems multiplied as Florence's condition worsened and he was unable to attend for duty. On 24 February 1908, the Mayor of Indian Head wrote in complaint to the Police Commissioner, informing him that Arthur Richardson and his family were living on the parish as welfare claimants, and that there was no job 'in which he could be trusted ... to perform'. The mayor further qualified his dismay by maligning Arthur and Florence, accusing them of being opium addicts.

Laudanum, tincture of opium, was widely prescribed for all manner of ailments from the common cold to cardiac complaints, to relieve pain, induce sleep and to soothe and allay irritation. It was available as a patent medicine, and its use was widespread in North America and Europe, being cheaper to buy than a bottle of gin or wine. Florence Richardson was prescribed laudanum to ease her pain and discomfort: she was probably highly dependent on it. And perhaps Arthur used it himself, for he suffered too, and was depressed and run down with the burdens he carried. But to claim the Richardsons were opium addicts was a wicked calumny.

In the autumn of 1908, Arthur returned to England to seek improved medical treatment for Florence. His homecoming went unnoticed, and he took up residence at 81 Cantsfield Street, off Smithdown Road, living for two years in dire poverty. According to correspondence between Leonard Dunning, Chief Constable of Liverpool at the time, and the Police Commissioner in Canada, Arthur Richardson and his family lived off the parish as welfare claimants. He could not work while caring for his wife and daughter, and his only source of income, beside his pension, was the charity of the elders of the city. Leonard Dunning sat on one of the Board of Guardians which dispensed the largesse, and he was naturally concerned about the distressed and parlous state into which this brave man had fallen. However, there was no mention of opium addiction in the letters.

There was no mention either of Mrs Carrie Richardson, a very wealthy woman, or of Richardson's well-to-do siblings, all of whom could have aided him in his desperate plight. By his own admission he made no contact with the family, choosing to fend for himself: to him, the breach with his mother was permanent and could not be healed, and he would not broker a truce or reconciliation, even for the sake of his wife and daughter.

On 24 May 1910, Florence Elizabeth Richardson died of tuberculosis of the spine at home in Cantsfield Streeet at the age of 37. She was laid to rest by her husband and daughter in the cemetery of St James Mount, Liverpool's oldest cemetery, behind the Cathedral Church of Christ in Liverpool, the city's beautiful Anglican Cathedral.

Released from his duty, Arthur Richardson VC now had time for himself. He found employment with Liverpool Corporation Tramways, at the Edge Hill depot of the Tramways Maintenance Department, and for the next fourteen years, until 1924, nothing more was heard of the real Arthur Herbert Lindsay Richardson VC, tramway labourer. If he had been an opium fiend, then the addiction never manifested itself in Liverpool, where he laboured daily on the streets for many years without any complaints from his superiors and was promoted to foreman of his gang. In all weathers, any time of the working day, he could be found on the streets and roads of Liverpool, maintaining and repairing the tram lines, digging out and replacing damaged track and making good any loose, supporting setts. No one at the depot knew his true identity, had no inkling of his history or bravery. He was the quiet man who kept to himself and laboured selflessly for his daughter.

When Dorothy was 13 she went away to school at St Margaret's School, Convent of Mercy, in Midhurst, West Sussex, though no records can be found of her stay there. After completing her education, she took the position of companion and governess to the family of Doctor Hamilton, of Queen's College, Belfast. But she did return to Liverpool, eventually, and lived with her father at 297 Queen's Drive, Knotty Ash, until his death in 1932.

For two weeks in April 1924, Richardson was prominently reported and pictured in the pages of the *Liverpool Echo*, following the death of the imposter from Aberdeen. He became a celebrity, plucked very reluctantly from obscurity and became the focus of much unwanted attention. He was stopped in the streets by well-wishers wherever he went, and was inundated with marriage proposals and requests to speak at a wide variety of functions, all of which he declined. His home in St Domingo Vale became a magnet for the curious, so much so that he could not leave or enter the house without running a gauntlet of back-slapping and handshakes; and he was forced to move home secretly to Knotty Ash. Wherever he worked with his tramway gang, the pavements were lined with admirers, eager to catch a glimpse of 'the shy VC', as he was dubbed. His supervisor had to take him off the streets and give him work at the depot until 'all the fuss and bother', as he called it, died down. Only then was he able to resume his work.

When reporters could not discover why he had not contacted his wealthy mother in more than sixteen years, a reunion between son and mother at her palatial home in Mannering Road, Sefton Park, was suggested. At first, Carrie Richardson was unwilling and reluctant to see her long-lost son, and told the press he would have to make the first move. After more than thirty years, the estrangement was as deep as ever. However, she relented, and Arthur Richardson VC was invited to call on 4 April.

Following the meeting with his mother, Arthur was asked whether reports were true that he had been nervous and shaking with fear before entering her home. He disarmed his interlocutors with a reply that summed up his creed: 'I have never been afraid of anything in my life.' Never daunted by what fate threw at him, he always fought back in his own inimitable, courageous manner, when winning the Victoria Cross, when struggling to build a life in the wilds of Canada and when caring for Florence and Dorothy.

He refused to speak of what occurred during the reunion, and the hope of a sensational story for the *Liverpool Echo* was stillborn. There was no reconciliation, however, between mother and son: he left her home, never to return, never to see her again. For the remaining eight years of his life, he continued in his self-imposed obscurity, resuming the life he had chosen for himself, working as a foreman labourer without help from anyone.

Arthur Richardson VC was to surface briefly once more, on 9 November 1929, when he attended the Victoria Cross Reunion Dinner, hosted by the Prince of Wales, the future King Edward VIII, at the Royal Gallery, House of

Lords. There he met for the first time the Liverpool contingent of holders, Ernest Wright Alexander VC, Donald Dickson Farmer VC, George Edward Nurse VC, Arthur Procter VC, William Ratcliffe VC and Ronald Neil Stuart VC, who had just returned from a trip to Canada. Perhaps they put their heads together and shared experiences. The imposter 'had had a good time with my medal', he explained when asked why he had attended the dinner, 'and I felt it was my turn to enjoy it.'

On Tuesday, 13 December 1932, he arrived home from his labours suffering with severe abdominal pain, and was rushed into Mill Road Hospital. The spectre of an illness which had haunted his early days was about to enshroud him: he had watched a comrade die of appendicitis in 1900, in the Cape Town hospital where his leg mended; and two years later in London, he was on duty when his king had been laid low with the same complaint. Richardson was diagnosed with acute appendicitis, but too late to save his life. The swollen, diseased appendix ruptured, and peritonitis set in. He died on Thursday, 15 December. Dorothy was by his side.

He had requested a private funeral, and Dorothy complied with his wishes. There was no military presence, no 'Last Post' and 'Reveille' sounded, no volley fired over the grave. The only concession to his heroic status was the Union Jack draped over the coffin. Canon Campbell Baugh conducted the service and Dorothy led the family mourners. A wreath of white chrysanthemums, shaped in the letters 'V' and 'C', from 'number 5 Gang, Edge Hill', was left at the graveside. Arthur Richardson VC was interred with his wife Florence in St James Mount Cemetery.

Four years later, the cemetery was closed. Over the years it fell into a state of dereliction, and a decision was taken to convert it to a Garden of Rest: the gravestones were removed, but many were retained and now line the pathways. But the last resting place of Arthur Richardson VC was lost and so was his headstone. In 1994, the Commonwealth War Graves Commission erected a headstone to Arthur Richardson VC on the grassy verge on the left of the path leading to the main entrance to the cathedral. A wreath of red poppies adorns the headstone every Armistice Day to honour 'the shy VC'.

No records of Dorothy can be found after 1932; it is not known if she married and had children. Her father's Victoria Cross, together with his Queen's South Africa Medal and clasps are held by the Canadian War Museum, Ottawa.

Donald Dickson Farmer VC
(1877–1956)

The Magaliesburg Mountains of South Africa are some of the oldest peaks in the world. They range for seventy-five miles due east from Pretoria to the town of Rustenburg, separating the high veld grassland of the south from the bush veld savannah in the north. During the Boer War, they were of great strategic value to both sides of the conflict. For the British, two vital supply routes between Pretoria and Rustenburg crossed the range, while from the heights, Generals Smuts and De la Rey, two of the wiliest Boer commanders, launched their guerrilla campaign, supported and sustained by the farmers of the mountain valleys.

The highest point of the Magaliesburg range is Nooitgedacht, which rises to a mile in height. From its cliffs cascade streams of pure mountain water which feed a long, fertile valley below. Known to the Boers as the Moot, this beautiful vale was an oasis of peace for most of the war. But, for three months in the late summer of 1900, as part of Kitchener's design to deny and deprive the Boer commandos of sustenance, Major General Clements and his 12th Brigade rampaged up and down the Moot, breathing fire and smoke, burning farms and crops, driving off stock and rounding up women and children.

Sergeant Donald Farmer was a member of the Mounted Infantry Company (MIC), of the Queen's Own Cameron Highlanders, under the command of Captain R.L. Aldercron, attached to the 12th Brigade. At the age of 23, he already had nine years under his belt as a regular soldier, and was a veteran of the Sudan campaign, in which he had fought alongside Major Paul Kenna VC at the River Atbarah and Omdurman. He was one of a new breed of soldiers, very different from the likes of John Kirk, who had passed most of his time in the bars and brothels of his various postings. Farmer had readily espoused the ethos of the newly formed Army Physical Training Corps, which, through its rigorous programmes of callisthenics and sports, sought to produce and maintain fit and healthy men in uniform. He was a robust and keen footballer and captained the battalion's team; and when not on duty, he could be found with a few friends kicking a ball around.

He had been in South Africa for several months and had seen action at Johannesburg, Blomfontein, Pretoria and Diamond Hill, and had been mentioned twice in dispatches. But the campaign of farm burning in the Moot left a bitter taste in his mouth. 'It was boot and saddle ... off we would go and surround a farm. If we found any ammunition, or rifles ... the place was burned down and the womenfolk put into Concentration Camps. ... And so it went on, fighting, raiding and destroying farms. ... It was a sorry business and we soldiers did not like it.' And like many of the mounted Camerons, he did not wear a uniform, but dressed in whatever came to hand, slouch hat, shirt and jacket, moleskin trousers, so that in appearance he resembled a fighting Boer. It was a ruse that saved his life.

On 9 December, the 12th Brigade set up camp at the foot of Nooitgedacht and for three days the men rested and watered their animals. The mood in the camp was relaxed: Clements knew Smuts and De la Rey were on the prowl somewhere in the area, but were not strong enough to mount a full-scale assault. Pickets were duly posted around the main camp in the valley, and 300 men of the Northumberland Fusiliers under Captain Yatman were positioned on the crest of Nooitgedacht. A bridle-path ran down the face of the mountain, and halfway along their descent, in a *kloof*, or ravine, Lieutenant Sandilands and Sergeant Farmer established lines for the MIC. But Clements's scouts had failed to ascertain that Smuts had been reinforced recently by 1,500 men of General Beyer's Commando; and Clements lingered a day too long in the camp. In the early morning of Thursday, 13 December, the Boers paid him a visit to give him a wake-up call.

In the Moot, through the half-light of dawn, De la Rey's men charged the main camp from the west, and Smuts came in from the south to block the only exit. On Nooitgedacht, Beyer's commandos assaulted Captain Yatman and his guards and drove them into the breastworks. Woken by the blast of firearms, Lieutenants Sandilands and Murdoch led Sergeant Farmer and thirteen Camerons from the *kloof* up the bridle-path to a small ridge beneath the summit to give supporting fire to Yatman's beleaguered pickets. From their vantage point, the vastly superior Boer forces saw them coming and opened up a deadly fire. Lieutenant Murdoch was killed instantly, a second Cameron was shot dead, and five more, including Lieutenant Sandilands, fell wounded to the rocky ground. Sergeant Farmer took command, and under his leadership the Camerons kept up the uneven fight for several hours, pinned down beneath the ridge by the awesome firepower of the Boers. The pickets on top were finally overrun; and with ammunition running low among the Camerons, their plight became desperate when the Boers began to edge forward down the bridle-path towards their position. Sergeant Farmer had to act.

Picking up the helpless Sandilands, he slung him across his shoulders, and for a half a mile, assailed by relentless fire, he stumbled and staggered under the dead weight of his lieutenant, down the rugged, stony bridle-path to reach the safety of a dressing station. Not wasting a minute after leaving the unconscious man in the hands of the medics, Sergeant Farmer picked up a box of ammunition and headed back to his comrades on the ridge.

In his own account of the engagement, Sergeant Farmer said he was unable to return to his men, who were dispersed by the advancing Boers. Instead, he positioned himself in some rocks and engaged them. 'I noticed a lot of them [Boers] coming down the bridle path – I had an exciting time potting them before they discovered me.' With the Boers to his front and the main camp below under attack, Sergeant Farmer decided to retreat and collect together whatever men he could find and try to make a dash for the defensive perimeter General Clements was setting up on Yeomanry Hill in the Moot. 'I made for a farm and was suddenly challenged by a very young Boer several yards away.' The Boer opened fire on Farmer. 'Luckily, an old Boer knocked the rifle out of his hands and the bullet just missed my head. After being taken prisoner, I found out because I was wearing civilian trousers and a slouched hat, they thought I was a Boer.'

For outstanding courage under fire when rescuing a wounded officer, Sergeant Donald Dickson Farmer was awarded the Victoria Cross. His citation reads:

> Donald Farmer, Sergeant, 1st Battalion Cameron Highlanders. Date of Act of Bravery: 13 December 1900. During the attack on General Clement's camp at Nooitgedacht, on 13th December 1900, Lieutenant Sandilands, Cameron Highlanders, with fifteen men, went to the assistance of a picquet which was heavily engaged, most of the men having been killed or wounded. The enemy, who were hidden by trees, opened fire on the party at a range of about twenty yards, killing two and wounding five, including Lieutenant Sandilands. Sergeant Farmer at once went to the officer, who was perfectly helpless, and carried him away under a very heavy and close fire to a place of comparative safety, after which he returned to the firing line, and was eventually taken prisoner.

'The Boers assembled us in a field and were kind enough to feed us on our own rations of biscuits and bully-beef. They kept us for a couple of days, and then put us on the way to Rustenburg.' Returning to Pretoria in the New Year, Farmer was greeted with the news that Lieutenant Sandilands had survived his wounds. The two men became friends for life, and James Sandilands would have an illustrious career in the army, attaining the rank of major general.

Notice of Donald Farmer's award appeared in the *London Gazette* of 12 April 1901. In August of that year, the Duke and Duchess of Cornwall and York, the future King George V and Queen Mary, during their grand tour of the British Empire aboard the converted liner HMS *Ophir*, paid a visit to Pietermaritzburg, the capital of Natal Province. Two officers and fifty men of the Queen's Own Cameron Highlanders were detailed as escort to the royals. They were on hand to witness the first presentation of the Victoria Cross to a member of the regiment when the duke bestowed the honour on Sergeant Donald Farmer during a ceremony in front of Government House on 15 August 1901.

Donald Dickson Farmer was born at 5 Winchester Row, Kelso, Roxburgh-shire, on 28 May 1877. He was the son of Thomas Farmer of Edinburgh, a journeyman pastry cook, and Joanna Clark, an Englishwoman from London. A journeyman was a qualified tradesman who worked for another tradesman, but Thomas Farmer chose a literal interpretation of the term, wandering throughout Scotland in search of work. After marriage to Joanna in Edinburgh on 23 August 1876, he moved on to Kelso where his son was born. Donald's memories of his childhood are of a family in transit: Dundee, Pitlochry, Carnoustie and Perth were his homes until his parents settled finally in Edinburgh, at 24 Bread Street.

He was the eldest, followed by Joan, Euphemia, Marion, Violet, Jane and Thomas. Thomas Farmer senior eventually set up shop for himself as a pastry cook, at 48 Cross Causeway, and ran the business with his daughter Marion following the death of his wife in 1900. Donald's first ambition was to work as a pastry cook with his father, but in 1887, after enlisting in 12th Edinburgh Company, the Boys' Brigade, his sights changed. The brigade was run on military lines, and the uniform and disciplined ranks appealed to young Donald Farmer and placed him on course for a life in the army. He was the first former member of the Boys' Brigade to win a Victoria Cross.

To keep him at home, his father apprenticed him to an engineering company in Edinburgh when he left school in 1889, but young Donald would not be sidetracked from his ambition. By the age of 14, he had grown to his full height of 5 feet, 7 inches, and he left home to train for seven weeks in the militia at Glencorse Barracks, the depot of the 3rd Battalion, Royal Scots. With that experience behind him, he tramped to Leith Fort, a few miles north-east of Edinburgh, took the Queen's shilling and a railway voucher to the depot of the Queen's Own Cameron Highlanders, Inverness, arriving on 29 March 1892. He was two months short of his fifteenth birthday, but at the initial muster in the 1st Battalion, he was passed as 3201 Private Farmer to carry a rifle, aged 18 years and 1 month, to serve seven years with the colours and five years on the reserve list.

After six months of hard training in Inverness, he was posted to Fort St Angelo, Malta. Despite his youth, he quickly impressed his officers with his maturity, and within nine months he received his lance corporal stripe. In the sunny climes of Malta, he excelled on the sports field and quickly became an established member of the football team. His next posting was Gibralta, where he spent two years deployed along the frontier with Spain, and where his fitness was put to the test nightly, chasing and apprehending tobacco and whisky smugglers.

In April 1897, he was promoted to corporal; and, amid rumours of a campaign in Africa, he was encouraged to apply for re-engagement for a further two years for a bounty of £3. He was accepted, and within weeks the regiment was ordered to Cairo to join the Anglo-Egyptian Expeditionary Force under

Kitchener. After five years of peace-time service, Farmer spent the next five years in a state of constant war, marching and riding over 3,000 miles through Sudan and South Africa. For his services in Sudan, he received the British Medal and Khedive Medal and clasps, Atbarah and Omdurman; and for South Africa, the Queen's South Africa Medal, with clasps, Johannesburg, Wittenburg, Diamond Hill and Cape Colony, the King's South Africa Medal, with clasps 1901, 1902, and silver oakleaf. Thankfully, his broad chest could accommodate all the awards.

With the end of hostilities against the Boers, the Cameron Highlanders returned to Fort George, Inverness in the autumn of 1902 for a much-welcomed furlough of six weeks. And Sergeant Farmer VC was quickly into his old routine: up went the goalposts, out came the shirts, shorts and boots, and the season kicked off under his captaincy. At stake, the Army Challenge Cup, one of the oldest competitions in the footballing calendar, which Farmer set his mind on winning. 'We held our own in the soccer world, military and local competitions, cups and medals in plenty and we were unlucky when we failed several times to win the Army Cup final. On looking back I am afraid I must have been a Jonah.' And between games of football, there was always plenty of other sport, particularly fishing in the North Sea. Besides the fish, he netted and landed a wife.

On 28 August 1903, Sergeant Donald Farmer VC joined the 'army of benedicks', the ranks of the married. At the University Hotel, in Chambers Street, Edinburgh, he married Helen Hall Menzies Bonnar, daughter of Archibald and Marion Bonnar, and sister of his best friend in the battalion, Sergeant Robert Bonnar. The best man was the man whose life he had saved, the newly promoted Captain James W. Sandilands, and the ceremony was conducted by Helen's uncle, the Reverend J.M. Bonnar. After a short honeymoon, the happy couple were installed in married quarters in Fort George, and Sergeant Farmer VC was to spend three years there with nothing more onerous to concern him other than his duties and winning the cup. In February 1904, he was granted an extension for a further nine years to make twenty-one years with the colours. His first child, Muriel Joan, was born at Fort George in August.

The following year he was promoted to the rank of colour sergeant and was posted for two years to the Royal Barracks in Dublin, where a second daughter, Olive Marion, was born in October 1905. At Tidworth Camp on Salisbury Plain, a third daughter, Hilda Margaret, was born three years later. But Farmer was by now a worried man: he began to think he would be without a son.

In 1909, he took the decision which brought him and his family to Liverpool. With less than four years of service to complete, he decided to spend them with the new Territorial Force. He was appointed permanent staff instructor and was transferred as Colour Sergeant Donald Dickson Farmer VC to the 10th (Scottish) Battalion, the King's (Liverpool) Regiment, with head-quarters in Fraser Street, in the city centre.

On 31 July 1909, the Farmer family arrived in Liverpool, taking up residence in Duddington Avenue, Sefton Park: 'my wife had to get busy buying household essentials. We hadn't a stick of furniture to call our own. . . . It cost us something but we knew we were building our home.' Over the next five years, Farmer not only built a home but also a highly trained and active battalion of part-time territorial soldiers, the 'terriers', as they were known. He was a man of authority, but never an authoritarian, and he was ever willing to share his knowledge and vast experience with his men who had nothing but the highest regard and respect for him. And at home, his persistence was rewarded with the birth of a son in July 1910, who was christened with his own name, Donald Dickson Farmer; and he would grow to be the image of his father.

In May 1914, at the age of 37, Farmer had to face the inevitable, and retired from the army. Luckily, he received help from a friend in finding employment, and the transition into civilian life was eased. He found employment at the Jacob's biscuit factory in Long Lane, Aintree, though found it difficult to adjust to office work, far removed from all he had known since the age of 14. However, the army, reluctant to lose a man of such wide experience, came to his rescue, and he was persuaded by his former commanding officer to join the Liverpool Scottish as a territorial on special, overage enlistment. And within weeks of doing so, hostilities erupted. Bidding both his family and the civilian job farewell, he was mobilized immediately in C Company of the 1st Battalion, the Liverpool Scottish, as 10742 Private Donald Farmer VC. He would fight on the Western Front, his third campaign for his country.

Posted to King's Park, Edinburgh under the command of Lieutenant Colonel W. Nichol, he was promoted to sergeant and then sergeant major, before moving into billets at Tunbridge Wells, where he became acting regimental sergeant major. In November, the battalion embarked on SS *Maiden* at Southampton for Le Havre, and when landed, marched off to take up positions near Mount Kemmel, south of Ypres. The battalion's medical officer was Lieutenant Noel Chavasse.

The Liverpool Scottish moved into the Ypres Salient, and on 16 June 1915, went over the top for the first time at the Battle of Hooge, known officially as the first action at Bellewaarde Lake. The battalion was in the second wave, attacking towards Bellewaarde Farm, where it met stout German resistance before withdrawing to consolidate the gains made earlier in the first-line trenches. Such was the ferocity of the battle that of the twenty-three officers and 519 other ranks who charged the German lines for a gain of 1,000 yards of mud, only two officers and 149 other ranks survived unscathed. Recalling the battle in later years, in which another Liverpool hero, Bill Ratcliffe, also fought, he spoke only of Noel Chavasse: 'our Medical Officer . . . the bravest man I ever knew. He was missing for two or three days after the Hooge battle and it was found he had attended all the wounded in no man's land and he even dressed the wounds of the Huns. He was entitled to the VC then.'

The Hooge offensive was the only major offensive in which he fought during the First World War. He was commissioned lieutenant and quartermaster in the newly formed 2nd Battalion, Liverpool Scottish, stationed in Ashford, Kent, and later filled the role of captain and adjutant. When the 2nd Battalion was amalgamated with the 1st, Captain Farmer VC was posted to a château near Boulogne, where he helped to induct and familiarize the newly arriving American forces. This accomplished, he moved on to the divisional reception camp, where battle-weary troops were retrained to take over relief duties in the lines.

His good work was recognized with promotion to temporary major; and when the Armistice was declared, he was made second-in-command of III Corps Concentration Camp, where demobilizing troops were gathered prior to repatriation. He succeeded to full command of the camp and was promoted to temporary lieutenant colonel in April 1919. Altogether, 50,000 men passed through his hands with the minimum of fuss on their way home. 'And so my job was ended and it only left me to demobilise myself which I did in May 1919. So thus I finished the 1914–18 war with not a scratch in this, my third campaign, nor in either of the two, preceding campaigns ... I wondered what FATE had in store for me. I always have been a fatalist and I am a living example. The Gods are on my side.' To have survived nine years of campaigning in Sudan, South Africa and on the Western Front without sustaining a wound or an injury was miraculous. It appears that the only hard knocks and injuries he suffered during his army life were on the football pitch. For his war services, he was awarded the 1914–15 Star, the British War Medal and the Victory Medal.

After twenty-eight years with the colours, fate brought Donald Farmer home to Liverpool and his family. His father had been ill for some time and he travelled to Edinburgh to be with him in his last moments. But 'the Land' forgot Donald Farmer VC, and for the next six years he was to find himself in and out of work: Lloyd George's promise of a land fit for heroes did not materialize. He went back to work at Jacob's biscuit factory and settled into civilian life, but the pay was poor and insufficient to meet the expenses of a growing family.

In 1921, he took the chance of changing jobs, despite a worldwide trade slump and growing lines of unemployed, and joined the the newly formed Army, Navy, Air Force Institute, the NAAFI, as a military representative. But he was made redundant after only a year and ended up on the dole. He held various other low-paid jobs over the next four years until fate, in the form of a brewing company, smiled kindly on him. He was employed as a representative by WilliamYoungers and Company, the Edinburgh-based brewery, which was seeking to expand its business in Liverpool. Youngers had only one premises in

Liverpool at the time, the Clock Inn in London Road, which became his operational base. Coincidently, the pub was just around the corner from the Fraser Street barracks of the Liverpool Scottish, and so for some years, Farmer was able to combine business with pleasure, the pub becoming the battalion's unofficial mess.

Donald Farmer was a genial man, full of humour, with an engaging personality, who could converse with anyone on a wide variety of subjects, particularly sport, and he left an indelible impression on all who met him, including the Prince of Wales. He enjoyed the life of a representative and salesman: he was his own boss and his success with the pub landlords of the city, many of them Scottish and Irish ex-servicemen, was guaranteed. 'It was . . . the happiest time of my life in the commercial world,' he reported.

Besides keeping contact with the Liverpool Scottish, he made a point of attending the Victoria Cross reunions. He was present at the afternoon party for holders at Buckingham Palace, hosted by King George V, on 26 June 1920, and there he met for the first time Gabriel George Coury VC, who would become a good friend. Together, they attended the Victoria Cross Reunion Dinner on 9 November 1929, hosted by the Prince of Wales at the Royal Gallery, House of Lords. And Donald Farmer VC demonstrated his humorous side, causing an uproar when he bypassed the queue of autograph hunters lining up in front of the Prince of Wales. 'I was determined to get the Prince's autograph on my menu card,' he said. 'I decided to adopt novel tactics . . . I got down on all fours and crawled beneath the tables to where the Prince was sitting. Suddenly I confronted him with the menu card poked up in front of his nose from beneath the table. There were howls of laughter, and the Prince himself was highly amused. My effort took the trick for I got his autograph.'

At the outbreak of the Second World War, he joined the Home Guard and was offered a command. But he could not give the necessary time to such a position and even refused to take a lance corporal stripe. He offered his services for 'teaching the troops the art of pressing the trigger', as he described it, but with his brewery customers to see, some of whom had been bombed out of their premises, his time with the Home Guard was to last but eight months. He was 62 years of age and he felt he had seen enough of war. He became a fire-watcher during the Liverpool *blitz*, which commenced in August 1940 and was to continue until January 1942.

Meanwhile, his son Donald was following in his illustrious footsteps. At the age of 15 he joined the Liverpool Scottish as a cadet, and served with the 'terriers' until the Second World War began. He was mobilized on 1 September 1939 with the 1st Battalion, Liverpool Scottish, and was commissioned as second lieutenant with the 10th Battalion, Highland Light Infantry, City of Glasgow Regiment. On joining B Company he was promoted to lieutenant and served in north-west Europe.

In the early hours of 24 March 1945, his platoon was in the van of B Company, tasked with clearing a defensive line, a bund, half a mile in length along the west bank of the River Rhine. The bund was invested with two heavily armed German Parachute Companies, which repulsed the first two attacks by B Company. Casualties in his platoon were high, but Lieutenant Farmer showed the way. Armed with a sten gun, smoke and hand grenades, he charged across 100 yards of open ground under fire and single-handedly elimated a post of eight Germans. Following his example, B Company cleared the bund, and the Royal Engineers were able to move in and build bridges across the river.

For his outstanding courage and leadership, Lieutenant Donald Farmer was awarded the Military Cross. It is doubtful whether there was a prouder father in Liverpool than Donald Farmer VC, when news of his son's award was published in the *London Gazette* on 7 June 1945.

Donald Farmer MC lived at 53 Walshingham Road, Childwall and before the war had worked in the South Castle Street branch of W. & T. Glover and Company of Salford, manufacturers of electrical wire and cables. And he returned to his position after demobilization, rising to become the manager for Merseyside and North Wales. In 1959, when the company was integrated into a larger, sister group, British Insulated Cable Company, he was made redundant. He and his wife moved to Southampton where he worked as a sales clerk for Pirelli. On retirement, he moved to Shawford, near Winchester, and lived at Coombe Dower Cottage until his death on 26 July 1995, at the age of 85.

When the Second World War ended, Donald Farmer VC retired from work. In August 1953, Donald and Helen celebrated their golden wedding anniversary at their new home in 6A Waverley Road, Sefton Park. The event was recorded in the local press, and he was pictured standing proudly beside his wife wearing his full array of medals, his shoulders thrown back, ever the soldier, even at the age of 75. In spite of his many years in Liverpool, he never lost his gentle, Scottish burr, and he spoke proudly of his Scottish heritage and of being a member of the Liverpool Scottish.

As the oldest living holder of the Victoria Cross, he was present at the Centenary Review of holders in Hyde Park on 26 June 1956. What should have been a happy occasion was marred for him by the absence of his friend, Gabriel Coury VC, who had passed away. He had paid his last respects to him at the graveside in St Peter and Paul's Cemetery, Crosby, in February.

Donald and Helen Farmer moved to a new home at 165 Greenhill Road, Mossley Hill not long after the Hyde Park Review. There he took ill and was diagnosed with cancer. He was admitted to the Radium Institute in Myrtle Street, for radiotherapy. But, on Sunday, 23 December 1956, at the age of 79, Lieutenant Colonel Donald Dickson Farmer VC died, attended by his wife and children.

On 28 December, the funeral service with full military honours was held at the crematorium chapel of Anfield Cemetery, conducted by the Reverend Bell, Minister of the Church of St Andrew's, Rodney Street. The coffin, draped in the Union Jack, and bearing his Victoria Cross and eleven other decorations, was carried by eight serving warrant officers and sergeants of 1st Battalion, Liverpool Scottish. Following cremation, his ashes were scattered in the Garden of Remembrance at the Crematorium. A small wooden plaque on the trunk of a tree, placed there by Bob Halliday, a worker at the crematorium, is all that commemorates the last resting place of this brave soldier.

Helen Farmer outlived her husband by twelve years, passing away at the age of 91 in 1968. On 9 May 1992, a plaque was erected to her husband by the Royal British Legion at Kelso War Memorial in the grounds of Kelso Abbey, and it was unveiled by her daughter, Hilda. The medals of Lieutenant Colonel Donald Dickson Farmer VC were presented by his children to the Highlanders Regimental Museum, and are on display at Fort George, Inverness.

Ernest Wright Alexander VC
(1870–1934)

Ernest Wright Alexander was born to a wealthy Liverpool family on 2 October 1870, at 87 Everton Road. From an early age, he set his mind on a military career and became a professional soldier. A thinker and an innovator, he was a gentleman of great personal charm, compassion and loyalty, a soldier's soldier who considered the men serving under him his greatest asset. He fought with great distinction during the First World War and his military career progressed solely on merit at the behest of a keen intelligence, and he rose rapidly through the ranks to become major general. His father Robert called him a 'dacent boady', a good and honourable man, as he himself was.

Robert Alexander was an astute businessman whose dealings were tempered with a whimsical streak as wide as the Irish Sea. Born in Belfast in 1837, he came to Liverpool in his teens to work as a ship broker and manager with Young, Liston and Company of Castle Street. Diligent and industrious, within a decade of his arrival he was the owner of one of the city's great shipping companies. He leased a ship here, bought one there, and built up a small fleet until he was able to branch out on his own as Robert Alexander and Company with offices in Tower Buildings, North Water Street. Unlike his friend, Henry Lafone, he steered clear of blockade-running during the American Civil War, and traded successfully in Australia and India. In 1874, he established a second shipping line, the Sun Shipping Company, which Liverpudlians were quick to nickname the Hall Line.

He named his vessels after the stately homes, mansions and halls of the great families of Britain. The *Eaton Hall*, named after the home near Chester of the Grosvenor family, the Dukes of Westminster, was one of the first, as was the *Haddon Hall*, after the manor of the Manners family in Derbyshire. Knowsley Hall, home to the Earls of Derby, and situated on the outskirts of Liverpool, did not escape his attention either. The *Knowsley Hall*, an iron ship of 2,000 tons, came into service in 1874 for the passenger run to the Antipodes.

Robert married Annie Greggan, daughter of James Cranston Greggan, a Belfast businessman, in 1861. Their first child, Arthur, was born in Madeira during a business trip. Robert, like his vessels, was always on the move, and he had several business and private addresses in Liverpool as his shipping interests prospered and his family grew: Alice, the only daughter in the family, and Ernest, were born in Everton; the youngest children, Austin, Philip and Frederick, arrived when Robert and Annie were living at 11 Beach Lawn, Waterloo, which stood on the River Mersey. The family then moved to Homesefton, 37 Aigburth Drive, where Ernest spent his formative years.

In 1890, Robert had a grand idea, an Irish whimsy, purchasing his own hall, a mansion and an estate on the outskirts of Liverpool, Woolton Heys, Woolton, after which he planned to name one of his vessels. But he was afflicted with gallstone problems; and with his eldest son Arthur making his own way as a shipowner, Ernest set on a military career and his younger sons too inexperienced to assume control, he decided to sell up and retire. He sold out in 1901 to the Ellerman Line, another notable Liverpool shipping company, for £450,000, a colossal fortune for the times, and retired to one of the city's most delightful and prestigious addresses, 13 Abercromby Square, off Oxford Street. A close friend and neighbour at No. 19 was the Right Reverend Francis James Chavasse DD, Lord Bishop of Liverpool and father of Noel Chavasse.

Ernest Alexander began his education at the age of 6 at Beechfield Preparatory School, Malvern, but from the age of 11 he was taught at home; and it was not until September 1884 that he re-entered the mainstream and attended Harrow School. He studied there for only ten terms, leaving at Christmas 1887 for the Royal Military Academy at Woolwich in early January, having decided on a career with the Royal Artillery (RA).

The following year, he was commissioned as a second lieutenant to serve with the 9th Battery, RA, stationed in Fort Bovisand at the eastern approach to Plymouth Breakwater. In the summer of 1892, he was promoted to lieutenant and posted to India. His first station was Barrackpore, Calcutta, where William Connolly VC was stationed in 1837. He spent eight peaceful years on the subcontinent at the cantonment at Kamptee, in central India, where tiger-hunting and pig-sticking were the favoured sports of officers. Promoted to captain in the Royal Field Artillery (RFA), he returned to England in November 1900. He went into barracks and was not called upon for duty in the Boer War, which by then had moved on from set-piece battles to a war of attrition, wherein artillery was but a minor element.

While stationed at Farnborough Barracks, he met Rose Newcombe, daughter of the late Major Newcombe RA: they married at Aldershot Manor, Hampshire, on 1 September 1903. The following month, he returned to India with his new bride and lived for three years at Barrackpore and Umbala. Their first children, twins, were born on the sub-continent in 1905, and were named after their paternal grandparents, Robert and Annie.

Just before returning to England in 1906, his abilities as a leader were recognized and he was promoted to the rank of major. While awaiting another posting, he lived for a time at Brant House, Wimbledon Parkside with his brother, Frederick, and his father, who had moved to London following the death of his wife. Robert died of kidney failure in April 1911.

He was given command of 119th Battery, 27th Brigade, RFA, attached to the 5th Division, stationed at Newbridge Artillery Barracks on the River Liffey. Major Alexander lived with his family at 117 Ridgeway, Martinstown, near the Curragh, a beautiful house which Rose quickly turned into a home. And for the next seven years, life was all he could have hoped for.

He attended his duties assiduously, and he was rarely absent when his battery was training, on manoeuvres and on the gunnery range. He had an inquiring, scientific mind and applied it to the military field. An avid reader, he was well versed in artillery theory and practice, and he also kept abreast of new tactics, one of which he would champion in 1915. And on the home front, two more children blessed the family, George William and Mary.

On 2 July 1914, as the war clouds gathered, Alexander and Rose were struck down by tragedy when George William died at the age of 3 of complications from a tubercular abscess. He was buried in the military cemetery at the Curragh. A month later, with barely time to mourn his son, Major Alexander left Dublin for France: on 4 August, Britain declared war against the Central Powers, Germany, Austro-Hungary, Bulgaria and Turkey.

The embarkation of the British Expeditionary Force (BEF) to France began in great secrecy on 6 August. Fifteen days later, four infantry divisions and one division of cavalry were crossing the French border into Belgium, ten miles south of Mons, under the command of General Sir John French. The plan was to link up with the General Lanrezac's French Army near Charleroi, to the east of the city, and halt and push back the advancing Germans. But, in the early morning of 22 August, forward units of the BEF encountered elements of General von Kluck's First Army advancing towards the French border. Sir John ordered his force to take up positions in front of Mons, and he delineated a second line to the south, from Elouges to Frameries, as the fall-back position.

The 5th Division, under Major General Sir Charles Fergusson, stood in the centre of the British front; and on a wooded rise between the villages of Dour and Elouges, Major Alexander positioned the six, 18-pound field guns of his battery and prepared to give supporting fire. As dawn broke through a drifting, misty rain on Sunday, 23 August, General von Kluck launched 160,000 battle-ready troops against the 70,000 men of the BEF who were still digging in.

The fighting raged all day. The BEF put up a dogged and heroic opposition, but the sheer weight of the German forces steadily made inroads into the defences. At five o'clock, with the Germans threatening both flanks, Sir John French ordered his forces to fall back to the Elouges–Frameries line. The Germans paused their attack during the night and an orderly withdrawal was made by the BEF, with unit leap-frogging unit under cover of a rearguard. But when news arrived that the French army was in full retreat and could offer no support, Sir John ordered the withdrawal to continue further south, towards the town of Bavai.

Near Elouges, after the main body of 5th Division had retired and the rear-guard was following, Sir Charles Fergusson received a worrying message from the observer of a low-flying Avro of the Royal Flying Corps: four echelons of an entire army corps were heading his way in hot pursuit of his retiring division. He appealed for renewed cavalry support and the assistance of a small force of infantry and artillery to mount a second rearguard. Major Alexander answered Fergusson's appeal, and galloped his six guns, two ammunition wagons and 170 men of 119th Battery into Elouges. He would stand and fight as part of the rearguard of two infantry battalions and two troops of cavalry.

There was nothing to Elouges but a railway station, a chemical mine and factory complex, which had its own engines, trucks and narrow-gauge rail line to carry away spoil to a huge dump pit. Placing two guns of the battery close to the main railway station under the command of Lieutenant Preston, Major Alexander positioned the remaining four guns 500 yards to the east of the town, close to the embankment of the bridge which carried the spoil rail line above the main road. He corralled the horses and limbers in the lee of the embankment, then began registering targets and laying his guns to stem the German advance.

The two battalions of infantry had no time to dig in, and took what cover was available along a rise in front of Elouges. Just after noon, Major Alexander opened fire with his guns on the massing hordes of German foot-soldiers streaming south from Mons, intent on sweeping through the rearguard to swamp the 5th Division. As Alexander's shrapnel shells burst above the heads of the troops and thinned their ranks, the infantry opened up with rapid rifle fire of fifteen rounds a minute. The Germans were stunned by the sheer volume of lead and steel concentrated on their front ranks, and the attack faltered and recoiled, momentarily giving the defenders hope.

But the opening rounds were shrugged off and the advance resumed its momentum. And now the Germans began to retaliate. Three enemy batteries zeroed in on Major Alexander's guns and all hell broke loose. The position was pounded by shells and riddled with rifle and machine-gun fire, and the men of the 119th Battery began to suffer. Beneath a blanket of screaming steel and lead, and amid the rhythmic, roaring cacophony of discharging guns, the gunners were bowled over, dead, wounded, bloodied and dismembered.

Major Alexander moved calmly from gun to gun, oblivious to the flying lead and steel, clambering over bodies, and urging on his gunners to keep working, pitching in when needed and directing the fire over open sights as the charging Germans came into full view. But the situation was grave: the infantry began falling back from the rise, overwhelmed by weight of numbers; Lieutenant Preston's position near the railway station became untenable and he brought in his guns; and as the casualties mounted, Alexander's firepower began to fall away. In danger of being overrun, he sought to save his men and the guns. Forty-two men and many of the horses had been lost, so vicious and efficient had been the German counter-attack, and he called on the survivors to man-handle the guns to safety, to the lee of the embankment.

The ground was heavy and badly churned, turned to mud with rain and blood, and the exhausted men could only move the guns one at a time. As they struggled under fire with their burdens, Alexander noted a group of mounted men to his left, remnants of the 9th Lancers, who were rallying following a heroic but reckless dash against the Germans. He called them over to assist.

Despite the continuing German onslaught, the troopers dismounted and rolled up their sleeves. Officers and men toiled together, using manpower and drag ropes to extricate the guns from the muddy ground and haul them under cover. Once the guns were out of the line of fire, Alexander and his men harnessed up as many of the horses as they could find, put them in the limbers, hooked up the guns and, gathering up as many wounded as possible in the ammunition wagons, galloped away, heading south.

The rearguard action saved the 5th Division, purchasing sufficient time for the battle-weary troops to reach the lines at Bavai unhindered. In the mean-time, Sir John French had ordered a further withdrawal to the town of Le Cateau. But so relentless was the German pursuit of the BEF that by the time Major Alexander rushed the remnants of his men and his guns into the town in the evening of 25 August, the BEF was already falling back on St Quentin, twenty miles further south.

The muddy roads out of Le Cateau were clogged with men and bogged-down vehicles, and the 5th Division, part of II Corps under General Sir Horace Smith-Dorrien, had nowhere to go as the enemy closed on the town. Smith-Dorrien believed it impossible to retire without being overwhelmed. When orders were received at seven-thirty that night to retreat, he gave orders to stand and fight on the ridge to the west and south of the town.

The 5th Division dug in across the heights to the west of the valley where Le Cateau clung to the banks of the River Selle. In the time available, the infantry could only dig shallow trenches a mile and a half in length along the ridge towards Inchy, on the road to Cambrai. Three brigades of the divisional artillery, including Major Alexander's weary battery, were brought into the firing line among the infantry.

Through a heavy mist as the sun rose, the forward units of the Germans were spotted; and from the north their batteries, concentrated at Rambourlieux Farm in front of the village of Neuvilly, unleashed a devastating barrage. The British artillery replied as the Germans came on, and punished them severely. But on they came, turning both flanks. By ten o'clock, the batteries and the battalions of the 5th Division found themselves under heavy enfilading fire, which destroyed guns and inflicted heavy casualties. Alexander's depleted battery fought itself to a standstill, and again he distinguished himself under fire, driving his men to greater effort, boosting morale and keeping the guns in action, firing at point-blank range over open sights.

German aircraft overflew the British lines, and streamers were released directly above the batteries, highlighting their positions to the German artillery observers. Heavy artillery and machine-gun fire was brought to bear quickly on the British lines, aimed at the batteries, adding to the enfilading fire which was causing such havoc. In a very short time, the position became indefensible, and the order came through to evacuate the guns. Raked by fire from three sides, the gunners responded manfully and stood exposed to the assault to haul and drag out the guns. One of the men was knocked down by a shell splinter, and Major Alexander went to his aid. Returning under fire to the front line, he carried the gunner to safety and ensured he was carted off in an ammunition wagon when the gunners made their escape.

For dedication to duty and gallantry in the line of fire, Major Ernest Wright Alexander was awarded the Victoria Cross. His citation reads:

> Ernest Wright Alexander, Lieutenant Colonel, 119th Battery, Royal Field Artillery. Date of Act of Bravery: 24 August 1914. For conspicuous bravery and great ability at Elouges on 24th August 1914, when the flank guard was attacked by a German Corps, in handling his battery against overwhelming odds with such conspicuous success that all his guns were saved, notwithstanding that they had to be withdrawn by hand by himself and three other men. This enabled the retirement of the 5th Division to be carried out without serious loss. Subsequently, Lieutenant Colonel Alexander (then Major) rescued a wounded man under a heavy fire with the greatest gallantry and devotion to duty.

Early the following morning, the battle-weary troops streamed into St Quentin, where they grabbed a bite to eat and a few hours' rest before resuming the retreat, which was to take them all the way back to the River Marne, thirty miles from Paris. Here, in the middle of September, the BEF halted the Germans' advance and drove them back to the River Aisne.

The following month, Major Alexander was transferred temporarily to 7th Division to take charge of 22nd Brigade, RFA, responsible for twenty-four guns and approximately 800 men. He commanded the brigade at the First Battle of Ypres when the Salient was created. And when the battle was over, Major Alexander, an 'Old Contemptible' – one of the men who were under arms on 4 August and who fought in France and Belgium up to midnight of 22 November 1914, when the fighting at Ypres ceased – was promoted to lieutenant colonel (RA), and returned to the 5th Division, this time as commander of the 27th Brigade. His former command, 119th Battery, was a unit of the brigade, and he received a very warm welcome from his former comrades.

Notice of the award of the Victoria Cross to Ernest Wright Alexander was published in the *London Gazette* on 18 February 1915. He returned to England on leave at the beginning of March, and it is thought he was decorated by the king at Buckingham Palace later that month.

On his return to France, he barely had time to settle in to his command before he was given another. Douglas Haig personally promoted him to temporary brigadier general, and gave him command of more than 3,000 men in four brigades of field artillery, one brigade of garrison artillery and the divisional ammunition column of the newly formed 15th (Scottish) Division.

His new job was to advise on and coordinate the role of the artillery with the Divisional Commander, Major General McCracken, and his appointment came at a very opportune time. Planning for the Battle of Loos, the first 'Big Push' mounted by the Allies, was nearing completion, and he would, for the first time since hostilities commenced, command during an Allied offensive. He would also revive and champion the tactic known as the rolling or creeping barrage, which the Bulgarian artillery had first developed during the siege of Adrianople in 1913 during the First Balkan War.

The rolling barrage provided a protective curtain of artillery fire that was lifted and extended in controlled stages to match the advance of the infantry against enemy trenches. Designed to keep the defenders in their dugouts until the last possible moment, the barrage also created devastation and a pall of smoke and flying debris to obscure the advance, thereby allowing maximum numbers of infantry to reach the trenches before any effective resistance could be mounted.

Alexander promoted the rolling barrage as a potential solution to the stalemate of trench warfare: casualties would be reduced in no man's land, enemy lines would be more easily penetrated and captured, leading to the breakthrough the Allies sought. He employed the tactic at Loos, but it met with limited success: the infantry attacked on too wide a front and it proved impossible to coordinate the infantry advance with the artillery fire. In addition, the numbers and weight of the available artillery were insufficient to give proper support, and many of the shells were duds and supplies were quickly depleted.

Nevertheless, Alexander persisted in promoting the tactic, and when his talents and intelligence were recognized once more and he was promoted to officer commanding, RA, XV Corps on 24 April 1916, he found a ready convert in the commander, Major General Sir Henry Horne. Together, Alexander and Horne became the architects of the rolling barrage during the Battle of the Somme. Success was mixed: again the tactic failed when the infantry attacked on too wide a front when the precise coordination in timing and movement between advancing troops and the covering artillery broke down. But it succeeded in smaller assaults of limited scope, when targets and movement could be better defined, such as the storming of Guillemont in September 1916.

When he moved on from the Somme, Horne continued with the tactic, especially during small offensives on narrow fronts, and achieved great success in the last two years of the war, most notably with the Canadians at Vimy Ridge. It was not the decisive tactic to win the war that the generals were

The only known photo of Joseph Prosser VC

Joseph Prosser's headstone

The only known photo of John Kirk VC

John Kirk's headstone

The only known photo of Alfred Stowell Jones VC

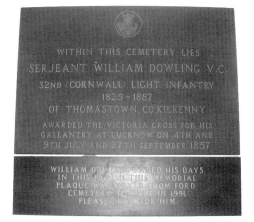

Memorial plaque to William Richard Dowling VC

Headstone of William Connolly VC   William Connolly's VC

The only known photo of George Hinckley VC   George Hinckley's headstone

Memorial to Paul Kenna

Paul Aloysius Kenna VC

George Edward Nurse VC

George Nurse's headstone

Arthur Herbert Lindsay
Richardson VC

Arthur Richardson's
headstone

Donald Dickson Farmer VC

Arthur Herbert Procter VC

Ernest Wright Alexander VC

Gabriel Coury's headstone

Gabriel George Coury VC

David Jones's headstone

David Jones VC

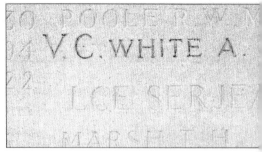

Albert White VC commemorated on the Arras memorial

Albert White VC

Ronald Neil Stuart VC

Ronald Stuart's headstone

William Ratcliffe's headstone

William Ratcliffe receiving his VC

Alexander Lafone commemorated on the Knockholt memorial

Alexander Malins Lafone VC

Hugh McDonald McKenzie VC

Cyril Edward Gourley VC

Cyril Gourley's headstone

Frank Lester VC

Arthur Evans VC

hoping for, but it did enjoy some success, and it certainly saved many lives. Nowadays, Horne is generally credited with the development of the rolling barrage, though he readily conceded at the end of the war that much of the success was due to the innovations of his artillery commander, Ernest Alexander VC.

In March 1917, wearied by months of fighting, Alexander took leave to see his wife and family. When he returned to the front on 31 May 1917 it was as Commanding Officer, RA, with the XI Army Corps. This command took him to the Southern Front, to Italy, where he helped to shore up the Italian artillery brigades following the Battle of Caporetto on 24 October 1917, when the Italian army had retreated in disarray in the face of a combined Austro-German offensive.

Alexander returned to the Western Front with XI Corps in March 1918. He found himself once more in Ypres, near Bethune, in company with the Portuguese Independent Artillery Corps (CAPI), and two divisions of the Portuguese Expeditionary Force (CEP), attached to the First Army under the command of his old friend General Sir Henry Horne. The Portuguese had come to France in 1917 but had never settled, hating the cold weather and British rations, and were on the verge of mutiny when Alexander arrived. The CAPI was brought under his command, the 2nd Division, CEP, was incorporated into the XI Corps, while the 1st Division was taken out of the line to be replaced by the West Lancashire Division, among whose ranks were Private Procter VC and Lieutenant Cyril Gourley VC.

At this time, General Erich Ludendorff was putting the finishing touches to 'Operation Georgette', part of his 'Spring offensive', the last-ditch attempt by the Germans to win the war. On 9 April, four German divisions smashed into the reluctant CEP at Neuve Chapelle, inflicting more than 7,000 casualties in a matter of hours. The situation became desperate very quickly: Horne's left flank became exposed when the CEP collapsed, and the British divisions struggled to close the gap. They were soon falling back towards the River Lys. By nightfall, the Germans had advanced more than four miles.

Horne whisked Alexander away from XI Corps and promoted him to temporary major general, RA, at First Army Headquarters, commanding thirty-six brigades of artillery, and tasked with halting the German onslaught. By 11 April, the Germans had made gains of up to ten miles and Field Marshal Sir Douglas Haig issued his famous 'backs to the wall' order of the day, for the Allies to stand and fight. By the end of the month, Ludendorff's thrust was brought to a standstill by the combined efforts of Alexander's artillery and the infantry, most notably the men of the 55th West Lancashire Division at Estaires.

The spring offensive was the last throw of the dice for the Germans, and became the prelude to the 'Hundred Days Offensive', the final, Allied 'Big Push', launched in August, which led to the Armistice of 11 November. Major

General Alexander VC continued to command the artillery of the First Army throughout the final offensive, and he finished the war near Mons, where he had fought his first engagement in 1914.

During the war, Alexander was mentioned nine times in dispatches, seven of which were recorded for actions against the enemy, and for which he received the single oak leaf in silver. Following the Armistice, further honours and awards were granted in recognition of his war service. He had already been appointed Companion, Order of St Michael and St George, CMG, in the King's Birthday Honours List of 23 June 1915, and he was made Companion, Order of the Bath, CB. From the French came the Croix de Guerre; from the Italians, Knight of the Military Order of Savoy; and from the Portuguese, Grand Officer of the Military Order of Aviz. As an 'Old Contemptible', he was awarded the 1914 Star with clasp and rose, the British War Medal, the Victory Medal. He also received the Coronation Medal, King Edward VII.

On 2 June 1919, Ernest Alexander was promoted to colonel, and three days later he took command of the Royal Artillery, Southern Area, Aldershot, with the temporary rank of brigadier general. In 1920, at the age of 50, he retired from the active list with the rank of major general with thirty-one years of service, and went home to his wife and children.

He first task was to find a home, and because Rose had family and friends in Devon, that was where he set his sights. His father would have been proud of him: he decided on an old country hall and estate in Devon, Horsewell House, South Milton, near Kingsbridge, which he purchased from Miss Ilbert, one of the two principal landowners in that part of the county.

He had retired from the army but not from work. There was a great deal of improvement to be made around the house, the garden and parkland, and he rolled up his sleeves and began work. Like his father, Robert, he was an intensely loyal man, and he showed this quality when three former members of 119th Battery, who had fought alongside him at Elouges, came to live and work at Horsewell House. Thomas Williams, who had been his batman, was employed as a gardener, together with Thomas Doyle, his groom, and William McCullen, his trumpeter. The four old comrades transformed the estate. On the death of their former leader, the three men received annuities in his will.

In retirement, Ernest Alexander VC remained a man of duty and service, and was very active in community affairs. He was President of the local Royal British Legion, a Justice of the Peace, a member of the Rural District Council, and he was elected for the parish of All Saints to the Kingsbridge Guardians Committee, which oversaw the provision of relief to the poor. And on 17 July 1931, he was appointed Deputy Lord Lieutenant of the County of Devonshire. He was known in the area as a quiet, modest man who much preferred to be known as Mister rather than General.

In later life, he was persistently troubled, as his father had been, with gall-stone problems. However, the complaint was not diagnosed as serious, and certainly not life-threatening. Generally, his health was good and he continued to spend most of his time outdoors. But in August 1934 he was taken in to South Hams Hospital where he was diagnosed with acute cholecystitis, inflammation of the gall bladder caused by the impaction of a gallstone in the neck of the gall bladder. A routine operation to remove the obstruction found that the gall bladder had perforated; he died in the hospital on 25 August.

The body of Ernest Wright Alexander VC was cremated and the ashes were buried alongside his father in the family plot at Putney Vale Cemetery, Wandsworth. Modest to the end, his name only is inscribed on the headstone: his rank and the long list of post-nominal titles were omitted, as he had instructed. Today the stone is in a state of poor repair, and it is to be hoped that something may be done in the near future to remedy the situation and highlight for all to see the last resting place of this brave soldier.

Undone by the death of her husband, Rose Alexander died six months later. Very little is known of the Alexander children. They left Horsewell House in 1936 and the estate was sold. Robert Alexander served as a lieutenant with the Royal Navy, and his twin sister, Annie, married Lieutenant Colonel W.P. Akerman. Of Mary, nothing has been heard.

On 25 February 1999, Ernest Alexander's Victoria Cross was put up for auction by Dix, Noonan and Webb. It was knocked down to the Michael Ashcroft Trust, the holding institution for the Michael Ashcroft Victoria Cross Collection. The Trust hopes to display the medal and others in the collection once a suitable venue has been found.

Arthur Herbert Procter VC
(1890–1973)

Before the turn of the last century, approximately 65 per cent of the working population of Liverpool were part-time workers, whose employment was directly or indirectly dependent upon the port and the sailing and docking of passenger and cargo vessels: 'no ships, no work, no pay'. Chief among those workers were the thousands of clerks, who, with bills of laden, ledgers and notebooks, tallied and recorded goods, services and cash on ships and quays, and in warehouses, markets, offices and shops. It was essential, but poorly paid work, giving barely enough to tide a man over the periods of unemployment when the port was quiet. Nevertheless, family traditions grew up, and son often followed father into the occupation. Arthur Procter's family had such a tradition, and it could be said that clerking was in his blood.

Arthur Herbert's grandfather, Richard, worked as a clerk with one of the several large timber merchants that crowded Derby Road, parallel to the Dock Road, and which dealt in lumber from the Brunswick, Hornby, Huskisson and Canada Docks. He married Emily Tyerman in 1863 and the couple lived in Irlam Lane, Bootle. His eldest son, Arthur Richard, born in 1864, began his working life as a clerk. But he had ambition and sought permanence and stability in his chosen profession, away from the vagaries of the port-dependent employment. By the time he married Sarah Ellen Cumpsty in 1886, he was a full-time clerk with Parrs Bank, in their branch at 55 Church Street, on the corner with Derby Road.

Sarah Ellen Cumpsty was born in Preston but had grown up in Bootle and lived at 216 Rimrose Road. Her mother, Bridget, was from Galway, Ireland, and her father, John, hailed from Lancaster. He worked as a clerk and book-seller before moving via Preston to Liverpool, where he started up in business for himself as a book-binder. Sarah, the youngest of seven children, was known by her second name, Ellen, within the family.

Arthur and Ellen Procter lived in a small apartment above the bank premises, and they had four children: Ethel, Arthur Herbert, born on 11 August 1890, Clarence and Ernest. Ethel and Arthur Herbert were educated at St Mary's Church of England Primary School in Waverley Street, a few minutes' walk from their home. But, before he was 9, Arthur Herbert was sent away from home to live at 3 Elm Grove Terrace, Exeter, with his father's younger brother, Herbert, and his great-aunt, Mary Tyerman, sister of Emily.

His father lost his position with the bank and took to the drink, turning his home into a battlefield. The brunt of his drunken outbursts was carried by the young Arthur Herbert; and Ellen, whose health was failing following the birth of her fourth child, could not protect him from her husband's outrages. When he found employment as a clerk with Lever Brothers of Port Sunlight, one of the world's largest manufacturers of soap and was preparing to take the family over the Mersey to live at 8 Boundary Road, New Ferry, it is believed that family on both sides intervened to save the boy from further harm and removed him to Exeter. Only Arthur Herbert suffered at his father's hands; Ethel, Clarence and Ernest continued to live with their parents.

As Herbert Procter was a travelling salesman and was absent from home for long periods of time, it fell to Mary to care for the traumatized boy. She was a spinster in her sixties when Arthur Herbert came to live with her, and in her he found a loving and affectionate woman, a home-maker and a devout Christian. In her custody, Arthur Herbert, distressed by his father's abuse and by the separation from his mother and siblings, was comforted and nursed back to health. She instilled in him the Christian faith which not only filled the void of separation but also became the bedrock of his life, sustaining him on the battlefield and leading him into the Church.

It is alleged that Arthur Procter was educated at Exeter Training College and that when Mary died in 1901, he was taken in by a Dr Barnardo home, the Marfords, in Bromborough, not far from where his parents were living. Here he remained until 1904, when he left to find employment, having completed his education at a local school in Port Sunlight. However, the Marfords did not open its doors as an orphanage until 1937. Further research indicates that Arthur Procter was not in fact taken in by a Dr Barnardo home – with both parents alive he would not have been eligible for admission. Nor did any school or establishment by the name of Exeter Training College ever exist. There was an Exeter Diocesan Training College, in Heavitree Road, Exeter, an institution for the education and training of teachers. But the lower age limit for entrance was 15, and Arthur Herbert was too young to qualify. It is certain Arthur Herbert did not return to live with his family in 1901, and his whereabouts are a mystery until he went into digs at 68 Derby Road, Tranmere, the home of Charles and Alice Codd in 1904.

Charles Codd, a native of Lincolnshire, trained as a chemist and druggist. He came to Liverpool in the 1880s and lodged at 16 Ceres Street, Kirkdale, working in various local pharmacies, before opening his own premises at 87 Hale Road, Walton. He married Alice Jones from Flintshire in 1893, and at the turn of the century, he moved his pharmacy to Tranmere. His only daughter, Hilda May, fell in love with the new lodger; in time they would marry and become lifelong companions.

Arthur Herbert began work as a clerk with the firm of Wilson Brothers and Company of 11 Temple Street, wholesale fruit and produce dealers, and a member of the Liverpool Produce Exchange in Exchange Buildings, Victoria Street. He quickly became a familiar face in and around Temple Street, a very busy thoroughfare off Dale Street, full of small warehouses and office chambers. His work took him to the docks, to the warehouses and markets of the city, Cazneau Street market in particular, where Frank Lester sold his produce, checking and accounting for the produce as it was landed and sold on to dealers and shopkeepers.

He impressed with an amiable personality, hard work and a stout Christian outlook on life. But he was not the man who would join his workmates in an office joke or a night on the town. His free time was spent at his church, St Paul's Presbyterian Church, North Road, Tranmere, and at the Mission close by in Stuart Road, where, for nine years, he attended Bible class and taught Scripture to children at the Sunday School. With some prescience, he trained in workplace first-aid with the St John Ambulance Association, acquiring skills he would one day utilize on the battlefield.

His marriage to Hilda May was put on hold when war was declared and he answered the clarion calls of Lord Kitchener and Edward George Villiers, 17th Earl of Derby. Arthur Procter was fortunate, if not blessed, when he enlisted. Any one of Kitchener's New Army battalions, or one of the four Liverpool Pals battalions raised by Lord Derby, made up of white-collars workers, many of whom were clerks, were open to him. Instead, he enlisted in the Territorial Force, in 5th Battalion, King's (Liverpool) Regiment, as 3156 Private Arthur Procter at the depot in St Anne Street. Kitchener's New Army and the Liverpool Pals would be swallowed up and annihilated on the muddy killing field of the Somme in 1916.

Arthur Procter fought in some of the most fiercely contested engagements of the war, Festubert, Loos, Arras, the Somme and Ypres, when thousands of young men were needlessly sacrificed. He was in the trenches for more than three years, but remained a private throughout and was never considered for promotion: when death and injury took its toll, younger and less experienced men were given the stripes over him. The black humour of the trenches, the joking and joshing, was not for him. As in the workplace, he was serious-minded and sought solace in the words and works of his Christian faith: his comrades were uncomfortable in his presence and he was seen as an outsider. He was never wounded in action but was wounded in a lull between battles. Similarly, he won the Victoria Cross not in the heat of battle but on a quiet section of the front, in the wake of a small raid that went disastrously wrong.

Following the Allied failure to capture Aubers Ridge in May 1915, the 5th Liverpools were held in reserve at Bethune, four miles west of Festubert, where the next blow was to fall on the enemy. Bethune was an important railway and hospital centre and was relatively free of enemy bombardments. But, as preparations were being made for the attack, the Germans began disruptive bombardments to hinder the work, and their big guns landed several 'overs' on the town, and several high-explosive shells struck the 5th Liverpools. Procter was wounded in the arm by flying shards of metal and his commanding officer, Captain Richardson, was hit also. Both men were evacuated down the line by the battalion field ambulance unit to the seaside town of Le Touquet.

Recovered from his injuries, he was back with the 5th Liverpools in January 1916 when they were made part of the 55th West Lancashire Division; and the following month the division took up positions three miles south-west of Arras. The Liverpools filled trenches near the small towns of Wailly and Bretencourt, facing the Germans lines close to the towns of Blairville and Ficheux to the east, in what was a relatively quiet sector of the front. But small raids were mounted to harass the enemy and to take prisoners in order to garner intelligence. Each battalion in turn provided a company of men to raid, and at the beginning of June, it was the turn of the 5th Liverpools.

Careful plans were laid to infiltrate the enemy trenches near Ficheux under cover of an artillery barrage. The company of Liverpools consisted of two officers and eighty-seven other ranks. Private Arthur Procter was given the role of stretcher-bearer. The attack would be in broad daylight and the Divisional RFA batteries would provide the bombardment. Among the men manning the big guns was Bombardier Cyril Gourley.

On Sunday, 4 June, the two officers led the men over the top and deployed them across open terrain: they would wait for the barrage to stop before dashing forward to engage the enemy. Despite the thorough planning, however, there was a deadly miscalculation: when the guns opened up, the initial salvo landed short, falling among the Liverpools as they crouched in no man's land. The 'friendly fire' killed and wounded several men.

Alerted, the Germans brought machine guns to bear on the hapless victims: they were stranded in no man's land, trapped between two murderous fires. It was some minutes before the gunners realized their error and ceased firing, and it was only then that the survivors, having collected their wounded, could scramble back to the safety of their own trenches, leaving behind nine dead – or so it was thought. The raid was abandoned and for the rest of the day, the Germans kept up intermittent fire on the Liverpools to forestall further assaults.

In the late afternoon, Private Procter peered through a periscope and observed movement: 75 yards in front, and lying out in the open, two men, assumed dead, were showing signs of life. Resolved to help, he reported what he had seen to an officer. 'Procter insisted on going to cheer them up,' said the officer. 'It was pointed out that it was almost certain death to venture out . . . that didn't deter him. He went . . . [and] as soon as he showed his nose above the trench parapet he was fired on. The enemy snipers all tried their best to get him.' Slowly, Procter inched forward towards the wounded men as the ground around him was peppered with lead from machine guns and rifles. Miraculously, he was not hit. Reaching the two men, he now had to find them cover from the relentless Germans' fire. But, God was on his side that evening. Procter dragged the nearest man into the lee of a shallow bank. 'It was slow work, and all the while he was exposed to a merciless hail of bullets ... to us watching it seemed like an eternity before he succeeded. Then he started the game of leap-frog with death all over again in order to reach the second man. This time the Germans ... had made up their minds that he was not to get off safely, but his splendid luck never deserted him ... and he soon made the second man comfortable beside his mate.'

Behind the shelter of the knoll, Procter dressed their wounds as best he could, making use of the first-aid skills he had learnt with the St John Ambulance Brigade. One of the wounded men was a Bootle boy, Private William Jones, who lived at 20 Bank Road, a two-minute walk from where Procter had been born. Making them as comfortable as possible, and covering them both with some of his own clothing, he left them with a firm promise of rescue when darkness fell. 'Then he had to pick his way back to the trenches under a perfect tornado of fire. The snipers took potshots at him from every hiding place. Shells were bursting all round as well, and Procter really had to make his way through hell's flames to get back ... he fell in a shell hole and a shell exploded at his feet, but still he made it.'

For outstanding gallantry under fire in going to the aid of two wounded men in no man's land, Arthur Herbert Procter was awarded the Victoria Cross. His citation reads:

> Arthur Herbert Proctor, Number 3156, Private, King's (Liverpool) Regiment (Territorial Force). For most conspicuous bravery. Private Proctor, noticing some movement on the part of two wounded men who were lying in the open in full view of the enemy at about seventy-five yards in front of our trenches, went out on his own initiative, and, though heavily fired at, ran and crawled to the two men, got them under cover of a small bank, dressed their wounds, and, after cheering them with a promise of rescue after dark, and leaving with them some of his clothing for warmth, regained our trenches, again being heavily fired at. At dusk both men were brought out alive.

Procter's surname was misspelled 'Proctor' on his citation, and it was given as such in one of the most authoritative records of Victoria Cross heroes and their deeds, *The VC and DSO Book*, edited by Sir O'Moore Creagh VC. And years later, on invitations to the several Victoria Cross celebrations he attended, the error persisted, a source of some irritation to him. It is believed that even his Victoria Cross medal was engraved with the misspelling.

Procter's battalion was pulled out of the Arras sector on 25 July. Thankful to be leaving behind the heavy mud of Flanders, the men marched south with a fresh spring to their steps into the chalky landscape of Picardy. Their thanks were premature: they took up positions opposite the village of Guillemont, on the north bank of the River Somme.

On 5 August 1916, the *London Gazette* announced the award of the Victoria Cross to Private Procter. Three days later, the 1st, 5th, 8th and 10th Liverpools moved forward in readiness to assault Guillemont, the second of three attempts to take the fortified village. However, as the opening shots of the assault were fired, Private Procter was plucked from the trenches and deposited in the peace and tranquillity of Querrieu, Fourth Army Headquarters of Lieutenant General Sir Henry Rawlinson. 'I was told to report to General Headquarters, and within the hour I was in the presence of the King,' Procter told the *Liverpool Daily Courier* on his return home. 'I felt very nervous, dazed.'

On 9 August, a huge assembly of the brass, overseen by the French and British Commanders-in-Chief, General Joseph Joffre and Sir Douglas Haig, watched as Private Arthur Herbert Procter was decorated by King George V. He was the first soldier ever to receive the Victoria Cross from the hands of a sovereign on the battlefield. 'The King shook hands and spoke with me. I then felt quite at ease. He said he was very proud of me indeed. ... Then he pinned [the] Victoria Cross on me and the Prince of Wales handed me the box in which the medal goes. Sir Douglas Haig also shook hands with me and said I had done very well.' Fourteen days of home leave followed.

He arrived at Lime Street Station at four o'clock on Friday, 18 August, and was met by his aunt Edith, his mother's sister, and her husband, Arthur Field. Also present was Captain Richardson, still recuperating from the wound he had received at Bethune. Only a small crowd of well-wishers gathered because he was not expected until the following Monday, and Private Procter VC and his welcoming party were able to walk unnoticed to the barracks of the 5th Liverpools in St Anne Street, where they took tea. It was one of the few times he was able to walk through the city unmolested.

That evening, he visited his aunt's home in Garmoyle Road, off Smithdown Road, where his younger brother, Ernest, was living. Here, in an emotionally charged atmosphere, he met and was reconciled with the man who had blighted his childhood, his father. Also present, to his great surprise, was his sister, Ethel. She had married Dr Robert Kelly in 1915, and had been living in Brighton. Dr Kelly was attached to the Indian Army, and was stationed in Mesopotamia.

On Saturday morning, Procter's return was widely publicized in the Liverpool press, together with the news that he would be guest of honour at a special celebration in the St Anne Street barracks at three o'clock, Monday afternoon. The Lord Mayor of Liverpool, and the 'soldier's friend', Lord Derby, would attend also. However, Procter received a message from Lord Derby's secretary on Saturday afternoon informing him the Earl could not attend on Monday because of a prior enagagement. Nevertheless, he did want to meet Procter, and suggested a rendezvous in Liverpool at the home of a friend.

On Saturday evening, Private Procter VC arrived in Abercromby Square and was ushered into No. 19, the palace of the Lord Bishop of Liverpool, the Right Reverend Francis James Chavasse DD. The two Lords, spiritual and secular, welcomed Private Procter VC. There can be little doubt of the direction the conversation took that evening.

Francis Chavasse DD, shepherd of Liverpool's Anglican flock, was the man to whom distraught families turned for comfort and guidance in those harrowing days when loved ones fell in battle; and his indefatigable pastoral work in the city made him one of the best loved of all the holders of that great office. He was a father himself, and his three sons, twins Christopher and Noel, and Aidan, were on the Western Front. He had just received news that Noel had been badly wounded at the Battle of Guillemont, the fight Procter had missed. From Private Procter VC the worried Bishop wanted to hear a more prosaic description of life on the Western Front other than those he gleaned from the anodyne, censored reports of the daily press. Noel Chavasse won the first of his two Victoria Crosses at Guillemont. Sadly, the Lord Bishop would lose two of his sons to the war.

Procter was kept very busy during his leave in Liverpool, and he would always reminisce fondly over the tremendous and emotional receptions he received on Merseyside in 1916. At the celebrations in the St Anne Street barracks, where he was welcomed by the Lord Mayor of Liverpool, Alderman Matthew, he spoke modestly of his achievement, saying he had been in the hands of God; and he claimed the Victoria Cross for all of his comrades in the 5th Liverpools. To rousing cheers from the assembled throng, he was taken from the hall with his father and hoisted aloft and carried shoulder-high along Islington down to Victoria Street to the Produce Exchange where former workmates greeted him.

But perhaps the most poignant meeting occurred on the Wednesday, at Bootle Town Hall, Oriel Road. The mayor, Dr John Pearson, introduced him to a grieving mother, Mrs Annie Jones, whose son, William, he had aided at Ficheux, but who had subsequently died of his wounds. In the evening, he called at her home, where he met her husband, Eddie, and offered them spiritual comfort for the loss of their son, and prayers for their other sons, John and David, who were fighting in the trenches.

He managed only a few hours with Hilda May during his leave, but sufficient for them to sketch very tentative plans to marry the following year. However, on his return to the front at the end of August, those plans must have appeared highly unlikely for he once more found himself in front of Guillemont, which was still in German hands despite the valiant efforts of the Liverpools. In September, he took part in the third assault and saw the village captured at last, saw action at Ginchy and Morval, before the battalion tramped north in October, into the mud of Ypres. And, having survived unscathed some desperate encounters, miraculously he would later claim, he was granted leave. On 23 May 1917, he married Hilda May Codd at St Paul's Church on North Road, his friend, the Reverend MacPherson officiating.

Private Arthur Procter VC took part in the 'Hundred Days Offensive', which culminated in the Armistice, and he finished the war near the town of Tournai, north-east of Arras. He was demobbed in the spring of 1919, and he returned to Merseyside and his wife, who was living with her parents in Tranmere. He took up his former position with Wilson Brothers in the fruit and vegetable trade, and after a couple of years was able to afford a home of his own. Mrs and Mrs Procter went to live at 42 Kingfield Road, Walton, where a son, Cecil Charles, was born in 1921. And, having found a new home, he found a new job also, despite the long dole queues: George Wall and Company, Provision Merchants, an old and respected firm with offices in Liverpool and West Kirkby, hired him as a travelling salesman for operations in the south of the city.

In between new jobs and houses, he found time to attend the Garden Party at Buckingham Palace on the afternoon of 26 June 1920, when he met other holders of the Victoria Cross from Liverpool: Gabriel Coury VC, Donald Farmer VC, Cyril Gourley VC, and the phoney Arthur Richardson. And on Thursday, 11 November of the same year, he was the city's sole representative in the Guard of Honour of seventy-four Victoria Cross holders at the unveiling of the Cenotaph in Whitehall and the interment of the Unknown Soldier in Westminster Abbey.

On Saturday, 19 July 1924, he again met King George V, who would recall their meeting on the Somme in 1916, the occasion being the review of the 55th West Lancashire Territorial Division in Wavertree Playground: Arthur Procter VC and another Liverpool hero, Cyril Gourley VC, were two of nine Victoria Cross holders presented to King George V and Queen Mary. The following day, the king and queen attended the consecration of the Cathedral Church of Christ in Liverpool. The city's Anglican Cathedral, built from sandstone quarried at Woolton, would not be completed until 1978, but it would serve Arthur Procter VC when he turned his back on the secular for the spiritual.

In 1925, he moved to Garston in the south of the city with his wife and young son to reside at 24 Blomfield Road. And it was here he took the decision to enter the Church. On his return from war, he had resumed his old contacts with the church in Birkenhead, and forged newer ones in Liverpool. His faith had sustained him through a difficult childhood and through the bloody miseries of the Western Front. This latter experience and the deaths of so many young men had scarred him, and he had been deeply affected by the death of Noel Chavasse, a true Samaritan. He would now serve God to ensure that similar horrors were not visited upon future generations.

Arthur Herbert Procter VC entered St Aidan's Theological College, Shrewsbury Road, Birkenhead, in 1926 to study for Holy Orders. And on 18 December the following year, he was ordained a priest in the Church of England in the Lady Chapel of Liverpool Cathedral, the founding and construction of which had originally been in the hands of Francis James Chavasse DD.

A lowly, compliant private in the army of the king, commissioned in God's battalion, he was reborn as an authoritative man of peace, who stamped his influence on the parishes he served, vigorously spreading his personal creed, the saving grace of the Word. Upon ordination, he was appointed deacon to the parish of St Mary-the-Blessed-Virgin, Bryer Road, Prescot, and he descended with full throttle, his first Sunday there, propitiously, being Christmas Day. He quickly re-established and taught Bible classes, concerned himself less with the ceremony of the Church and more with pastoral work, and his robust commitment made him a popular figure with the congregation. In 1931, he was uprooted from Liverpool, never to live there again, and was given his own parish, St Mary the Virgin, in the village of Bosley, near Macclesfield. It was a stay of only two years: again he gathered admirers, even though the occasional thorn appeared when his authority was questioned.

His new home was Flowery Field, Newton, near Hyde, on the outskirts of Manchester, vicar of St Stephen's parish, a living he held for eleven years. But from 1941 he divided his ministry between the parish and the RAF, where he served as chaplain with the rank of squadron leader in the Voluntary Reserve. His decision to volunteer for wartime duty may have had something to do with the loss of his son, Cecil Charles.

Cecil enlisted in the RAF at the outset of the war as 990753 Aircraftman Cecil Procter. After training, he was posted to 86th Squadron, Coastal Command, stationed at RAF North Coates, Lincolnshire, and rose to the rank of sergeant. At 0210 hours on 21 July 1941, he took off in a Bristol Beaufort from RAF North Coates on a mine-laying operation in the North Sea. The plane and the crew of four were lost off Schiermonnikoog, off the coast of the Netherlands, and no trace of the men or the aircraft was ever found. Cecil Charles Procter is remembered on the RAF Memorial, Runnymede.

The Procters soldiered on following the death of their son, and the Reverend Arthur Procter VC continued with the chaplaincy until 1946, when he resigned his commission. He was awarded the Defence Medal and the War Medal for his work during the Second World War. The same year, he was appointed as rector of St Mary's Church in Droylsden, Manchester, where he remained until 1951. He tried always to attend Victoria Cross celebrations, and he was present as a holder, along with Bill Ratcliffe VC, at the Second World War Victory Day Celebration Reception at the Dorchester Hotel on 8 June 1946. He also attended the Victoria Cross Centenary Review of Holders at Hyde Park in 1956. And as a founder member of the Victoria Cross and George Cross Association in 1958, he made a point of travelling up to London for the Association's biennial dinners, making his last visit the year before he died.

He was an unselfish and untiring, if perhaps an irascible, servant to his flocks, more so in his later years, believing he was chosen to do God's work, a legacy no doubt of his Presbyterian upbringing. After the war, he served for twelve years as vicar of the parish Church of St Peter, Claybrooke cum Wibtoft, Leicestershire. And he gave no thought to retirement when, at the age of 73, he was transferred to the south of the country, to Devon, where he ministered to the congregation of the Church of St John the Baptist, Bradworthy. However, in 1964, ill health forced him to retire.

It is thought he and Hilda lived for a time in Shrewsbury, before making a home in a bungalow for retired clergymen at 1 Cherry Close, Sheffield. He suffered with heart trouble but still managed to get about and lead an active life. However, his condition worsened, and he was admitted to Winter Street Hospital, where he died of cardiac arrest on 26 January 1973 at the age of 82. His lifelong friend Hilda May was present at his bedside. A private funeral service without a military presence, in keeping with his role as a trooper of God, was held five days later in the Chapel of St George, Sheffield Cathedral. Arthur Herbert Procter VC was cremated at the City Road Crematorium, and his ashes were interred within the Crypt Chapel of All Saints in the Cathedral.

Two blue plaques were erected to his memory by the Metropolitan Borough of Tameside, Manchester, one at St Stephen's Church, Hyde, the other at St Mary's Church, Droylsden. In 1995, Tameside erected a plaque at the town hall, Ashton-under-Lyme, to commemorate eight holders of the Victoria Cross associated with the area, one of whom was Arthur Procter VC.

Following the death of her husband, Hilda Procter took up residence in Shrewsbury again, where she passed away in 1983 at the age of 85. Seven years later, the full array of medals Arthur Procter VC had received, including the 1937 and 1953 Coronation Medals, came up for auction and were sold by Glendinings, the coin and medal dealers, to the Regimental Museum of the King's (Liverpool) Regiment. Today the medals are held by the King's Regiment Collection, at the Museum of Liverpool Life.

Gabriel George Coury VC
(1896–1956)

The Pioneer Battalions were the unsung heroes of the First World War. The battalions were attached to every infantry division, and were made up of men from the construction trades, tradesmen and labourers alike. They underwent basic military training, including the use of firearms, but they were usually armed only with shovels, spades, saws and hammers. They worked in the forward area on tasks not requiring the specialized equipment and expertise of engineers: they dug and shored up trenches, dugouts and saps and installed barbed-wire entanglements. During offensives, they laboured under fire, following the advancing infantry to dig communication trenches from their own lines across no man's land to captured German positions; and very often they were caught in the open during counter-attacks only lightly armed.

In his first and only encounter with the Germans on land, Second Lieutenant Gabriel Coury won his Victoria Cross in front of Guillemont on the Somme when serving with the 1/4th Pioneer Battalion, attached to the 55th West Lancashire Division. It was the fight that Arthur Procter missed, the same contest during which Lieutenant Noel Chavasse MC would win the first of his two honours.

In the week before the attack began, Coury and his Pioneers were at work in Trones Wood, which spread to within 1,000 yards of Guillemont. Under heavy fire, they dug saps and trenches forward from Arrowhead Copse, a small stand of trees on the eastern edge of the wood, towards Guillemont, to reduce the distance across no man's land the infantry would have to traverse. On the eve of the assault, these new lines filled with men of 1/4th Battalion, King's Own Royal Lancaster Regiment (KORLR), under the command of Lieutenant Colonel Joseph Swainson DSO.

At twenty minutes past four in the morning of 8 August, the assault commenced. But the summer weather, which had bathed the front for the past week, turned its face: a heavy mist, which mingled with the smoke and fumes of the artillery barrage, descended across no man's land and obscured the village. The infantry rose from the trenches and disappeared into an opaque smog. The Germans met the advance with everything in their arsenal, firing blindly into the mist, but knowing they would find targets in the narrow stretch of no man's land crowded with advancing troops.

Coury and two platoons of Pioneers from D Company set to work as soon as the 1/4th KORLR disappeared into the fog, digging furiously with their trenching spades into the sun-baked earth. 'He was the best officer I served under,' a corporal in the Pioneers was later to say of Gabriel Coury. 'The task given to the men under him was no soft one. To dig a trench in the thick of battle is a thing that requires some nerve, and a better officer than Lieutenant Coury could not have been chosen to direct the operation. He showed absolute contempt for death and made us all feel that a dozen deaths were as nothing compared with the necessity of completing the task given to us.'

Within an hour and a half, the offensive faltered and stalled. In a short time, the walking wounded, the dazed and the bewildered, began streaming past the point to which Gabriel Coury and his Pioneers had brought the trench. Lieutenant Colonel Swainson DSO had advanced his brave troops up to the German wire only to be met by fierce opposition. The men tried to dig in beyond bombing range, but were driven back; and together with the supporting battalion, they were forced to withdraw.

By mid-morning the sun finally broke through the smog and haze and restored visibility: no man's land was littered with the broken bodies of the dead and wounded. The Germans could now register their targets, the backs of the retreating infantry and the Pioneers who stood exposed in the open. Some of the fleeing troops sought refuge (in the Pioneer trench), where the brunt of the German counter-attack now focused. The shelling and machine-gun fire intensified all around the trench, and several casualties were taken. No thought could be given to withdrawing under such a barrage, and Second Lieutenant Coury moved among the men, calming nerves and keeping up spirits.

There were many wounded men lying out in no man's land without shelter from the incessant bombardment, and several unsuccessful attempts were made from the trench to try to bring some of them in to safety. 'It blew hurricanes of fire across the open and it seemed to invite certain death to go out there,' said the corporal. Then word came through to Gabriel Coury that Lieutenant Colonel Swainson was among the wounded, collapsed in the open, and that two, perhaps three, previous attempts to bring him in had resulted in the deaths of the would-be rescuers.

Peeking over the top of the trench, and risking a sniper's bullet or a shell fragment, Coury marked Swainson's position and resolved to bring him in. Leaving a sergeant in charge of the trench, he clambered over the top and set off across no man's land. 'He started out under fiendish fire. The enemy snipers were after him from the first, but he ran right on regardless of the shoals of bullets flying around him.'

Coury crouched low, and, weaving and dodging, he navigated a path between shell craters and pot-holes and through the enemy fire to reach the wounded officer. He took a few minutes to rest before hauling up Swainson across his shoulders and setting off back. 'The enemy redoubled their efforts to pick off the brave officer as he toiled painfully towards our trench. Once he stumbled and we gave him up for lost.' Coury collapsed under the weight of his burden, sliding down into a shell hole.

> We thought he would never rise again; but rise he did and resumed the terrible journey. Before he got back, the enemy's machine guns were turned on full blast, and it was nothing short of a miracle that the lieutenant was able to make his way through it all. . . . He stumbled again, but regained his footing and continued straight on. Then there was another furious gust of fire. Down he went again. . . . Enemy snipers took up the running, and bullets spat and spluttered all over the place.

Private Haworth of the Pioneers braved the enemy fire and climbed out of the trench to assist. 'Under heavy fire all the time, rescuer and rescued were helped into the trench, which was now being subjected to very severe artillery fire.' Exhausted but unhurt, Coury handed over the injured officer to the stretcher-bearers and barely took a minute to catch his breath. Then he mustered his Pioneers and the infantrymen and organized them into fighting units to defend the position, for he suspected a counter-attack was imminent. He was correct; and, when it came, he and his makeshift command were prepared, and the Germans were quickly repulsed and driven off in total confusion.

For gallantry in rescuing a wounded man under fire and in repelling a German attack, Second Lieutenant Gabriel George Coury was awarded the Victoria Cross. His citation reads:

> Second-Lieutenant Gabriel George Coury, South Lancashire Regiment. For most conspicuous bravery. During an advance he was in command of two platoons ordered to dig a communication trench from the old firing line to the position won. By his fine example and utter contempt of danger he kept up the spirits of his men and completed his task under intense fire. Later, after his battalion had suffered severe casualties and the Commanding Officer had been wounded, he went out in front of the advanced position in broad daylight and in full view of the enemy, found his Commanding Officer, and brought him back to the new advanced trench over ground swept by machine-gun fire. He not only carried out his original task, and saved his Commanding Officer, but also assisted in rallying the attacking troops when they were shaken and in leading them forward.

Coury's mission had been in vain: Lieutenant Colonel Swainson DSO succumbed to his wounds hours later. Coury spoke rarely of his actions in front of Guillemont, and when he did so, it was brief and modest:

> I had to do it because not only was he a CO but he was married and had children. When I went out to him he must have known that the three

others who went out before me had fallen, because he turned to me and said, 'For Christ's sake, go back.' I took him and ran. He weighed fifteen stones, and was 6 feet, 2 inches tall. All the way he begged me to tell him my name, but I didn't. An hour and a half after reaching our trench the poor chap died. What I did was nothing. It was my direct duty, and I should have to do it again under similar circumstances.

Gabriel George Coury was born in Liverpool on 13 June 1896, the son of immigrant parents, infidel *dhimmis*, non-muslim citizens of the Turkish Ottoman Empire, who came to England in the 1890s. His mother, Marie Dagher, was a French-speaking Maronite Christian, born in Lebanon in 1871, the daughter of a successful silk trader. His father, Raphael, was born in 1860, in Alexandria, Egypt's second city, where the Coury family, Coptic Christians, made a livelihood in the cotton trade.

During the American Civil War, the major ports of the Confederacy, Mobile, Alabama and New Orleans, through which passed the raw cotton destined for Liverpool and the hungry cotton mills of the Lancashire hinterland, were blockaded by the Union navy; and imports of the staple declined sharply. In response, the British government invested heavily in Egyptian cotton plantations to provide an alternative source, and so, throughout the war, millions of bales of Egyptian cotton were landed on the Liverpool quays, together with a clutch of Egyptian businessmen, dealers and clerks.

Born in 1840, Basil Coury came to Liverpool at the height of the Egyptian trade, taking diggings at 139 Granby Street, in the south of the city. He worked as a merchant's clerk, initially, but such was his drive and business sense that by 1891, he had established the firm of Coury and Company, General Merchants, of Oldhall Street, which dealt mainly in cotton. He never married, and when the time came for him to retire, he sought out Raphael to take over the enterprise. Raphael was either the younger brother or nephew of Basil, and was a businessman in his own right. And though he travelled extensively throughout the Ottoman Empire, trading in cotton and silk, he had settled in Alexandria with his new bride, Maria; and their first two children, Aimée and Charles, were born there.

In 1893, Raphael brought his wife and family to Liverpool and lived for several years at Basil's home, 16 Croxteth Grove, Princes Park. A second daughter, Louise, and another son, Gabriel George, were born there. When Basil retired, Raphael took over the running of Coury and Company and moved his growing brood to the greener pastures north of the city, to 51 Waterloo Park. There, two more sons, Maurice and Earnest, were born.

Gabriel Coury was brought up in a secure, middle-class environment, and lacked for nothing as a child: he learnt French at his mother's knee, and there were nurses and nannies, servants and tutors, to cater for all his needs. At the age of 5, he entered St Francis Xavier School in Salisbury Street. While there, he was traumatized by the death of his father, who passed away in 1903 at the age of 43. This loss of his father also meant the loss of the family business: Raphael's sons were too young to take over his mantle, and Marie was forced to sell out. The proceeds barely provided sufficient funds for the children's education and to maintain the living standards they had come to expect.

He studied at Stonyhurst College where Paul Kenna VC had been a student.There is nothing in his school record which hints of the redoubtable man he was to become, a man of great courage and fortitude, who would never be intimidated by anything life threw at him. He much preferred, as he would throughout his life, the freedom of outdoors to the confines of a classroom or office. Academically and on the sports field, he was adept rather than outstanding, and, except for four years as a rifleman with the Officer Training Corps (OTC), he passed his time at school without remark. However, a contemporary at Stonyhurst offers a clue: 'He was undoubtedly a general favourite with his contemporaries and full of high spirits and fun. ... His physique was quite exceptional. He had tremendous long and powerful arms, and had an exceedingly tough and wiry frame. Though invariably good natured and easy going, he was a formidable opponent if it came to a resort to arms, and I can remember one or two occasions when he demonstrated this in no uncertain fashion.'

When Gabriel graduated in April 1913, Charles was the sole provider for the family. He had established himself as a successful trader for the brokerage firm of Bazett Hooper and Company on the floor of the Cotton Exchange in Oldhall Street and, through his contacts, he secured an apprenticeship for Gabriel with Reynolds and Gibson, Cotton Brokers, which had offices in Tithebarn Street and Exchange Street East.

The family were now living at 22 The Esplanade, Waterloo, and from there it was but a twenty-minute daily train ride for young Gabriel to Exchange Street Station and the offices of Reynolds and Gibson, where he began to learn his father's trade. Business was booming in the cotton trade: annually, more than 5 million bales of cotton were landed on the Albert and Stanley Docks, and the Liverpool Cotton Exchange set the world price for cotton. Cooped up inside an office, Gabriel would have preferred to work as his father had done, in the open air, on the flag-stoned piazza behind the town hall known as Exchange Flags. Here, deals were struck with a wink, a nod or a handshake, and the air was always thick with white fluff and fibres released by the cotton samplers as they prodded and plucked the bales to draw tufts for inspection and testing. But that tradition had died in 1906 when the new Liverpool Cotton Exchange in Oldhall Street was opened by Lord Derby and the cotton traders were ordered indoors.

Gabriel took the first opportunity offered to escape the stuffy confines of his office routine: when war was declared, he enlisted at the age of 18 as 2482 Private Gabriel Coury in 6th Battalion, King's (Liverpool) Regiment. Eager to do his duty and serve his country, he was frustrated by months with the second-line unit of the battalion, moving up and down the country, from Blackpool to Margate, training and waiting on equipment. With nothing to lose except boredom, he put his time in the Stonyhurst OTC to good use and applied for a commission, which was granted in April 1915. Four months later, as Second Lieutenant Coury, he joined the 1/4th Battalion, South Lancashire Regiment, in the Ypres Salient. The following month, the battalion was re-designated a Pioneer unit; and in January 1916 became the labour battalion of the 55th West Lancashire Division. Towards the end of July, Gabriel Coury marched with his Pioneers down to the Somme, to Guillemont, where he won the Victoria Cross.

The announcement of his award appeared in the *London Gazette* of 26 September 1916. By that time, he had been promoted to full lieutenant and had traded his shovels and spades and the slog of tramping through mud for the unbridled freedom of the air. After Guillemont, he had transferred to the Royal Flying Corps (RFC) to train as an aerial observer with 13 Squadron, 3rd Brigade, stationed at Aubigny, ten miles north-west of Arras: while supervising his Pioneers, he had cast his eyes skywards and become enamoured of the soaring Farmans and Caudrons of the Aéronnautique Militaire and the Avros and De Havillands of the RFC. He wanted to fight his war in the air.

In November 1916, he made a brief visit home to receive his honour. His first port of call was Crosby, to see his mother and spinster sister, Aimée, who were living at 43 Canning Street, and caring for his brother Maurice. The Liverpool Cotton Exchange opened its doors to him on 14 November when he made a triumphal return to the city. Colonel James Reynolds DSO, senior partner of Reynolds and Gibson, welcomed him back, and he was granted the Freedom of the Exchange. The following day, he was honoured with a civic reception hosted by the Lord Mayor at the town hall. And on Saturday, 18 November, accompanied by members of his family, he was decorated with the Victoria Cross by the king in the forecourt of Buckingham Palace.

However, the main purpose of his leave was to finalize his wedding plans. He had begun courting Katherine Mary Lovell, seven years his senior, the daughter of William and Mary Lovell. William, known as Stuart in the family, was an insurance representative, and the family lived at 47 North Side, Clapham Common. His wife, Mary Powell, had been born in Liverpool in 1859 and brought up in Southport. Mary and William married in 1886, and later moved to London, where Katherine Mary, Kitty to her friends, was born in 1890. After agreeing a wedding date, Gabriel Coury kissed his fiancée adieu and returned to the front.

He flew as an observer for nine months in a De Havilland BE-2 biplane, the workhorse of the RFC, on photographic reconnaissance and artillery spotting missions over the front, until he qualified as a flying officer at the School of Military Aeronautics, Reading, on 20 September 1917. His first station was the aerodrome on Kenley Common, Croydon, attached to 7th Aircraft Acceptance

Park, where planes were assembled and tested for airworthiness before dispersal to the RFC. Coury test flew these new aircraft and ferried them across the Channel to the RFC stations at the front.

However, on 22 November 1917, he volunteered to fly in atrocious weather conditions to ferry much-needed replacement craft to France at the height of the Battle of Cambrai. As he took off from Kenley, one of the wings snagged a flag post, and it was torn free from the fuselage. The aircraft nosedived and crashed to the ground, bursting into flames on impact. Unconscious, he was pulled from the wreck, his hands, legs and face burnt and badly contused.

He spent two agonizing months recovering at the Royal Herbert Hospital, on Shooters Hill, Woolwich; and upon discharge, a medical board grounded him as 30 per cent disabled, unfit for general service, fit only for light duties on home service. It was thought his marriage to Kitty would have to be postponed because of his injuries, but the ceremony went ahead as planned. On 7 January 1918, Gabriel Coury VC married Katherine Lovell at St Mary's Church, in Park Road, Clapham, according to the rites of the Roman Catholic Church. The couple made their home at 21 Heath Street, Hampstead.

But, the indefatigable Gabriel Coury was not finished with flying. He was left physically and mentally enfeebled by the crash, and reported he was 'never much fit for flying ... and had no confidence at all'. Nevertheless, during the crisis of the German spring offensive, when the RFC was flying round-the-clock missions to find where the next blow against the Allies might fall, his overwhelming sense of duty would not allow him to remain idle, grounded on light duties: at the end of April, five months after the horrific crash, Gabriel Coury VC was passed fit for flying duties, and he took to the air again.

The following month he was found to be suffering with neurasthenia, a catch-all diagnosis at the time, which included a wide range of conditions from simple fatigue to anxiety, depression and chronic fatigue syndrome. Today, he would not have been allowed within a mile of an aeroplane. But, 'circumstances alter cases', and he continued to ferry aircraft across to France.

In June the inevitable occurred: he crashed at Kenley Common again, and was hospitalized for three months. Following his release, he went before another medical board on 21 August. His injuries had healed, but he was again diagnosed as suffering with neurasthenia. Declared unfit for further flying duties, he became a desk pilot with the Royal Air Force, which had been formed on 1 April 1918, working in the medical section of the administrative branch, with the rank of temporary captain from 20 September.

Ill health plagued him for the remainder of the war. He did not recover his hearty, outdoors self, and complained constantly of chesty coughs, stomach pains and fatigue. When the Armistice was signed, he continued in uniform during the demobilization process, despite his debilitated state, and left himself open to any prowling infections. In February 1919 he succumbed to the Spanish 'flu, which would claim more than 50 million lives worldwide.

He was treated at Mount Vernon Hospital, Northwood, but complications of pneumonia and pleurisy set in. On several occasions he was at death's door and received the last rites, but he fought back with the same indomitable courage that had carried him across no man's land in 1916. The birth of his first child, a daughter, Carmen, probably assisted the healing process. At the end of April, he was medically assessed as 20 per cent disabled, transferred to the unemployed list and demobilized. He relinquished his commission and returned to civilian life. For his services during the First World War, in addition to the Victoria Cross, he received the 1914–15 Star, the British War Medal and Victory Medal.

He gave up his London home and returned to Liverpool, settling down to civilian life, initially at 2 Merton Grove, Bootle, where two more daughters, Joan and Margaret, were born. Reynolds and Gibson welcomed him back as an employee, and he resumed his duties as a cotton broker. During the inter-war years, he led a very quiet, ordinary life, working to maintain his family. He regained his health slowly and began to take an interest again in outdoor pursuits, and he took up tennis after moving to live in Southport. In 1929, he attended the Victoria Cross Reunion Dinner in the Royal Gallery, House of Lords, where he met other Liverpool heroes, George Nurse VC, Arthur Richardson VC, Donald Farmer VC, Ernest Alexander VC, Arthur Procter VC and William Ratcliffe VC. He would become a close friend of Donald Farmer VC.

At the outbreak of the Second World War, he was living at 50 Queen's Road, Southport. He was 43 years of age, and considered himself fit enough to make an active contribution to the war effort. A colleague at Reynolds and Gibson, Lieutenant Colonel Allen Foulkes OBE, who had taken command of 4th Anti-Aircraft Unit, Royal Army Service Corps (RASC), supported his application for a commission, and on 9 September 1940, Lieutenant Gabriel Coury VC was posted to 913 Company, RASC, stationed in Eccles, Manchester, under the command of Major Alex Davidson.

After an absence of twenty-seven years, Coury returned to France during the D-day landings in June 1944. He saw service in France, Belgium, Holland and Germany, though he was not involved directly in the fighting. He had the time in which to visit some of the old battlefields of the First World War, most notably the Somme, where he had won his Victoria Cross. He was demobbed in August 1945, and was awarded the 1939–45 Star, the France and Germany Star, the Defence Medal and the War Medal.

Returning home, he joined the list of unemployed: the Liverpool Cotton Exchange had closed in 1941 and the new Labour government now controlled the price of cotton. Many brokerage firms and dealers went to the wall, including his former employer, Reynolds and Gibson. However, never a man to sit on his laurels, Gabriel quickly devised a new beginning for himself. In October 1945, he moved his family from Southport to Liverpool, and purchased a large house at 103 Brunswick Road, at the top of Islington. Converting the upstairs into an apartment, he developed the downstairs as a fish-and-chip shop: he would compete with the two Gianelli brothers from 'Little Italy', John and Frank, who sold the best fish and chips in the city from premises on the corner of Christian Street and Islington Place.

While the work was in progress, he gained experience in the trade at Naylor's chippy, 65b Moss Lane, Orrel Park. 'I could not wait for the re-opening of the Cotton Exchange, which is at present doubtful,' he told a reporter from the *Liverpool Echo*, who tracked him down to the shop. 'So, I have put my pride in my pocket ... receiving instruction in all branches of the business – the preparation of fish and potatoes, cooking, serving and so on.'

In November, he opened the doors of the 'Frying Pan', and it soon became popular with the locals. Known since his youth for his good humour, customers flocked to the shop to be served by this jolly, sociable man, who not only served excellent fish and chips but was also a hero. Many a young lad, clutching a couple of coppers, would ask for a bag of chips flavoured with a tale of derring-do from the Western Front; and Gabriel would always oblige. Not many people outside the Brunswick Road area could say their suppers were cooked and served by a holder of the Victoria Cross.

Business boomed, and became a family enterprise in which his wife Kitty took a leading role. A second 'chippy' was opened at 58 Everton Road; and Kitty opened a sweets and tobacco shop further down the road at No. 5. The latter shop would become the headquarters of a new Coury and Company, founded in 1950, from which was organized the catering concessions the Courys won for the cafés and kiosks along Otterspool Promenade and in Sefton, Calderstones and Reynolds Parks.

A successful businessman in the catering industry, his financial future secure, Gabriel could at last afford to relax. But, cotton was in his blood, and he yearned to return to the business he knew best. In 1952, he handed over the reins of the various enterprises to Kitty and took a salesman's job with cotton dealers George H. Way and Company, Harley Buildings, 11 Oldhall Street. He worked in Liverpool for more than two years, and no one in the city was more delighted than he, when, in May 1954, Lord Derby officially reopened the Liverpool Cotton Exchange. But, it was the last gasp of a dying era. 'King Cotton' was moribund, and Liverpool would never again be the pre-eminent force it had once been in the industry.

He had always been a heavy smoker, puffing his way through twenty or more a day of untipped cigarettes; and in 1955, his health broke down. He was taken in to Walton Hospital, Rice Lane, the former workhouse where William Connolly VC had been an inmate. He was diagnosed with cancer, and suffered greatly in his final days. Anointed with the last sacrament, he died of carcinoma of the bronchus and cerebral metastases on 23 February 1956.

His funeral took place two days later at St Peter and Paul's Church, Crosby. His mother was too old and infirm to attend, but more than 300 peole were present at the Requiem Mass, including his friend Donald Farmer VC, many senior Army and RAF representatives and a host of business associates from the cotton trade. The coffin, draped in the Union Jack, was carried by six National Servicemen of the SLR, and the 'Last Post' was sounded by a regimental bugler. He was buried behind the church in the family plot holding his father and brothers, Maurice and Ernest.

All the Coury men died relatively young, Raphael at the age of 43, Gabriel at 59, Maurice 27 and Ernest 38. Charles was the exception, passing away in 1960 at the age of 70. As for the women, the matriarch Maria died three years after Gabriel, at the ripe old age of 86. Aimée died in 1950 aged 58, and Louise, who lived an independent life in London for most of her life, working as a editor with a glossy women's magazine, died in 1982 at the age of 84. Kitty Coury soldiered on alone for a few years with the family businesses, but eventually sold off the second Coury and Company in 1958. She died on 6 August 1976, aged 86. Of Gabriel Coury's daughters, little is known. Joan marrried Peter Bird, who served with the RAF during the Second World War; Margaret married Peter Shepherd; and Carmen married Reginald Walden. But nothing is known of their families.

At the Grosvenor Hotel on Remembrance Sunday 12 November 1961, Kitty Coury presented her husband's Victoria Cross to the Regimental Association of the South Lancashire Regiment. The honour is held at the Regimental Museum, Peninsula Barracks, Warrington. Gabriel Coury's other medals were distributed among his daughters for safe keeping, but their exact locations are today unknown.

John Mulholland, a former pupil at Stonyhurst College, wrote a detailed account of the deeds of Gabriel George Coury VC for the *Stonyhurst Magazine*. He ends his story with a quote from an old friend of Coury's, which encapsulates the man's invincible spirit: 'My lasting recollection of Coury is his invariable good humour and cheerfulness. He loved a laugh, and if the laugh was at his own expense or to do with some aspect of his own appearance, then no one enjoyed it more than he. I saw him in hospital shortly before he died – he had only a week or two to live. But he had no complaint to make of the rather depressing surroundings of his hospital ward, and even then he managed to extract some fun from it, and he indulged as usual in a good hearty laugh.'

David Jones VC
(1892–1916)

Earlier in the day a German prisoner had given him a cigar, a cheap black cheroot, which he tucked away in his pocket. He decided to light it in the afternoon, during a lull in the ferocious fighting, a quick smoke before the awful business of the day resumed. He asked for a match and, puffing away slowly, kept a watchful eye over his position as the grey, acrid smoke rose and curled from his nose and mouth and drifted away into the mist and haze which covered the battlefield.

The tableau could be a scene from a film about the First World War, a door-die hero, a stoic Rudolph Valentino, cool and calm, prepared to acquit himself bravely against overwhelming odds. But this was no fantasy on celluloid. This was real life. The hero was a young Liverpool man of Italian descent, Sergeant David Jones VC. And when the fighting recommenced, he was last seen alive with the cigar clamped between his teeth, crouched low over his Lewis gun, firing at the advancing Germans. No one saw him fall.

That evening, when his comrades were relieved in the lines, someone asked where he was. In the misty twilight, a search was made among the dead, and the shattered body of David Jones VC was eventually found. Distraught comrades gently gathered him up and carried him to the rear for burial, weeping while they covered him with the sod. Mrs Jones received the news of his demise within a week, and she informed his mother, Jesse. And all over 'Little Italy' prayers were said for the soul of David Jones.

The neo-classic revival in architecture and the arts during the first half of the nineteenth century was characterized by an enthusiasm for classical antiquity and archeology, inspired by the excavation of Roman remains at Pompei and Herculaneum. Charles Robert Cockerell, who completed the interior of St George's Hall in Lime Street, one of the finest neo-classic buildings in Britain, was in the van of the movement. His work stirred and stimulated the wise and the good of the city to endorse and express its wealth and influence culturally through the generation of buildings designed and adorned in the style.

The demand went out from the city for skilled craftsmen who could sculpt in marble and create mosaics in the Roman style. In response, hundreds of Italian artisans and their families crammed the steerage holds of vessels in Naples and Genoa and sailed to England, where they poured into Liverpool to offer their skills. They made their homes in the warren of streets where Scotland Road began, around Gerard Street and towards St Anne Street and Springfield Street. The artisans were followed by butchers and bakers, grocers and ice-cream makers, musicians and performers; and within a very short time, names such as Volante, Ginochio, Capaldi, Lucchesi, Mancini, D'Annunzio, were as familiar along Scotland Road as those of Murphy, O'Brien, Flynn, O'Hanlon, names redolent of an earlier migration, and which had earned Liverpool the soubriquet 'the capital of Ireland'. The area around Gerard Street became known as 'Little Italy', and the Italians injected a breath of fresh air into the city, not only with their beautiful craftmanship, but with their zest for life, their music, restaurants and fish-and-chips shops.

One of the most famous sons of 'Little Italy' was Dom Volante, a great featherweight boxer famed during the interwar years.The sculptor Michael D'Annunzio, two of whose statues can be seen outside the Walker Art Gallery, was another. And David Jones, who won the Victoria Cross on the Somme in 1916, was a third.

Peter, or Pietro, Ginochio landed in Liverpool, possibly from Genoa, at the beginning of the Italian migration. He worked as a plaster-moulder and journeyman marble mason in the city, and his family believe he worked on the interior of St George's Hall. He married a widow, Sarah Ann Gasperina, in 1856, with whom he lived at 24 Spring Place, off Springfield Road, in the heart of the Italian quarter. They had three daughters, Elizabeth, Catharina, Jessie, and a son, Angelo. Catharina married a musician, Angelo Diodati, in 1880. Elizabeth married an Irishman, Michael Danahy, but on his death, she wed an Italian, John Vermiglio, an ice-cream seller. But Jessie Ginochio fell in love with an Englishman, David Jones.

He was an iron moulder by trade, from Oxton on the Wirral Peninsula, but worked as a cotton porter on the Liverpool Docks. Jessie and David married on 23 February 1885 at the parish church of Liverpool, St Nicholas. They set up home with Jessie's widowed mother at 3 Hutchinson Street, and had six children: Marguerita, Joseph, William, John Alfred, Samuel and David, who was born on 10 January 1892. The family later moved to 25 Elmore Street, behind Everton Terrace, where young David Jones grew up, attending the newly-built Heyworth Street School, now Everton Park School.

He had a happy if unremarkable childhood and progressed well at school, being noted as a cheerful and intelligent pupil, who was just as good with his hands as he was with the books. On leaving school, his good academic record secured him a much-valued apprenticeship, one in the forefront of modern technology: he began work as an indentured motor mechanic with the firm of Joseph Blake, of 148 Mount Pleasant, in the city centre.

Joseph Blake was a coach painter, who branched out to building coaches and carriages for the gentry. The advent of the internal combustion engine saw him establish one of the first maintenance and repair shops for cars and lorries on

Merseyside. He built up his business to be one of the most successful in the city, and in 1896 retired and handed over to his son-in-law, James Reece. The firm continued to prosper, and in 1910 the Ford Motor Company awarded its first Liverpool dealership to Joseph Blake and Company.

Workmates of David Jones remembered him as a conscientious worker, enthusiastic and dependable, who liked nothing better than a good laugh and to tinker beneath the bonnet of a car or lorry. He was of average height, 5 feet, 7 inches tall, and the only extant photograph of him shows a bright-eyed, alert young man, with open features and a mop of wavy brown hair. Popular with everyone, he impressed the management with his work ethic and when, in 1914, he decided to join Kitchener's New Army, James Reece gladly agreed to hold open his job until he returned from the front.

In his late teens David Jones had begun courting Elizabeth Dorothea Doyle. She was a Liverpool girl, born in 1890, and she lived nearby at 37 Mere Lane. Her parents, Michael and Elizabeth, were Irish, and she was the youngest of nine children. The couple made marriage plans but shelved them temporarily when David enlisted as 14951 Private David Jones in 12th (Service) Battalion, King's (Liverpool) Regiment.

The battalion was formed at Seaforth within days of Lord Kitchener's appeal to the nation, and was attached as divisional or army troops to the newly forming 20th (Light) Division, then assembling at Aldershot. On the train to Aldershot, David Jones met an old friend, Fred Austin, who lived in Wavertree, and who worked as a sign-writer for a local firm of coach builders. He introduced him to Francis Coxhead, from Kirkdale, and the three men became close friends. They were posted to 10th Platoon, C Company, of the battalion, and began their training together.

In January 1915, the 12th Liverpools were transferred to 61st Brigade of the division, and underwent additional training in trench warfare and weaponry. Before the formation of specialized machine-gun units, each infantry battalion carried a two-gun, machine-gun section. The most readily available and most reliable weapon at the outset of the war was the Lewis light machine gun, an American weapon, but manufactured under license in Britain by the Birmingham Small Arms Company. It weighed in at twenty-eight pounds, almost half the weight of the Vickers equivalent, and could be carried into battle over the shoulder and handled in action by one man only.

For David Jones, the Lewis gun was his weapon of choice. With the brain and aptitude of a good mechanic, it did not take him long to master the weapon and blindfolded he could strip and rebuild the gun in minutes. He learnt the basics of machine-gun tactics, of direct and indirect fire, and in the months to come in France he was rarely seen without his trusty Lewis gun slung over his shoulder.

At the beginning of May 1915, Jones was granted a fortnight's leave, and he returned to Liverpool. From his home in Aigburth Street, he put the final touches to his wedding preparations. Elizabeth Doyle was living at 55 Silverdale Street, Tuerbrook at the time; and from there, on 27 May, she married David Jones at the local church of St Cecilia. The couple made a home at 87 Heyworth Street before embarking on their honeymoon. 'Our honeymoon lasted eleven days altogther,' Elizabeth would later recall. 'And then, a few months later, they told me he was dead.'

Within days of his return to his unit, the division was inspected by the king at Knighton Down on 24 June 1915, and judged ready for war. By late July, David Jones was in the Artois region of French Flanders, the division concentrated on the town of St Omer. He was promoted to coporal, his intelligence, the ease with which he handled men and the cheerfulness he exhibited in the face of adversity, being quickly marked by his superiors as meriting the promotion.

On 25 September, the 12th Liverpools received their baptism of fire when they went over the top in support of the Meerut Division at Petrie, one of three subsidiary attacks made on the opening day of the Battle of Loos to divert German reserves from that battlefield. The assault was not well planned, no set objectives were set, and it petered out quickly. Nevertheless, it was a valuable experience for Jones and his comrades, and prepared them for the next round of fighting in the Ypres Salient, when their nerve would be tested by a mighty German onslaught.

In June 1916, the 12th Liverpools were in trenches in Railway Wood, east of Ypres on the Menin Road, close to the village of Hooge. On the right was the 3rd Canadian Division, which included Princess Patricia's Canadian Light Infantry (PPCLI), among whose ranks was Sergeant Hugh McKenzie. The Canadian lines extended south, along a wooded crest line topped by the heights of Tor Top and Mount Sorrel. The heights were the last dominating observation position in front of Ypres, overlooking the salient, the town, the railway line and the main approach roads. The Germans planned to wrest it from the Allies.

On 2 June, the Canadians on Mount Sorrel and Tor Top were blasted from their trenches by a devastating artillery bombardment and were overrun by the massed infantry assault of the XIII Württemburg Corps. The trenches of the 12th Liverpools also came under heavy attack, but the front held as the Germans were repulsed with heavy machine-gun fire. A counter-attack against the heights was launched the following day but was beaten back; and before another could be mounted, the Germans attacked again, near Hooge. Jones and the 12th Liverpools were in the thick of the action, supporting the Canadians, and repelled the enemy in fierce, close-quarter combat.

The front fell silent. The Germans dug in. The Allies brought in reinforcements and additional artillery support. Then, in the early morning of 13 June, the Canadians stormed from their trenches in heavy rain and slogged back up the slippery slopes to the high ground. Advancing from Railway Wood on the left of the Canadians, Jones's Division made four successful trench raids under cover of a smoke barrage. In the driving rain, Mount Sorrel and Tor Top were recaptured in two days of bitter fighting and the Germans were pushed back beyond their original lines of attack.

Corporal David Jones very quickly learnt the cut-and-thrust of trench warfare in his first two engagements, and his leadership and the manner in which he encouraged others to bring out their best, were rewarded with a further promotion to sergeant, in charge of a Lewis-gun section. 'He was a wonderful scout,' wrote his company commander, Captain Norman Millican, 'and did some magnificent patrol work, which combined brain and bravery to a high degree. His fearlessness had a very great influence for good on the men of his platoon and company.'

The division then moved south to the Somme, to the fortified village of Guillemont, which to date had defied the Allies in two attempts: on 30 July, Lord Derby's Liverpool Pals had been sacrificed there; and on 8 August, the 5th and 10th Liverpools had been badly mauled also. Noel Chavasse, Arthur Procter, Cyril Gourley and Gabriel Coury had all been in the lines in front of the intractable defences of the village. On 3 September 1916, the 20th (Light) Division and the 16th (Irish) Division, supported by the 7th Division, would be tasked to carry Guillemont.

The village stood six and half miles east of Albert, on the right flank of the British sector. Beyond it, to the north and east, stood a number of German strongpoints, Ginchy, Falfemont Farm, Leuze Woods, each providing protection for the other. The capture of Guillemont would open the way to these strongpoints and allow the French and British armies to combine finally on a straightened front and to push on towards the east. The 20th Division took up positions to the west of the village, and its lines extended to the north, toward the railway station. In addition to capturing the village, the division was to establish a perimeter 500 yards beyond, along a crossroads to the east. The men in the trenches waited in dread of going over the top, knowing what to expect from the formidable defences.

Under the cover and protection of a rolling barrage of 25 yards a minute, the infantry attacked from the north, west and south. The village was penetrated quickly, and trenches and dugouts were overrun. The fighting, however, was savage and ferocious, and the Germans sold every yard dearly. But, by half past one in the afternoon, Allied grit carried the day, and the 20th Division swept through Guillemont and began to establish its position to the east.

North-east of Guillemont, some units of the 7th Division had entered the outskirts of the village of Ginchy, another German stronghold, but enemy fire from the right enfiladed their position. David Jones and C Company of 12th Liverpools had been in the thick of the fighting and were hoping for a well-earned respite. No such luck: the men were ordered forward astride the Guillemont–Ginchy Road to drive out the Germans on the right. But the

Germans were recovering from the assault and were regrouping to counter-attack. Their artillery was ranging targets, and the advance of the 12th Liverpools was spotted.

Suddenly, the men of C Company were engulfed by a storm of exploding shells and crackling machine-gun bullets, and threw themselves to the ground to find cover. The company became dispersed across no man's land. 'We walked right into hell by the back door and suffered terribly,' reported a corporal of Jones's platoon. 'All officers bowled out. The men were like sheep without a shepherd. Things were all in a muddle. Nobody seemed to know what to do. Sergeant Jones sprang forward and gave orders.'

Sergeant Jones made the wounded comfortable and then collected together as many able-bodied men as he could find. 'The men quickly recovered from their temporary dismay and under his direction they resumed the push on the enemy's position. The machine guns played hell with us, but the Sergeant led us straight to the goal.' Utilizing what cover they could find, the men followed Sergeant Jones through the barrage, only to face a second when the Germans in the trenches turned their attention to his motley band. Without hesitation, Jones guided the men forward in a charge against the trenches. 'We carried the position with a rush though we were greatly outnumbered. The enemy fled in panic and we lost no time in making ourselves at home.'

As he supervised the position and mounted and positioned the Lewis guns, the Germans counter-attacked. Sergeant Jones and a small band of men drove them off. A second attack an hour later was repulsed also. 'All night long the enemy deluged us with shell fire and twice they attacked with great fury. They were determined to overwhelm us by their weight of numbers but under the orders of Sergeant Jones we put our backs into it and drove off the Hun each time.' But the situation was desperate. The men were cut off from their battalion, and as the Germans pressed to stem the Allied advance, they found themselves isolated, tucked away in a small salient of their own.

'We had neither food nor water and the circumstances were about as depressing as they could be, but Sergeant Jones never despaired. He was so cheerful himself that everybody felt ashamed to be anything else.' Day and night the Germans pounded the position, but the fortitude of Sergeant Jones could not be suppressed, and he continually rallied his men in the face of the enemy actions. 'So we held on like grim death for two days. We smashed up the enemy every time they tried to overwhelm us. It was hard fighting but the boys stuck it well until relief came.'

It was only when the Germans began to concentrate their attack on another sector after two days of vicious fighting that Sergeant Jones and his men were relieved. 'We had been given up for lost. Nobody ever expected to see us again. That we had come through the ordeal safe and with honour was due entirely to Sergeant Jones's handling of the men and no one will begrudge him the honour he has won.'

Francis Coxhead, who survived the war, later added his own comments in appreciation of the strength of character exhibited by his friend during the dark days of isolation on the front line: 'He ought to be an officer. He led us with great skill and completely baffled the foe at every turn. Nothing could dismay him. At times there was enough to make one's heart sink to the boots, but Sergeant Jones was as chirpy as could be and his cheeriness was infectious. We all felt sure that nothing could go wrong with us under his leadership and we were right.'

For conspicuous gallantry in leading his men to their objective and holding the position for two days while under constant attack, Sergeant David Jones was awarded the Victoria Cross. His citation reads:

> David Jones, Number 14951, Sergeant, 12th Battalion, Liverpool Regiment. For most conspicuous bravery, devotion to duty, and ability displayed in the handling of his platoon. The platoon to which he belonged was ordered to a forward position, and during the advance came under heavy machine-gun fire, the officer being killed and the platoon suffered heavy losses. Sergeant Jones led forward the remainder, occupied the position, and held it for two days and two nights without food or water, until relieved. On the second day he drove back three counter-attacks, inflicting heavy losses. His coolness was most praiseworthy. It was due entirely to his resource and example that his men retained confidence and held their post.

Exhausted, Jones led his platoon to the rear to rejoin the battalion. But there was little time in which to rest and recuperate. The fighting continued unabated, and the Liverpools continued to advance. Ginchy was taken on 9 September, and the division moved on in support of the Canadians and New Zealanders at the battle of Flers-Courcelette six days later. And by the end of September, with the capture of the town of Morval, the third line of the German defences on the Somme, the original objective on the opening day of the battle on 1 July, was finally in Allied hands.

However, the slow, arduous campaign on the Somme had gifted the Germans time in which to build a fourth defensive line along the Transloy Ridges, further east; and beyond that, a fifth and sixth line were under construction. The prospect of the much vaunted Allied breakthrough appeared as remote as ever. Field Marshal Haig was adamant, nevertheless, that it could be achieved, and he ordered another offensive to smash the Transloy line, giving the job to Lieutenant General Sir Henry Rawlinson and Fourth Army. Battle-weary, without sleep or a decent meal in days, unwashed, unshaven, their uniforms tattered and torn, the men of 12th Liverpools tramped into positions south-east of Gueudecourt to take part in the assault, under orders to capture a section of the opposing lines known as Rainbow Trench.

The Battle of Transloy Ridges opened in heavy rain on 1 October 1916. A seven-hour preliminary bombardment battered the German lines, but when the troops went over the top and slogged through the mud, they were met with fierce resistance. Casualties on both sides were high, and it took two days of fighting in dreadful conditions just to capture the first objectives, Le Sars, on the Bapaume Road, and Eaucourt L'Abbaye, from the enemy.

The weather deteriorated further, and the lashing rain became the enemy, reducing visibility to zero. The offensive became bogged down in the running mud and stalled. The 12th Liverpools had made very little progress and suffered many casualties; and the men hunkered down outside Gueudecourt, cursing the weather, waiting for the attack to restart. When the rain began to ease, orders were received that hostilities towards Transloy Ridges were to resume on the morning of 7 October.

The announcement of the grant of the Victoria Cross to Sergeant David Jones was published in the *London Gazette* of 26 October 1916. The same supplement also carried details of the award to Lieutenant Gabriel Coury and Captain Noel Chavasse MC. Sergeant David Jones was killed in action before the announcement was made, and it has always been assumed that he died without knowing of the award. However, his friend Francis Coxhead tells a different story: 'Colonel Vince sent for him to tell him that he had been awarded the Victoria Cross for his bravery at Guillemont a month earlier.'

In the evening of Saturday, 6 October, Sergeant David Jones was ordered to the rear and presented himself to his commanding officer, Lieutenant Colonel Vince. Having been informed that he had won the Victoria Cross, Sergeant Jones then made a fateful decision. 'The Colonel left it to Dave whether he went home on leave to receive the Victoria Cross, or go into the line next day. . . . Dave chose to go into action.' The Liverpools were in the middle of a battle: fighting would resume the next day. Honoured by the award, appreciative of what it meant, Sergeant Jones, nevertheless, decided that his duty came first. A dedicated soldier, he chose to stand with his men and fight rather than return to England.

On 7 October, Sergeant Jones VC jumped off with his platoon to the south-east, along the muddy track that had once been the road from Gueudecourt to Le Transloy. Progress was good, and the Liverpools advanced 500 yards under heavy fire and attacked the western section of Rainbow Trench. The German defenders were routed in vicious, hand-to-hand combat, and several prisoners were taken. One of them ingratiatingly offered Sergeant Jones a cigar. He accepted, and tucked it away in the breast pocket of his tunic.

The new position was consolidated and manned to face a possible counter-attack, and as the day wore on, with no sign of the enemy, plans were made to advance further; another sector of the German line, Cloudy Trench, 300 yards ahead fell within the remit of the Liverpools. But the Germans held the right-hand section of the trench and the Liverpools were in danger of enfilading fire from that postion if they advanced too quickly.

The Liverpools went forward cautiously and gained a foothold in Cloudy Trench. A German assault from the right was deemed likely, and the men dug in, alert to the danger. In the afternoon, Sergeant Jones lit his cheroot, minutes before the expected attack materialized. The Liverpools held fast and threw back the Germans with heavy casualties. At the height of the battle, Francis Coxhead caught a final glimpse of his friend: cigar in mouth, Sergeant David Jones VC was hammering the enemy with his favoured Lewis gun.

The 7th Battalion, Somerset Light Infantry, relieved the 12th Liverpools that night in the trenches. It is believed that Francis Coxhead and Fred Austin carried the lifeless body of their friend to the rear for burial. They marked his grave with his name and number carved into a simple wooden cross. Sergeant David Jones VC was later laid to rest in the British Cemetery at Bancourt, two miles east of Bapaume. Had he survived the assault, he would have gone home, received his honour and, in all probability, would have been commissioned and sent for officer training. His talents as a fighting man and his leadership qualities had marked him out as officer material early in the war, and his loss was keenly felt in the battalion.

Elizabeth Jones was living with her brother Joseph at 203 Smithdown Road when she received the news of her husband's death. A letter from the king would follow, in which His Majesty offered his condolences and expressed his sorrow over not being able to confer the honour of the Victoria Cross on her brave husband. Married for less than sixteen months, she had enjoyed no life at all with him; and the abrupt dashing of her dreams and hopes, of finally being reunited with him and starting a family, were very difficult for her to endure. She was inconsolable as she grieved for her loss with her in-laws.

She travelled to London to receive the award from the king at Buckingham Palace on 31 March 1917. The king requested she wear the honour above her right breast in remembrance of her husband, and she agreed to do so. Elizabeth wore the medal with pride on the streets of Liverpool, but she was embarrassed often when passing soldiers would come to attention and salute her; and she soon gave up wearing it in public.

On 3 April 1917, Elizabeth Jones and her mother and father-in-law attended as guests of honour a dedication ceremony in Heyworth Street School. A large crowd of local residents and friends and relatives from 'Little Italy' gathered around the playground, and Graham Blake Reece, Managing Director of Joseph Blake and Company, joined the platform. The pupils were assembled by the headmaster, and cohorts from the 12th and 9th Liverpools paraded as the Lord Mayor of Liverpool, Councillor Max Spratt, unveiled a brass plaque to honour Sergeant David Jones VC, which the children themselves had erected inside the school. A stone tablet, detailing the hero's brave deeds, and fixed into a wall, was unveiled in the playground. The band of 3rd Battalion,

Royal Welsh Fusiliers, closed the ceremony with the sounding of the 'Last Post'.

Elizabeth Jones subsequently married William Woosey, a plumber by trade, some years after the end of the war. They lived for many years at 138 Portelet Road, Tuebrook. This marriage, like her first, was childless. Her later years, following the death of William Woosey, were attended with some bitterness. She had loved David Jones very deeply and felt cheated out of a life with him: memories of their brief time together as husband and wife haunted her old age and much thought was given to what might have been. 'Our honeymoon lasted eleven days altogether. And then, a few months later, they told me he was dead,' was the acerbic comment she made to a reporter from the *Liverpool Echo* in the winter of 1958.

On 1 September of that year, it was announced that the King's (Liverpool) Regiment, which had stood in the city since 1685, would cease to exist, amalgamating with the Manchester Regiment to form the King's Regiment. Elizabeth Jones Woosey was incensed: the Victoria Cross and the Liverpools framed her memories of her beloved. She had intended leaving the honour to the regiment, but would not pass it on to this new formation, which she believed could not do justice to her brave husband's memory.

The reporter she spoke to that winter arrived with a ready-made solution. He told her a story: unknown to her, every year since the unveiling of the Cenotaph on 11 November 1920, Graham Blake Reece, and later his son Stanley, had sent a representative from the firm to Whitehall on Remembrance Day to lay a wreath at the Cenotaph in memory of David Jones VC. The former employee of the company, the hero from 'Little Italy', had not been forgotten.

At the head office of Joseph Blake and Company in Bold Street, Elizabeth handed over the Victoria Cross to Stanley Blake Reece. It held pride of place there for many years. The medal is owned by trustees of the company, and is on permament loan in the King's (Liverpool) Regiment Collection at the Museum of Liverpool Life.

Albert White VC
(1892–1917)

William Barclay was Secretary of Everton Football Club when it became a founder member of the English Football League in 1888. Following a dispute over the club's playing field at Anfield, he sided with the breakaway group wishing to retain Anfield, and in 1892 became Secretary of 'the other lot', Liverpool Football Club. He retired from football four years later to become governor, with his wife as governess, of the Liverpool Certified Industrial School at 33–35 Everton Terrace.

Industrial Schools were established in 1857 to provide education and training for what were known as the 'ragged' children of the inner cities, the orphans, the destitute, the homeless, the persistent truants beyond parental control and the tearaways who roamed the streets, children aged between 7 and 14 who had yet to commit a criminal offence but whose lifestyle, if it could be so called, was leading them into delinquency and probable confinement within a juvenile reformatory school.

These schools aimed to wean children away from troubled pasts, to instruct and educate, to bring out and develop latent potential and to instil the habit of work. There were more than twenty such schools in Liverpool, with pupil rolls totalling more than 4,000. They were financed by the government and from local rates, and were overseen by boards of governors drawn from, and aided by, the churches, charitable institutions and local dignitaries such as Lord Derby, James Nugent and William Rathbone.

William Barclay introduced a strong sporting element into the curriculum, both to provide a sense of belonging and as a means of curbing high spirits, and allowed boxing bouts and football matches on Saturday afternoons in the winter, and cricket and gymnastics during the summer. Everton Terrace competed annually against other industrial schools in gymnastics for the Melly Cup and the Cricket Cup, and although the school did not produce a winning team in any of the competions during its long history, it did turn out one outstanding individual winner, Albert White, who won the Victoria Cross in 1917.

Albert White was born on 1 December 1892, at 62 Teulon Street, not far from Goodison Park, which had recently become the new home of Everton Football Club. He was a high-spirited young lad, a tearaway, one of the tough nuts on his street at a time when every street of terraced housing and every court and cellar in the city typically produced at least one hard case. His eldest brother, Thomas Henry, with whom he had a close relationship, tried to curtail his waywardness, but the young lad could not be told. His reputation for toughness, for causing trouble, exaggerated no doubt by his cronies and rivals, followed him when the family moved to 124 Arlington Street, off Stanley Road. From there, it was a walk of ten minutes and a 'spot of bother' too much for him to pass through the gates of the industrial school at Everton Terrace.

The boys and girls lived in, sleeping in dormitories and eating together in the mess hall. The regime was strict and rigidly enforced: rising at six o'clock in the morning, seven days a week, the children followed a set timetable for school work and learning the rudiments of a variety of trades. Sundays were put aside for religious instruction, communal worship and monthly family visits. Thomas Henry persisted in exerting a calming influence on his troubled brother and, within the confines of the school, his visits had the desired effect. Always able to take care of himself in a fight, Albert lost the urge to prove himself; and, encouraged by his brother, and by applying himself diligently to his studies, he began to redeem himself.

After leaving the school, Albert did what generations of young Liverpool men had always done, including his grandfather Elias: he went to sea with the Merchant Navy. He found a berth on board SS *Laurentic* of the White Star Line, which owned the ill-fated RMS *Titanic*. Perhaps a little too rough and ready for the job of steward, the position his grandfather had filled, he was put to work in a tough job, a trimmer in the boiler room.

The boiler room was the heart of a steam-powered vessel, and the boilers were prepared and fed with coal by firemen, known as stokers in the Royal Navy. It was the job of the trimmer to supply the firemen. He would trim the coal forward with a deep, wide-bladed shovel from the bunker to within easy reach of the firemen to throw into the flames. Under full steam, a single boiler could consume up to fifteen tons of coal a day. It was exhausting, dirty, back-breaking labour for the firemen and trimmers working drenched in sweat in the sauna of the boiler room, where metal surfaces glowed red-hot, roasting exposed skin, and where fumes and dust congested the lungs.

But the work suited Albert White and he stuck to his task. He was of average height, approximately 5 feet, 7 inches tall, and below decks he quickly developed a strong, muscular frame. A strong-featured man, with dark eyes and a mop of brown hair, his face showed signs of the hard knocks taken on the streets and in the boxing ring at Everton Terrace. Home on leave every thirty days, he had money jingling in his pockets to treat his family and friends, and tales to tell of Canadian cities.

His father, Thomas, was born in Dundee in 1862, and came to Liverpool as a young man of 19. He lived in lodgings at 14 Lockhart Street with the Ingleby family, and found work as a railway porter. His mother, Eliza Ann Falls, was born in Liverpool in 1861. She was the daughter of Elias Falls, a ship's steward, and Ellen Hewitt, who had married in 1858 and lived at 9 Bailey Street, in the city centre. Ellen Falls supported her family working as a seamstress after she was widowed in 1879; and, when she was old enough, Eliza Ann made a contribution, working as a domestic servant in Upper Pitt Street. She married Thomas White on 26 March 1883 at St Nicholas Church, the parish church of the city of Liverpool.

The newlyweds' first home was at 23 Tillard Street, where three sons were born, Thomas Henry, Elias and Robert. After moving to Teulon Street, the couple were blessed with Albert and Jessie; and the family was completed in Arlington Street with the arrival of Edward and Florence. It was only after leaving Everton Terrace that Albert got to know his young brother and sister. He doted on them, making them his own special responsibility and always ensuring they had a few extra pennies to spend whenever he was on leave.

Home on shore leave from SS *Laurentic* just after the First World War began, Albert enlisted at Liverpool on 23 October 1914 as 43785 Private Albert White in the Royal Army Medical Corps (RAMC). He gave his age incorrectly as 24, and named his widowed father, Thomas White, then living at 58 Lamb Street, as his next of kin. Albert was not married, but he made a weekly allowance from his pay of eight shillings and seven pence to his sister Jessie on behalf of his siblings, young Edward and Florence.

It is thought that he was posted to 2nd West Lancashire Field Ambulance, under the command of Lieutenant Colonel Thomas Stevenson, the well-known ophthalmic surgeon of Rodney Street. In the military context, a field ambulance was not a vehicle, but a unit of men. Each unit was composed of ten officers and 224 men, divided among three sections, comprising stretcher-bearers, medics, orderlies, sanitary cleaners, cooks, drivers and grooms. Three field ambulances were attached to each infantry division, and the 1st, 2nd and 3rd West Lancashire Field Ambulances were attached to the 55th West Lancashire Division. The officers and men were responsible for the safe evacuation of the wounded, and went unarmed and carried no munitions on the battlefield.

Albert White was sent to Calderstones Park for induction, where he had his first taste of army life, living under canvas in the autumnal splendour of the park. The 2nd West Lancashire Field Ambulance was mobilized to Westerham, Kent, in November, to start training in basic first aid and bandaging. Early in 1915, Albert and the ambulance team was on the move again, to Tunbridge Wells, for three months of intensive training, before joining up with other units in Wye, Ashford, in preparation for the move to France.

It is not known why he enlisted in the RAMC, why he did not continue work as a mariner and serve his country in that capacity. In all likelihood, he joined up with a friend: a young man by the name of William Urmson, born in the same year as Albert, also enlisted in the same field ambulance unit. And a William Urmson was living in Arlington Street at the time Albert lived there.

However, life in the RAMC did not suit Albert, and on 1 June 1915, just before he was due to leave for France, he transferred to the 2nd Battalion, South Wales Borderers (SWB), as 24866 Private Albert White.

Returning to England from China in January 1915, the battalion re-equipped at Rugby and joined the 87th Brigade of the 29th Division, which brought together Regular Army units returning to England from all corners of the empire. The 29th Division became part of the Mediterranean Expeditionary Force. On 25 April, the division, under Major General Aylmer Hunter-Weston, and supported by HMS *Cornwallis*, landed on five beaches around Cape Helles on the southern tip of the Gallipoli Peninsula. The objectives were the village of Krithia and the nearby heights at Achi Baba to the north, but after three days of fierce fighting Krithia remained in Turkish hands.

Albert White did not join the battalion on Gallipoli until 30 June. By the time he entered the fray, a second and third assault against Krithia, in early May and the beginning of June, had failed also, and an abortive attack on the hill of Achi Baba was just coming to an end, with heavy Allied casualties.

In the sweltering summer heat, in the rough dugouts and trenches scratched into the rocky ground, Albert White was afforded time in which to acclimatize while the Allied Generals contemplated the next move to secure Gallipoli. The 2nd Battalion was allowed a month in which to recover from the rigorous campaign and to re-equip for the next phase, the final, bloody assault of the disastrous campaign, the landing at Suvla Bay and the attack on Scimitar Hill.

Major General Beauvoir de Lisle took command of 29th Division when it was transported along the coast to Suvla Bay. On 21 August, the assault on Scimitar Hill began. The preliminary artillery bombardment, which both looked and sounded impressive, had little effect on the Turkish defences, and ultimately hindered the advance by setting fire to the landscape. And, amid the inferno, Albert White went over the top for the first time. The 2nd Battalion, SWB, advanced in the teeth of a vicious Turkish counter-fire of exploding shells and chattering machine guns. The men charged up the hill blindly to engage the enemy. Elements of the battalion fought their way to the summit, as did others of the brigade, but were unable to consolidate the gain. Even with the Mounteds of Brigadier General Paul Kenna VC in the support, they were forced back in disarray in the face of a resolute Turkish defence, tumbling back the way they had come, stumbling over the shattered bodies of friends, and gathering up the wounded as they went.

When the battle was over and the division regrouped, the 2nd Battalion roll call told a sorry tale: 300 men, a third of the strength, had been lost on the burning slopes of Scimitar Hill. But Albert White had survived without a scratch or a burn. He returned to the lines battered and bloodied like his comrades, choking and gasping for air, his lungs full of the acrid smoke which would hang like a pall over the battlefield for days to come. There would be no more fighting on Gallipoli. The 2nd SWB spent the following five months in crude dugouts freezing in the depths of a severe winter while the generals and politicians dithered over their next move. On 8 January 1916, the 29th Division was evacuated from Gallipoli, and for the 2nd Battalion, the move was from the frying pan to the fire, from the horrors of Gallipoli to the bloody slaughter on the Somme.

In April, the battalion was introduced to the Western Front, and went into lines to begin training for the rigours of trench warfare in preparation for the assault on the village of Beaumont Hamel on the opening day of the Battle of the Somme. Albert White was promoted to corporal. His experience was much needed in the battalion as it absorbed new faces, bright, inexperienced and unknowing, new blood that had to be readied for the horrors to come.

Beaumont Hamel, six miles north of the city of Albert, in the northern sector of the front, and north of the river Somme, was situated within the German front line. Lying in a cleft in a narrow valley, the village had natural protection: one arm of a Y-shaped ravine guarded it from the east, and the second ran parallel to the British front line, before rising to the heights of Hawthorn Ridge, on top of which the Germans had constructed a formidable redoubt. The 2nd Battalion, SWB, occupied positions south of the village on the forward slope of the most westerly of a series of ridges overlooking the Y-ravine. The battalion would lead the assault against the Germans.

On 24 June, an intense preliminary barrage opened against the German lines. It rained hellfire on the defences for five days; and when inclement weather forced a postponement of the attack, it continued creating havoc for a further two days until 1 July. That Saturday morning broke bright and clear, ideal for battle, and the golden sun seemed to signal the prospect of a great Allied victory. Haig and his generals were highly confident of success, believing little resistance could be offered by the enemy following such a bombardment, and that the troops would simply waltz through the enemy positions.

Albert White readied himself in the jump-off trench just after dawn, sucking in air to calm his nerves, fussing at the sixty-six pounds of equipment that he, like all the men, would hump into battle that day: food, extra ammunition, trenching tools; all deemed necessary for the consolidation and defence of the expected gains. The generals had thought of everything – everything except the ingenuity of the German engineers who had constructed the defences.

Zero hour was seven-thirty in the morning. But, ten minutes before the appointed time, 40,000 pounds of high explosive ammonal were prematurely detonated beneath Hawthorn Ridge. The massive explosion, which was heard in London, stunned the combatants at Beaumont Hamel, and alerted the Germans all along the front. And, while Albert White and his comrades recovered their senses, the preliminary bombardment lifted and rolled on to the second line of the defences. Then, at seven-thirty, the officers blew their whistles and the men climbed from the trenches.

But the ten-minute interval was crucial. The German engineers had done their job well: despite the bombardment, the defences were still intact, and the battered defenders crawled out of their dugouts and manned the ramparts. When the whistles blew, their shrill cries were answered by the metallic rasp of machine guns being cocked.

In the van, down the grassy slope, came 2nd Battalion, SWB, walking in lines as instructed towards the Y-ravine. Albert White and his comrades were enveloped in a blanket of flying lead. Out in the open, they were cut to shreds by machine-gun fire from the Ravine. The carnage was beyond belief. Within minutes, from a strength of 599 officers and men, 246 were killed and 153 were wounded, sprawled in heaps in the long summer grass: the 2nd Battalion virtually ceased to exist. Some brave men did manage to reach the wire but could go no further in the face of such resolute resistance, and died yards from their objective.

Chaos ensued. 1st Battalion, King's Own Scottish Borderers, supporting the 2nd Battalion, was mown down also. Major General Beauvoir de Lisle mistook German flares requesting more ammunition as a signal that the trenches had been stormed, and ordered forward further support units. Two more battalions entered the killing field, and when the German artillery joined the slaughter, the men were knocked over like ninepins. At ten o'clock, the attack was called off, and the shell-shocked survivors staggered back to their lines with their wounded. The waltz the generals had anticipated had turned into a *danse macabre*.

The division suffered more than 5,000 casualties in less than three hours of fighting. The dead littered the slopes of that 'idle hill of summer' until the middle of November, when Beaumont Hamel fell finally to the Allies, and burial parties were able to recover the remains. Albert White was one of the fortunate ones, not only surviving the attack but doing so without injury. The remnants of the battalion were taken out of the line and sent to the rear to await reinforcements. On 2 July 1916, as he struggled to come to terms with the loss of so many friends following the nightmare of Beaumont Hamel, he was pro- moted to sergeant in D Company of the battalion. A seasoned campaigner now, his talents and abilities would be needed to help restore the fighting spirit of the battalion before it went into action again.

In February 1917, Albert White was granted a week's home leave, and he returned to Liverpool and his family, who were living at 58 Lamb Street, Kirkdale. Welcomed as a hero, a sergeant of his battalion, a brave soldier who was doing his duty, he had come a long way from his early days as a tearaway on the streets of the city; and the admiration and respect of family and friends and neighbours was all the more heartfelt.

His brother and best friend Thomas Henry was home on leave from the Merchant Navy. He had married Agnes Reid in 1911, and their first child, another Thomas Henry, had been born just as Albert went off to war. Albert White never married, but he was a family man, and, in the short time he had at home, his two-year-old nephew became the apple of his eye. But he still kept the soft spot for Edward and Florence. 'Wait until the war's over,' he told them, 'and we will have a fine time.'

But, as the day drew near for him to leave his loved ones and return to the front, he brooded. Never one to pull his punches, he spoke forthrightly to Jessie: 'If I am killed, what about it? I am only one of them, and they're all as good as me.' He had no pretensions about himself, no inflated ideas about his own worth: he had found a niche for himself in the army and he was a tough, rugged, uncomplaining, dedicated soldier. But too many friends, ordinary, working-class men like him, good soldiers also, had perished, and he knew fate would catch up with him sometime. On the day he departed, he was accompanied to Lime Street Station by his father and the two Thomas Henrys. But, when bidding his final farewells, a sense of foreboding overcame him, and he confided in his aged father: 'I will not come home.' He was proved correct.

Back at the front, his battalion was sent to the Arras sector, where the formidable Hindenburg Line began. In recognition of his abilities, he was offered a commission and posted to the rear to commence initial training: the young tearaway from the city streets, the trimmer from the boiler-room, was to rise above his past and become an officer and a gentleman. However, he did not complete the introductory course: the expenses of being an officer, the cost of uniforms, the mess bills, were too high. He wrote to his sister, Jessie: 'If I get a commission I should have to stop my eight-shilling and seven pence allotment to you, so I intend to give up the commission and keep on the allotment to you.' He would see his family cared for regardless of the personal cost.

Returning to the battalion with the same rank of sergeant, he spent a miserable six weeks in the trenches, reminiscent of the awful days on Gallipoli, when snow storms, hail and freezing rain engulfed the Artois region. But it was soon to warm up, as the Allies schemed to break the Germans and finish the war by the end of the year.

The Arras offensive in the spring of 1917 aimed to break the deadlock of trench warfare once and for all by pushing through the German lines and beyond, out into the open plains of Douai, where the numerically inferior German army could be engaged and defeated in a war of movement. Simultaneous attacks would be made against Vimy Ridge, at Arras and further south at Bullecourt, supplemented a week later by a huge French offensive on a front of fifty miles, from Soissons to Rheims. The Allied High Commands expected the combined operations would end the war before the end of the month. At Arras, the immediate objectives were to draw German reserves away from the sector of the French attack while advancing beyond Arras, and to take the high ground along Vimy Ridge to the north-east.

On 9 April 1917, the Arras offensive opened beneath a downpour of snow and sleet and a rolling barrage along the twelve-mile front. The 29th Division, part of General Allenby's Third Army, was held in reserve initially, to the south of the city. The fighting around Arras would be inconclusive, and the offensive would break down into a series of minor battles which would rage until May. Only at Vimy Ridge would there be success.

In what became known as the First Battle of the River Scarpe, Allenby attacked on either side of the town of Arras and the River Scarpe, and advanced two miles on the opening day. However, south of the river, progress was slower, and the Germans were able to hold up the advance at the fortified village of Monchy-le-Preux, perched on top of a conical hill, four miles east of Arras. But the weather was the arbiter in this contest, and when a blizzard descended upon the battlefield, the killing halted for three days.

As the flying snow reduced visibility to zero, 2nd Battalion, SWB, came forward into positions west and to the south of Monchy-le-Preux, taking over the right-hand section of the front which ran down to the left bank of the River Cojeul. Albert White held a position from which another Liverpool hero, Arthur Evans, would advance to win his Victoria Cross seventeen months later. When Monchy fell to the Essex and the Newfoundland Regiments, the 2nd Battalion fought in the Second Battle of the River Scarpe and the advance to the industrial town of Rouex. But very little progress was made in the appalling weather, and the battalion barely advanced 600 yards in the face of strong enemy resistance.

At the beginning of May, the 2nd Battalion occupied lines half a mile north-east of Monchy when the Third Battle of the River Scarpe began. On the left of the position was a sunken road, Bit Lane, and 200 yards along the track, Arrow Trench emerged, into which ran at an oblique angle the heavily fortified Devil's Trench. Even though the Arras offensive officially ended on 17 May, fighting continued in isolated pockets for several days, particularly near Monchy-le-Preux.

On 19 May, behind a rolling barrage, Captain Davies, Second Lieutenant Jones and Sergeant White led forward D Company of the 2nd Battalion, supported by A and B Companies, to capture Arrow Trench at the junction with Devil's Trench. Just before the barrage lifted, a bombing squad from D Company went into action against the German wire, attempting to blast a passage through the entanglement for the men to exploit. But when the barrage crept on, the enemy were alerted, and the defences were rapidly manned. The German artillery retaliated, pounding no man's land, and machine-gun fire opened up from the left, from Bit Lane and Arrow Trench. A heavy toll was exacted from the men of D Company. They struggled across no man's land, which the melting snows had turned into a quagmire, wading knee-deep through the slushy mud, all the while under constant fire.

Captain Davies led the charge into Arrow Trench, and the German defenders were routed. But Davies was killed, together with Second Lieutenant Jones. The attack faltered as the remnants of D Company wavered, pinned down in the waterlogged trench by a withering hail of machine-gun fire from Devil's Trench. Sergeant Albert White stepped into the breach created by the loss of the two officers: he rallied and steadied the men, and organized them to continue the advance. Scouting the lie of the land, he discerned the only option was a frontal attack on the machine guns hindering progress. He focused on one gun to the left which was causing most of the damage. Leading by example, and supported by Corporal Newell, he climbed from the safety of Arrow Trench, dashed out into the open and charged the machine-gun nest.

The enemy must have been astonished to see this lone man bearing down on them like a raging bull, for they hesistated momentarily, allowing him to get in close. Shooting dead three of the defenders and bayonetting a fourth, he turned to continue his charge on the machine gun; and he was within a few feet of it when the gunner fired off a burst. Sergeant White collapsed to the muddy ground, mortally wounded. He died in the mud moments later.

For outstanding courage and leadership under fire in the face of the enemy, Sergeant Albert White was honoured with the grant of the Victoria Cross. His citation reads:

> Albert White, Number 24866, Sergeant, late 2nd Battalion, South Wales Borderers. For most conspicuous bravery and devotion to duty. Realizing during an attack that one of the enemy's machine-guns, which had previously been located, would probably hold up the whole advance of his company, Sergeant White, without the slightest hesitation, and regardless of all personal danger, dashed ahead of his company to capture the gun. When within a few yards of the gun he fell riddled with bullets, having thus willingly sacrificed his life in order that he might secure the success of the operation and the welfare of his comrades.

Albert White's self-sacrifice went unrewarded on the battlefield near Monchy-le-Preux. The Germans kept up a relentless fire on the trench sheltering D Company, and the men could progress no further. They remained pinned down until darkness fell and the German fire eased. Of the 116 officers and men of D Company, 2nd Battalion, SWB, who took part in the abortive attack towards Devil's Trench that day, fewer than half, many of them wounded, crawled back to the safety of their own lines.

Sergeant White's body disappeared beneath a sea of mud. The body was never recovered, like thousands of others from the Arras offensive, and his final resting place is unknown. Arras proved to be the greatest killing ground of the war, greater than the Somme, where daily casualty rates were 4,000 compared with 3,000 on the Somme.

The posthumous award of the Victoria Cross to Sergeant Albert White was gazetted on 27 June 1917. 'Sergeant White was a splendid type of man, and one can hear nothing but praise of him,' reported the *Liverpool Express* the following day. 'Everything he took in hand he did well, and his progress in the army was exceptionally rapid.'

Albert's father travelled to London to receive the Victoria Cross from the hand of King George V at Buckingham Palace on Saturday, 21 July 1917. He passed away in 1922, but not before he was photographed wearing proudly the Victoria Cross his son had won. Albert's brothers, Thomas Henry and Robert, both served with distinction throughout the war in the Merchant Navy on the Atlantic convoys, and survived the German submarine menace. On 26 June 1956, by invitation of the queen, Thomas Henry White, then aged 70, travelled with his sister Jessie to London to honour their brother at the Victoria Cross Centenary Review held at Hyde Park. He died in 1964, six months before Jessie passed away.

A second member of the White family also made the ultimate sacrifice for his country. Albert's younger brother, Edward, to whom he paid the allotment from his pay, enlisted at the outbreak of the Second World War in the King's (Liverpool) Regiment, and later transferred as 3763878 Private Edward White to 1/9th Battalion, Manchester Regiment. As part of the British Expeditionary Force, the battalion was sent to France in 1939, and Edward was promoted to the rank of corporal. By the time the Germans launched the *blitzkrieg* which opened the Battle of France on 10 May, the 1/9th Manchesters had advanced into Belgium, close to the town of Tournai.

The battalion withdrew towards Arras and, like his brother, Edward fought at the River Scarpe and during the defence of Arras. When orders came on 25 May for the BEF to withdraw from France and to fall back to the north and the coast, he fought in the rearguard actions which established the thirty-mile corridor between Poperinge and Dunkirk through which the BEF escaped. But, on 27 May 1940, as the evacuation from the Dunkirk beaches began, Corporal Edward White fell in the fighting near Poperinge. He was buried in Dozinghem Military Cemetery, thirty miles north of Arras.

Thomas Henry White, who accompanied Albert to Lime Street Station at the age of 2 in February 1917, served as a sergeant with the Royal Artillery during the same conflict, seeing action in Palestine and Crete. He died in 2004, aged 90. Jessie's son, Edward McArdle, fought with Allied Special Forces, the Chindits, under Major General Orde Wingate DSO, when the fight was taken to the Japanese in the north of Burma. He survived two years in a Japanese prisoner-of-war camp.

Sergeant Albert White VC is remembered on the Arras Memorial in the Faubourg-d'Amiens Cemetery in the Boulevard du General de Gaulle, Arras, together with twelve Victoria Cross holders who also perished during the war and who have no graves. His name is recorded on a wooden panel in the chapel of Brecon Cathedral, the Church of St John the Evangelist, alongside those of four other men from the South Wales Borderers who won the Victoria Cross during the First World War.

Great-nephews and -nieces of Albert White VC live in Liverpool today, and his memory is revered. His Victoria Cross, his Victory Medal and British War Medal are in private hands.

Ronald Neil Stuart VC
(1886–1954)

It is appropriate that Liverpool, with its long maritime history, was home to one of the most highly decorated navy men of the First World War, Ronald Neil Stuart. He was the city's only naval Victoria Cross winner during the conflict. In a jocular piece in the *Sunday Mirror* of 3 March 1935, he was referred to as 'Alphabet Stuart' because of the fourteen initials, eleven of them post-nominals, which followed his name: he was an officer of the Royal Naval Reserve (RNR), and in addition to winning the Victoria Cross (VC), he was made a Companion of the Distinguished Service Order (DSO), and was awarded the American Navy Cross (USNC), and the Royal Naval Reserve Decoration (RD).

Ronald Stuart was of seafaring stock on both sides of his pedigree. A willing hostage to his heritage, his life was the sea, and he would allow nothing to loosen or prise open its embrace. He witnessed the golden age of the great passenger liners, the opulent palaces of steel, the swift ocean greyhounds, which criss-crossed the seven seas from Liverpool to the Americas, Australasia and India, floating microcosms of society with names such as *Majestic, Lusitania, Montezuma, Corinthian*, the pride of the White Star, Cunard, Canadian Pacific and Allan Lines. He saw the era sail off and disappear into the sunset and only swallowed the anchor because it was the last one remaining.

His maternal grandfather, John Andrew Banks, was a second-generation master mariner of 27 Cambridge Street, Wavertree, who married Mary Park of Flookburgh, Lancashire, in 1846. The couple lived at 29 Chester Street, Toxteth, and had five children, James, John, Sarah, Jane and Mary Harrison Banks, the eldest daughter, born in March 1849. On the paternal side, his grandfather Ronald was a mariner also and brought up a family of three girls and seven boys on Prince Edward Island, Canada. His fourth child, Neil, born in June 1838, followed in his wake, and ran away to sea at the age of 14. Family tales tell of Neil blockade-running for the Confederacy during the American Civil War and crewing on windjammers down to Australia and South America.

Neil Stuart probably first came to Liverpool during the Civil War, and he may have crewed aboard one of the Liverpool-built blockade-runners in which Henry Lafone had a share. On one of his visits to the city, he met Mary

Harrison Banks. At the time, she was running a dressmaking business from lodgings at 17 Miller Street, Dingle. Her father had died in 1856, her mother in 1869, and she was head of the family, responsible for her younger sisters, Sarah and Jane, her two brothers having gone off to sea.

In 1874, Neil and Mary crossed the Atlantic and married in Montreal, where they had decided to live. Their first child, Mary Catherine, was born there two years later. However, they did not settle, but moved across the border to America, where Neil worked as a riverboat captain on the Mississippi. But when Mary fell pregnant again, the couple decided on Liverpool for a home, and returned to live at 40 Claribel Street, near Princes Park. Daughters Ethel, Lillian, Amy and Agnes arrived before a son, Ronald Neil, was born on 26 August 1886, at 31 Kelvin Grove.

Ronald was brought up in a middle-class home and received an excellent private education at Liverpool Collegiate Institution, in Shaw Street, Everton. But his childhood could best be described as dysfunctional, and probably accounts for his later comment to one of his sons that he 'hated Liverpool and had no particular affection for the the place.' While at school, his father, who was somewhat eccentric and impecunious, moved the family from the fashionable area of Kelvin Grove to the less salubrious addresses of Underley and Wordsworth Streets, off Smithdown Road; and when he died of carcinoma of the kidney at the Liverpool Royal Infirmary in 1898 at the age of 55, his family was left 'quite poor but absurdly proud'.

Ronald was left to cope with a household of women, and he was desperate to escape and put to sea, and so fulfil the demands of his pedigree. It seems that his mother prevented him from doing this, probably for financial reasons, and put him to work in an office in the city centre. Here he languished, angry and frustrated, for almost a year until he was rescued by one of his mother's sisters, who secured for him an officer-apprenticeship in the Merchant Navy. He first went to sea in February 1902, on board the iron sailing barque *Kirkhill*, owned by the Kirkhill Ship Company and managed by Joseph Steel and Son, of Water Street. Steel and Son were merchants who traded in Caribbean sugar and rum to South America and Australia.

The skipper of the *Kirkhill*, John Howell, was 'a right fine seaman ... and a hard case, too', a firm taskmaster who cut no slack for anyone on board. Stuart was the dogsbody of the vessel, at the beck and call of everyone, put to work at the most difficult and dirtiest of tasks, literally learning the ropes from top to bottom. Much of what he did learn, both in maritime skills and the handling of men, came from the lessons he absorbed under Howell's command. Stuart was stern, direct and frank, the archetype, bluff naval officer who brooked no nonsense, intervention or interference. Short and stocky, with fair hair and steely blue eyes, he commanded his bridge with authority, and his voice, a look, or a gesture, could turn a crewman's knees to jelly.

In the spring of 1905, the *Kirkhill* foundered and sunk while beating back to the Falkland Islands after trying to round the Horn. All on board reached the safety of the lifeboats and spent several hours adrift in the South Atlantic before being picked up and landed at Port Stanley. The terrifying experience instilled in Stuart a healthy respect for the awesome power of the sea, but did not deflect him from his ambition. Arriving back in Liverpool some weeks later, carrying only his father's sextant – all he salvaged from the sinking vessel – he quickly found another berth and put to sea again. He completed his apprenticeship in 1906 and six years later, after completing his Master's Certificate, he joined the Montreal Ocean Steamship Company, better known in Liverpool as the Allan Line, and sailed passenger liners regularly between Liverpool and Montreal.

When war was declared he was working as second officer on the newly launched *Alsatian*, at 18,481 tons the largest and most luxurious liner operating between Britain and Canada and the pride of the Allan fleet. The vessel was converted to a troop-ship, and Stuart could have remained on board to serve; but he reasoned that if he was to be at sea during hostilities, it would be best to be aboard a warship. He joined the Royal Naval Reserve, and on 1 September was posted to the destroyer HMS *Opossum* as probationary second lieutenant.

In 1914, it could be said without fear of contradiction that Britannia ruled the waves. But Britannia also waived the rules, when Winston Churchill, First Lord of the Admiralty, ordered the naval blockade of Germany, the 'hunger blockade', in an attempt to starve Germany into submission. Churchill later declared the North Sea a military area, and, in a secret memo, waived the Cruiser Rules, long-standing, international controls for belligerents at sea. A warship could not capture, attack or sink an enemy merchant ship without first making provision for the safety of its civilian crew; and to qualify for protection of life under this protocol, the merchant ship, once challenged, could not attempt to flee, act in a hostile manner or fly false colours. Churchill's memo sanctioned the use of false colours and the arming of merchant vessels.

It was the *Unterseeboot*, the submarine, and the measures adopted by the Admiralty to counter its threat, the 'mystery ship' or 'Q-ship', which sank Cruiser Rules. In September 1914, submarine warfare came of age when the German submarine *U-9* sank three armoured cruisers of the Royal Navy off the Dutch coast with the loss of 1,500 lives. Once the Germans had discarded their rule book, unrestricted, all-out war at sea commenced.

The 'mystery ships' sailed under false colours and acted as decoys to lure U-boats, operating under Cruiser Rules, onto their guns, which were hidden, disguised and camouflaged behind lifeboats, under canvas, in false steering and engine housings. They were known as mystery ships because their names did not appear in Lloyd's Register of Shipping; and their designation as Q-ships referred probably to their operating base, Queenstown, now Cobh, in County

Cork. Ronald Neil Stuart won his Victoria Cross on board the Q-ship, HMS *Pargust*, in June 1917.

The basic plan of action for a Q-ship was simple: the vessel would steam the Western Approaches in the hope of being challenged by an enemy submarine. When challenged, the crew of the ship would go into a well-rehearsed routine, panicking as if in great danger, and taking to the lifeboats. Meanwhile, the gun-crews would lie hidden on deck, waiting for the submarine to surface and come in close to accept surrender. Once the vessel was within range, the captain would signal the gunners who would pull away the false coverings around the guns and open fire. The initial point of attack was usually the base of the conning tower: if holed there, the submarine could not submerge and escape.

For the first twenty months of the war, Ronald Stuart served in the limbo of Plymouth Sound on board HMS *Opossum*, 'a clapped-out destroyer', according to him; and when not reporting on 'stray logs and boarding Dutchmen' he was twiddling his thumbs in the dockyard while repairs were made to the vessel. It was not until he had pestered the Admiralty to the point of rudeness that he was given a more active posting. In May 1916, he joined the mystery ship HMS *Farnborough*, *Q-5*, as first officer, under Commander Gordon Campbell, a fearless sailor cut from the same mould as Drake and Hawkins.

The vessel had made its first kill on 22 March 1916, sending to the bottom the crew of *U-68* under the command of Captain Guntzel. *Q-5* put to sea again in June, and Stuart employed all his know-how and expertise in rigging the vessel to resemble an old tramp steamer, carefully camouflaging the guns, and running the deck crew under normal watch conditions. But it was not until 1917, after a round trip to Canada via Bermuda, that the enemy were encountered.

On 17 February, as she cruised the Western Approaches, *Q-5* was holed by a torpedo fired from *U-83*, commanded by Captain Bruno Hoppe. The designated panic party went into action, abandoning ship. But, as Hoppe brought in his vessel to inspect his work, Campbell's gun crew opened fire and sent her to the bottom. Following the action, *Q-5* began to heel over and was abandoned. Ronald Stuart and a damage control party remained on board while she was towed into the Berehaven, Bantry Bay, where she was beached at Mill Cove. For his part in the action and for remaining on board as damage control officer during the hazardous tow, First Officer Ronald Stuart was made a Companion of the Distinguished Service Order. The award was gazetted on 23 March 1917.

Campbell and Stuart quickly found another berth, the *Vittoria*, an old tramp steamer of 3,000 tons, which was armed as a Q-ship at the dockyard on Haulbowline Island opposite Queenstown, and her holds were filled with Canadian spruce. She was blessed with the rather uninspiring name of HMS *Snail*, but just before Campbell put to sea at the end of May, the name was discarded in favour of HMS *Pargust*. Within days, she was in action.

Dawn on Thursday, 7 June 1917, was heralded by a heavy squall as HMS *Pargust* headed east through choppy seas ninety miles off the south coast of Ireland. Visibility was poor and no one saw the silver streak of the torpedo on the starboard side until it bobbed clear of the water and smashed into the engine room. Petty Officer Isaac Radford was killed outright in the explosion. A tremendous gash 30 feet across was blown in the side of the vessel, the starboard lifeboat was blasted to smithereens and one hold and the engine and boiler rooms were flooded.

The crew were staggered and stunned by the unexpected explosion and the sudden lurch of HMS *Pargust* as she shipped water. But all hands responded as trained and manned their positions. There was no sign of the submarine, but Campbell ordered away the panic party boats while the gun crews lay in wait, the men tense and shaken but ready to fight. The periscope came to surface 400 yards off the port side, and the submarine stalked the *Pargust*. She was a mine-laying submarine, *UC-29*, and her wary master, Captain Rosenow, was waiting to see what would unfold. Half an hour passed, during which all hands suffered an agony of anxiety. Then the submarine surfaced astern. She passed to the starboard quarter, then round to within 50 yards of the port beam. But no one appeared in the conning tower; and Campbell, wanting to catch the submarine with its 'lid' open, bided his time as the suspense mounted.

The lifeboats pulled towards the stern, and the submarine began to shadow them. Then the hatch in the conning tower was opened, and an officer emerged. The U-boat came in slowly and presented a good angle on the beam. Campbell ordered the men to open fire: the White Ensign flew with a snap to the masthead as the guns were uncovered, and they delivered a shattering broadside to the submarine. In just four minutes, the crew discharged thirty-eight shells into the doomed vessel. When sailors were seen leaping from the forward hatch and conning tower, waving their arms in surrender, Campbell ordered a ceasefire. But Captain Rosenow sealed the fate of his vessel and its crew: he attempted to escape, turning out to sea into the heavy mist. Campbell had no option but to open fire again. Several more salvoes from the guns caused the U-boat to explode, and she sank stern first within minutes. Only two survivors were found.

Campbell and Stuart now turned their attention to their own plight. HMS *Pargust* was holed, without power and shipping water. But the badly damaged vessel did not sink. With all hands employed, and the Canadian spruce in the holds doing its job, she wallowed until help in the form of the sloop HMS *Crocus* appeared and towed her to Queenstown, where she arrived the following day.

The king approved the award of two Victoria Crosses to the crew of HMS *Pargust*, one to an officer and one to a man from the lower deck, under Rule 13 of the Royal Warrant. First Lieutenant Ronald Neil Stuart was elected by ballot from among the officers, and Seaman William Williams was chosen from below decks. On 20 July 1917, the *London Gazette* published the citation, which simply said: 'Honours For Services In Action With Enemy Submarines.' The following day, on the forecourt of Buckingham Palace, Lieutenant Ronald Neil Stuart DSO, received the Victoria Cross from the hand of his grateful sovereign. His citation reads:

> Lieutenant Stuart and William Williams were selected by the officers and ship's company respectively of one of HMS Ships to receive the Victoria Cross under Rule 13 of the Royal Warrant dated 29 January 1856.

This is the shortest and least informative of all Victoria Cross citations, necessitated by the secrecy under which the Q-ships operated, and the desire to prevent vital intelligence falling into enemy hands. A fuller citation, detailing the daring action of HMS *Pargust*, was published in the *London Gazette* on 20 November 1918.

In recognition of his service, Stuart was given his first Royal Navy command, HMS *Tamarisk*, a flower-class sloop of 1,250 tons. She was tasked, in conjunction with squadrons of American warships, with convoy escort and protection in the Western Approaches, in particular the shepherding of American troop-ships carrying the fresh blood destined for the Western Front. On the bridge of HMS *Tamarisk* Ronald Stuart was to distinguish himself again with his seamanship and courage.

In heavy weather, on 15 October 1917, the escort destroyer USS *Cassin*, captained by Commander W. Vernon, spied the conning tower of a U-boat twenty miles south of Mine Head Lighthouse, Waterford, at the entrance to St George's Channel. She promptly gave chase, driving the submarine away from the convoy. But, in the early afternoon, the U-boat turned on her attacker and fired off several torpedoes. One of them struck the destroyer, port side aft, and the explosion caused a fire. Gunner's Mate First Class Osmond Ingram was killed while attempting to jettison munitions, the first American casualty of the First World War. The detroyer's rudder was blown away and her stern extensively damaged: she began to circle, and as the weather got up to gale force and dusk gave way to total darkness, she was in dire straits.

Stuart shadowed the destroyer during the pursuit and was aware of her predicament. In total darkness, in heavy seas and strong winds, and with great skill and composure, he brought HMS *Tamarisk* alongside the incapacitated vessel; and, after several unsuccessful attempts, managed to secure a line to her at two o'clock in the morning. Despite the dangers of further submarine attack, Stuart began to tow the destroyer at four knots towards the haven of Queenstown. When the hawser parted, Stuart again brought in HMS *Tamarisk* to rig another line, and finally successfully towed her to safety with the assistance of two tugs and another destroyer.

Five months later, HMS *Tamarisk* was part of a squadron escorting a convoy of troop-ships off the south coast of Ireland when, in very heavy seas, the destroyer USS *Manley* rolled and collided with the auxiliary cruiser HMS *Montague*. The collision detonated eighteen depth charges on board the *Manley*, destroying her stern and killing thirty-four crewmen. Shrapnel pierced two drums of petrol and two tanks of alcohol, and the flammable liquids ran along the deck and were ignited, enveloping the vessel in flames. Stuart stood off while the American sailors extinguished the blaze, then came alongside and made several attempts to send over a line. The weather prevented him from doing so, but as the sun rose, two tugs managed to take her in tow, and brought her in to Queenstown.

These two remarkable feats of seamanship, performed under such adverse conditions, showed Ronald Stuart for what he was, a brave, resolute and highly accomplished seaman. But it would be ten years before America belatedly recognized his heroism. On 14 October 1927, President Calvin Coolidge consented to grant him the Navy Cross, the announcement coming in a special feature in the *New York Times* the following day.

Ronald Stuart VC ended the war as lieutenant commander, RNR, and came home to Liverpool to continue his career with the merchant marine. He returned to duty on the luxury liners, sailing from Liverpol to Montreal, Halifax and Quebec with a new company: in his absence, the Hall Line had merged with the Canadian Pacific Railway Company and now operated under the name of Canadian Pacific Ocean Services (CPOS). And more changes were afoot. The White Star Line had moved its operational base for first rate, transatlantic crossing from Liverpool to Southampton before the war. Cunard would make the same move in 1919; and CPOS would follow suit also. With the loss of so much sea traffic, Liverpool began to decline as a major seaport.

Stuart's mother and sisters were living again in the old family home at 31 Kelvin Grove, but he preferred a place to himself when on shore leave, and resided at 25 Carlingford Street, a small thoroughfare off Upper Parliament Street. Across the way at No. 12 lived William Wright and his family. A native of Manchester, William had served his time as a blacksmith and began his own business in Norbury, Derbyshire. In 1884, he married Hannah Redfern, and the couple had four children: James, Annie, Ethel and Evelyn, who was born in 1893. The family moved to Liverpool not long after Evelyn's birth. On June 1919 at St Clement Church, Dove Street, Toxteth, Ronald Neil Stuart VC DSO married Evelyn Wright. The couple took a house on the other side of the Mersey, at 21 Haydock Road, Liscard, Wallasey; and, with no thought of settling down to married life ashore, he returned to his first love, the sea.

Rising steadily through the ranks, in 1922, the year after CPOS became Canadian Pacific Steamship Ltd (CPS), he was promoted to staff captain aboard the flagship *Empress of Australia*. In August of that year, she carried

HRH, Prince of Wales, the future King Edward VIII, and British Prime Minister Stanley Baldwin to Canada for an official tour. The Prince marked the occasion for Ronald Stuart VC with the gift of a silver cigarette case emblazoned with the royal crest set in gold.

Six years later, he was given his first command, captain of SS *Brandon*, and later served as master of SS *Minnedosa*. At 20,000 tons, the *Duchess of York*, launched in 1928, together with her sisters, *Duchess of Atholl*, *Duchess of Bedford* and *Duchess of Richmond*, was designed to give the CPS fleet the leading edge in the highly competitive service between England and Canada. After she was commissioned the following year, Stuart was given command. He would serve her for five years and make her the pride of the fleet.

However, whilst pursuing his Merchant Navy career, he did not neglect his association with the RNR. He regularly attended for requalifying training and was granted a special Ensign Warrant in May 1927, authorizing him to fly the Blue Ensign on any vessel under his command. On 30 June 1928, he was promoted to commander RNR, and the following year, was awarded the reserve officers' decoration. His final promotion within the RNR was to captain, which came on 1 July 1935.

At home, Ronald and Evelyn began a family. Five children were born to the couple, Ronald, William, Ian, Evelyn and Hazel. Ronald tired of living on the Wirral side of the Mersey and brought his family to Liverpool, taking a house at 19 Watergate Lane, Woolton. His stay there, however, was traumatic and short-lived: on 5 January 1931, Evelyn died.

It was several months before he came to terms with the loss of his wife, and he took extended leave to console and care for his motherless children. But it was only a temporary arrangement: his life was the sea and he would not relinquish it even for the sake of his family. His sisters were the answer to his predicament: they would care for the children in his absence. And into their hands he commended his offspring. It was an ideal arrangement for him, but not for his children, who endured and survived a difficult upbringing at the hands of their aunts.

Mary Harrison Stuart had died in 1924, and Mary Catherine had taken over as householder at Kelvin Grove, where she was the dogsbody to her sisters. Ethel, like Ronald, was highly intelligent, and taught for twenty years as headmistress of the infant section of the King David Hebrew School, on the corner of Pilgrim Street and Hope Place. She made the home another class-room. Amy, short and stocky like her brother, but 'vicious and vindictive', ruled the roost, sternly dictating the pace of family life, and showing little sympathy to her nephews and nieces. Her compassion had probably been exhausted during the First World War, when she nursed wounded and dying men on the Southern and Western Fronts, and was awarded the Associate of the Red Cross Medal for her dedicated nursing services. Lillian had died in

1927, and Agnes worked abroad for several years as a children's nurse in Canada and would retire to live in Kent with her brother.

In 1933, at the age of 47, Ronald Stuart VC achieved the highest rank within the Merchant Navy when he was promoted to commodore of the CPS, and given command of the company's flagship, the 42,500-ton *Empress of Britain*, the most luxuriously appointed liner of the era. He commanded the vessel for two years, on monthly sailings from Cherbourg and Southampton to Quebec in the summer, and during the winter sailed her as a cruiseship across the globe. But, the days of the luxury liner were fading fast. The Great Depression and the slump in the world's economies during the interwar years resulted in a huge fall-off in trade and manufacturing capability: vessels were not refitted or more modern ones built, and there were very few passengers who could afford the high costs of fares even for a transatlantic journey never mind a world cruise during the winter.

Seeing which way the wind was blowing, in 1936 Stuart very reluctantly gave up the sea. Appointed CPS superintendent in Montreal, he returned to England a year later as general superintendent, and later general manager of CPS British Operations, based in London. In this capacity, he oversaw the company's operations during the Second World War, in particular facilitating the transfer of more than thirty vessels of the fleet to the Royal Navy for war duty. Two of his former commands, the *Duchess of York* and the ocean grey-hound *Empress of Britain*, became troop-ships. Both were sent to the bottom by enemy action.

Many liners on troopship duty were sunk during the hostilities and were not replaced by the major lines after the war: fleets became smaller but passenger numbers continued to decline and the problem was exacerbated by the growing popularity of air travel. In 1951, Commodore Stuart VC, with very few vessels at his command, retired and went to live at Beryl Lodge in Charing, Kent, with his sisters Amy and Agnes. But not long after taking up residence, he was diagnosed with multiple myelomatosis, a cancer afflicting the bone marrow. On 8 February 1954, at the age of 67, he died of pneumonia and the cancer.

All Ronald Stuart's children possessed his keen intelligence, and two of his sons continued the seafaring tradition. The eldest, also named Ronald Neil Stuart, joined the Merchant Navy with the Brocklebank Line. During the Second World War, he was commissioned as a sub lieutenant in the RNR, won the Distinguished Service Cross on board HMS *Foley*, and saw out the war on submarines. He continued to serve until the 1950s, retiring as lieutenant commander, RN, when he became a Trinity House Pilot. His daughter is the theologian, Dr Elizabeth Stuart, Professor of Christian Theology at the University of Winchester, and founding chair of the Centre for the Study of Christianity and Sexuality. In 2006, she was consecrated Archbishop of the Province of Great Britain and Ireland of the Liberal Catholic Church International.

William Stuart, the second son, began his naval career as a cadet on HMS *Conway*, the merchant marine training ship, which was originally moored in the River Mersey at Rock Ferry. He joined the Royal Navy in 1939 as a midshipman and saw action in the Atlantic and Indian Oceans and in the Mediterrranean and Adriatic Seas. He was mentioned in dispatches for his part in rescuing survivors from the harbour at Bari, after the American liberty ship *John Harvey*, carrying a cargo of mustard gas, was bombed by the Luftwaffe.

After the war, he transferred to the Royal Canadian Navy and took part in the Korean War, and was awarded the Canadian Forces Decoration (CD). In the 1960s, on board the fleet replenishment ship HMCS *Provider*, he brought a Royal Canadian Navy (RCN) squadron to Liverpool, where he and his crew were entertained by the Lord Mayor and one of the city's great Members of Parliament, Bessie Braddock. He became Chief of Staff, Combat Readiness, for the RCN, with the rank of captain, and upon retirement was appointed director of the Canadian Coastguard, spending most of his time in the Arctic. He died on Remembrance Day 1998.

The youngest son, Ian, served in the ranks of the Scots Guards for six years, three of which were spent on active service fighting Communist-led insurgents during the Malayan emergency. After spending a further four years in the country as a planter while the emergency continued, he returned to England and became an archaeologist, and worked until retirement as an inspector of ancient monuments for the Department of the Environment and English Heritage.

Ronald Neil Stuart VC was buried in Charing Cemetery, four miles from Ashford, in Kent. Over the years the headstone on his grave decayed and the inscription thereon faded. Several other monuments and memorials honouring those who fought for their country also suffered a similar fate, and concerned citizens, among them Ian Warner and Neil Clark, formed a pressure group, Ashford Fallen, to rectify the situation and to have them restored. After almost two years of pressurizing the Royal Navy, Ian Warner secured a new headstone for the grave of Ronald Stuart VC, which was erected in February 2005.

In addition to the Victoria Cross, the DSO, the USNC and the RD honours, Ronald Stuart also received the 1914–15 Star, the British War Medal, the Victory Medal, and two Coronation Medals, 1937 and 1953. His medal collection is held by the National Maritime Museum, Greenwich, London.

William Ratcliffe VC
(1884–1963)

On 7 May 1915, RMS *Lusitania*, a passenger liner of the Cunard Steamship Company, was torpedoed off the Old Head of Kinsale Lighthouse, Ireland, by Captain Walter Schweiger of the German submarine *U-20*. She sank within eighteen minutes taking more than 1,100 passengers and crew, many of them from Liverpool, to a watery grave. Among the dead was Peter Ratcliffe, who worked as a fireman in the boiler room.

At the time of the sinking, which brought waves of angry protests to the streets of the city, the vessel's home port, Peter Ratcliffe's younger brother Bill was serving in Flanders with 2nd Battalion, South Lancashire Regiment (SLR). He heard of Peter's death in June, just before going into action at Bellewaarde Lake, and told his comrades the Germans had robbed him of his brother and he had nothing more to lose. Over the next three years, during some of the most vicious and bloody fighting on the Western Front, in the Ypres Salient and on the Somme, Bill Ratcliffe exacted retribution for the loss; and the fearlessness he displayed in battle, which became a byword in his battalion, would be rewarded with the grant of the Military Medal and the Victoria Cross.

Bill Ratcliffe was a tall man for the times at 5 feet, 10 inches, and a large head and prognathous jaw commanded a soldierly set to a wiry frame, and gave him the appearance of a stern, no-nonsense type of individual, a man not to be confronted or crossed when his dander was up. According to his family, however, he was quiet, shy and retiring, a gentle man who kept very much to himself, going about his business without making calls on anybody. He worked on the docks after the First World War, and his co-workers coined a phrase to describe a particular difficult task on the quays: 'It's going to be as hard as getting a word out of Bill Ratcliffe.' But revenge is a dish best served cold: and coldly, methodically and stealthily, did he dispense his vengeance.

William 'Bill' Ratcliffe came from a poor and humble background. His father William was a docker, a corn porter, whose job was to pick up from the quayside, weigh and store, the sacks of grain packed by the bushellers in the holds of the grain ships at East Waterloo Dock. It was a part-time job, poorly paid and insecure employment; and the twin spectres of hunger and poverty were never far from the door. His mother, Mary Ann, née Kelly, worked as a chip dealer to supplement the family income, buying up scrap wood and chopping it into kindling chips, which she sold in small bundles on street corners.

Like most dock labourers, William Ratcliffe senior lived within walking distance of his work. And that meant a home of two or three rooms in one of the infamous courts off the Dock Road, terraced dwellings two or three storeys high, built around a small, central courtyard in which was situated the only water supply, usually a hand pump, and communal toilets. Underfed, shoeless urchins, many of whom would not attain adulthood, scampered in the bare, damp rooms, along the dark, musty corridors and down through the rat-infested alleyways connecting the cramped courts, pursued by dysentery, measles, diphtheria, whooping cough and scarlet fever. These squalid homes had the deserved reputation of the worst slums in Europe, surpassing in notoriety those of Gardiner Street in Dublin and the Gorbals of Glasgow.

Bill Ratcliffe was the second youngest of a family of five, and was born on 18 February 1884 at 38 New Hall Street, off Upper Parliament Street. Shortly after his arrival, the family made a home at No. 7 Court, house 5, Blundell Street, which ran down to the King's Dock. Sarah, who helped her mother sell the wood chips, was the eldest, and then came Peter, Mary Jane, Bill and Alice. It was not unusual in those days for families to be constantly on the move, in search of healthier or cheaper or larger accommodation, depending upon circumstances: after the birth of Alice, the family moved on to Fisher Street and later Head Street.

All the children attended St Vincent de Paul's Roman Catholic School in Norfolk Street. But the dire circumstances in which the family lived determined that schooling was always a secondary consideration: an empty stomach and a bare covering of clothing, particularly in the winter, were not conducive to learning; and a day of truancy could mean a farthing, a halfpenny or a penny earned on the streets to buy a crust of bread, a twist of tea or a spoonful of jam. The environment bred tough individuals who learnt from a very early age to live by their wits.

Mary Ann died in 1892 and Sarah assumed her role as matriarch, while Peter followed his father onto the docks. Mary Jane left home at 16 to marry Peter Rowen, and the Ratcliffe family upped sticks and moved in with them, into very spacious accommodation at 13 Upper Parliament Street, where William Ratcliffe senior died in 1910. Bill Ratcliffe left school at the age of 11, and, too young to work as a docker, he earned his keep at the Pier Head, working for coppers as a messenger boy and luggage handler. His ambition was to work alongside his father and brother as a porter, the better of the two dock-labouring jobs. The majority of dockers were lumpers, offloading cargoes to the quays for the porters to carry off. The porters returned the favour, carting goods to the lumpers to load on the vessels. The pay was the same, but the porter's job was cleaner and less hazardous. It is believed that Bill Ratcliffe did work on the docks as a youth, but from 1899 until the outbreak of the First World War his life is something of a mystery.

In 1914, he was 30 years of age. He enlisted in 2nd Battalion, SLR, and was posted to Tidmouth, assigned to 16th Platoon, D Company. Though long in the tooth, he was also long on experience apparently, for he claimed to be a veteran of the Boer War. The younger soldiers and new recruits looked to him for advice and assistance; and one of the men he took under his wing was a bright young Liverpudlian, Hugh Higgins, with whom he became fast friends. In 1916, Hugh Higgins was promoted to sergeant at the age of 19, and he relied greatly on Bill Ratcliffe for his expertise and common sense: 'Bill was an old soldier and was in my platoon ... and with his experience and my precocity we managed along.' The two pals landed in France in the first week of December 1914, but had to wait until 16 June 1915 to go over the top for the first time, a few days after Bill Ratcliffe heard about Peter.

The battalion moved into the Ypres Salient just after the Second Battle of Ypres ground to a halt and made ready to fight. The German defences beyond Railway Wood on the eastern side of Lake Bellewaarde were the targets, and it was during this offensive the Ratcliffe legend was born. Supported by several other units, including the Liverpool Scottish, Bill Ratcliffe and his battalion dashed across no man's land through a withering hail of machine-gun fire. Despite heavy casualties, the men captured the first line of trenches and rapidly took the second in fierce hand-to-hand fighting. The next day, the gains were consolidated and a new front was established.

Throughout the fighting, Bill Ratcliffe was intrepid and relentless in pursuit of his mission, cutting swathes through the enemy with his bayonet. After the battle, as he quietly took his ease, his comrades whispered and nodded and winked admiringly behind his back, acclaiming his prowess. In another dug-out, not far from where Bill was relaxing, the reputation of another hero was cemented: Lieutenant Noel Chavasse was recommended for the Military Cross for his services during the fight.

From Railway Wood, Bill Ratcliffe brought his crusade to the Somme, and fought courageously at Thiepval, Ovillers and Pozières. However, he would return to Ypres in 1917, and in the horror that was the Third Battle of Ypres he would win his Military Medal and Victoria Cross. Third Ypres was Sir Douglas Haig's grand design of another 'Big Push' to smash the stalemate of trench warfare and break out into open country. But before he could launch the offensive in July 1917, a long-standing thorn in his side had to be surgically removed: in the southern sector of the Ypres Salient, the Germans held the Messines–Wytschaete Ridge from where they dominated the Allied lines. The operation was placed in the hands of General Sir Henry Plumer, whose engineers and pioneers tunnelled twenty-two mine shafts beneath the enemy lines on the Ridge, and packed them with more than 1,000,000 pounds of high explosives.

At the beginning of April 1917, Bill Ratcliffe and his battalion tramped north from the Somme to new lines near the hamlet of Wulverghem, a few miles west of Messines. The sector was quiet at first, but as the finishing touches were applied to Plumer's plans, the Germans on the Ridge, alerted by furious activity of the Allied troops, began to harass and disrupt Plumer's preparations with constant sniper fire and sporadic artillery bombardments. Platoons from 2nd Battalion, SLR, were deployed in working parties near Wulverghem, but their labours brought them within sniper range from the Ridge. The German marksmen took a heavy toll and the essential work was disrupted. In response, Sergeant Hugh Higgins organized a handful of men, among them Bill Ratcliffe, into a counter-sniping unit to suppress the enemy fire.

Armed with a rifle, Bill Ratcliffe concealed himself in a covered position and set to with a vengeance. Coolly and methodically over the course of the day, he counter-sniped at the German sharpshooters. He came under retaliatory attack himself and was forced to change his location several times as the enemy hunted him out. But he was undaunted, and held out until evening, until the work parties complete their allotted tasks. When he returned to his billet, he was credited with seven kills.

For his actions at Wulverghem, for his marksmanship and courage under fire, Bill Ratcliffe was awarded the Military Medal. News of the award came through on 20 June and was entered in the battalion war diary at the end of the month, though it did not appear in the *London Gazette* until 28 July. However, celebrations within his unit were soon overtaken in the euphoria which erupted almost immediately when it was learnt he had been recommended for the Victoria Cross for bravery during Plumer's stunning victory on Messines Ridge on 14 June.

At ten past three in the morning of 7 June, Plumer's mines beneath Messines Ridge were detonated. The Ridge was totally destroyed, and more than 10,000 German troops disappeared from the face of the earth, vaporized or buried beneath thousands of tons of cascading earth and mud. Within three hours, all the objectives in the southern sector of the Salient were taken. In response, the Germans brought up reserves and counter-attacked, and the battle ebbed and flowed in the sweltering summer heat for a further seven days. Bill Ratcliffe's battalion was held in reserve and did not participate in the initial assault. But, on 12 June, he moved forward into the front line to attack the extensive German fortifications beyond the ridge from which the enemy were drawing reserve strength.

There were no trenches in the advanced position, so the men dug their own to give some shelter from the enemy shelling. It was arduous work: the ground, which only weeks previously had been oozing mud, was now baked rock hard by the summer sun. The following day, while the trenching continued, the men came under sniper attack. Bill Ratcliffe and his friend Sam Calvery were ordered to act as stretcher-bearers, and all day were kept busy ferrying the wounded to the first aid station. In the evening, orders came through to advance.

On Thursday, 14 June, the battalion moved forward on a line between Ferme de la Croix and Steignast Farm. Bill Ratcliffe and D Company jumped off from their trenches at half past three in the afternoon and advanced across open terrain in pairs at intervals of thirty paces. There was no wind, and a summer haze persisted, mingling with the smoke of battle to reduce visibility. Under fire, the men crouched and hurried forward, keen to reach the safety of their new positions. Casualties were light, however, but Bill Ratcliffe and Sam Calvery still had their work cut out to carry back the non-walking wounded to the aid post which had yet to come forward.

Just after five o'clock, D Company reached its objective. However, the battalion's advance had been so rapid that some of the platoons had lost contact with their neighbours because of the poor visibility, and gaps arose between them. In some sectors, the move forward had gone unnoticed by the enemy; and small pockets of isolated Germans, hidden in pillboxes and shell holes, were now intermingled with the platoons. As the men dug in, they came under artillery fire from the front and sniper and machine-gun fire from the flanks and the rear.

Sergeant Hugh Higgins takes up the story: 'Then a headquarters' orderly came to us and said there was a German pillbox full of Huns behind us. Immediately, Bill took a rifle and bayonet, plus a couple of Mills bombs, and went back to find it. He was away some time and when he returned he hardly mentioned what he had done.' The sergeant should have known: Bill was still on a mission, and a group of intrusive Germans demanded his attention.

It wasn't until later we found out that he had single-handed and on his own initiative rushed the machine-gun position and bayoneted the crew. He then brought the gun back into action in our front line. Meantime, we were still trying to dig into the thick clay. Bill lent a hand until he was knocked out by a machine-gun bullet in the shoulder. I dressed it and sent him down the line.

If Bill Ratcliffe had had his way, nothing more would have been said of his action. He shrugged it off and would not speak of it, refusing even to confide in his pal Hugh Higgins. But the attack was witnessed by several officers and men who were astounded not only by its swiftness and ferocity, but by the complete and utter disregard he showed for his own safety. His gallant action was immediately reported to battalion headquarters, and the story quickly spread up the line to Brigadier General Sir Douglas Bird. He had heard of Bill Ratcliffe and knew him as an 'old sweat' and fearless warrior. In all likelihood it was the brigadier who recommended the award.

For bravery in the face of the enemy, William Ratcliffe was granted the honour of the Victoria Cross. Notification of the award appeared in the *London*

Gazette of 2 August 1917. His citation reads:

> William Ratcliffe, No. 2251, Private, South Lancashire Regiment. For most conspicuous bravery. After an enemy's trench had been captured, Private Ratcliffe located an enemy machine gun which was firing on his comrades from the rear, whereupon, single-handed and on his own initiative, he immediately rushed the machine gun position and bayoneted the crew. He then brought the gun back into action in the front line. This very gallant soldier has displayed great resource on previous occasions, and has set an exceptionally fine example of devotion to duty.

Bill Ratcliffe's shoulder wound was serious. The field ambulance moved him down the line to the casualty clearing station, from where he was transported across France and carried to England by hospital ship. He was a patient at Hampden-in-Arden Military Hospital, Warwickshire, where he remained under doctor's orders until the end of August. Mary Jane Rowen visited him there: 'He talked about everyone else in the ward but himself,' she recalled, 'pointing out other soldiers whose wounds were much worse than his. When I insisted he tell me about himself, he said his leg was fine. When I reminded him he had been wounded in the shoulder, he then continued to tell me about the other patients. He would never talk about himself.'

News of the award was widely reported in the Liverpool press: 'the Dockers' VC', as he was dubbed, became an overnight celebrity. Word he would make a visit to Liverpool after leaving hospital spread like wildfire through the courts and terraces of the Dock Road and was greeted with a delight that verged on hysteria. In and around Brindley Street, where he was to stay with Mary Jane, the residents eagerly anticipated his arrival: grimy windows were washed and polished, encrusted steps scrubbed and sandstoned and scallywag children shaken and sponged. Not even the paving flags escaped this bustling, extravagant lavation: they, too, were brushed and buffeted, before the flags, streamers and bunting were hung and strewn to decorate and adorn the houses.

On Tuesday 28 August, Mary Jane and her two sisters, Sarah and Alice, gathered at Lime Street Station, watching the trains from Coventry, one of which they believed would carry home their brother. But Bill Ratcliffe was working to a different schedule, no doubt one that he hoped would bypass the planned reception. The following day, they waited again, but in vain. And it was not until the Thursday, when a telegram from the commandant at Hampden-in-Arden arrived, informing them Bill Ratcliffe had boarded the ten past nine train from Birmingham to Liverpool, that the women knew for certain that the celebrations could begin.

Just before noon, the Ratcliffe sisters proudly greeted their heroic brother as he stepped from the train. Among the welcoming committee was an old friend, Bob Devalve, Secretary of Number 5 Branch, the Dockers Union. Ratcliffe was carried shoulder high from the station and paraded through Lime Street, the procession bringing traffic to a standstill. It is believed that the Lord Mayor's coach was made available to ferry him to the town hall for a civic reception.

But Bill Ratcliffe quickly dampened the enthusiasm of his fellow Liverpudlians. He went to earth at Mary Jane's home and kept a low profile, declining all offers to attend further celebrations in his honour, very rarely venturing out and shunning any untoward contact with an admiring local populace. She reported he entered and left her home by the back door on his rare forays onto the streets because he did not want to be 'stared at by a parcel of women'. His only concession was to his old *alma mater*, St Vincent de Paul's School in Norfolk Street. At the beginning of September, he was welcomed back; and from a specially constructed platform in the playground, the current crop of schoolchildren sang his praises.

Billy, Billy Ratcliffe, you are a great, brave-hearted man,
A credit to your country and all your native land.
May your arm be ever steady and your aim be ever true,
God bless you, Billy Ratcliffe, here's your country's love to you.

But he could not lock himself away for ever. On Saturday, 29 September 1917, he was decorated with the Victoria Cross by King George V in the forecourt of Buckingham Palace. And he emerged from his seclusion again on Saturday, 13 October. In the afternoon, he kicked off a football match at Aigburth between South Liverpool and Tranmere Rovers. His presence at the game added 1,000 spectators to the gate, the crowd numbers climbing swiftly to 4,000 midway through the first half when it became known he was there. His team, South Liverpool, won 4–2.

That evening, he attended a celebratory dinner in his honour, one he would not have missed to save his life. It was hosted by the National Union of Dock Labourers. Lord Derby, then Secretary of State for War, gave the address. To much applause and laughter, Lord Derby said he would grant the hero as much leave as he needed so that he could earn a bar to his Victoria Cross by getting married. But Bill Ratcliffe did not take advantage of Lord Derby's largesse: he was a confirmed bachelor and never married.

It is not known whether, after convalescence, Bill Ratcliffe VC returned to the front before hostilities ceased in November 1918, for the record is incomplete. The 2nd Battalion, SLR, fought in several punishing actions on the Western Front in the last months of the war, returning to the Somme in the wake of 'Operation Michael' in the spring of 1918, before fighting its last major engagement at Courtrai, Flanders, east of Ypres in October.

Bill Ratcliffe was discharged from the army on 11 February 1919, when he returned to civilian life and his former job. On every morning of every working day, inconspicuous among the swarm of 30,000 dockers, he marched down to the Dock Road and beneath the 'dockers' umbrella', the Overhead Railway, and passed through the dock gates and into the hiring pens, ready for work, dressed in his docker's uniform of cap, silk scarf and long overcoat. He laboured for thirty-six years on the docks, hauling and carrying on the quays, quietly minding his own business, until forced to retire because of injury.

Along with another shy Victoria Cross holder, Arthur Richardson, he attended the reunion dinner held in the Royal Gallery, House of Lords, in November 1929. He was also present at the Dorchester Hotel on 8 June 1946 for the End of World War Two Victory Day celebration reception to honour the fallen. His last appearance at a Victoria Cross reunion occasion was on Tuesday, 26 June 1956 when holders were reviewed in Hyde Park by Her Majesty, Queen Elizabeth II, to mark 150 years of the award. He was accompanied by his sister Sarah's daughter, Margaret Walsh, and her daughter Noreen. It was reported a local tailor kitted him out in a new hat, suit and coat to attend the review because he had fallen on hard times. On that occasion, Bill Ratcliffe VC was the second oldest living holder of the Victoria Cross, the oldest being Donald Farmer VC.

Not long after his visit to the Dorchester Hotel, he was badly hurt on the quayside on Queens Dock, struck by a couple of heavy bags of castor oil seed which fell from a sling while being offloaded from a vessel. He sustained injuries to his neck, spine and pelvis, and he was left stone deaf. A family story says he was taken to the mortuary at Princes Dock and was pronounced dead. However, as in the case of Mark Twain, the report of his death was greatly exaggerated.

He was declared medically unfit for work after the accident, and retired to live on a pension of £2 a week from the Dock Board, supplemented by his Victoria Cross pension, which would have been substantially increased because of his inability to earn a living. Following the redevelopment of the Brindley Street area, Bill Ratcliffe went to live at 29A St Oswald's Gardens in Old Swan, and was cared for by Margaret Walsh and Noreen. He made new friends in the area, and maintained contact with Hugh Higgins; and he was often seen in the local pubs, sitting alone in a corner or listening to a friend reminisce.

Late in life, he suffered with senile dementia, Alzheimer's disease. His occasional drinking bouts, coupled with the illness, gave cause for concern to Margaret. Her fears were realized when he celebrated his eightieth birthday in February 1963. On his way home from the pub, he fell in the street and was taken to hospital. He was not seriously injured but he was bewildered and lost, and nursing staff were unable to elicit his name and address. It was not until the following day that Margaret was able to locate him.

Needing constant supervision, he was admitted to Kirkdale House, Westminster Road, a residential care institution for the elderly, where he was well looked after by the staff, who treated him as a celebrity, but his illness meant he had little understanding of his whereabouts and what was happening around him. A severe winter brought on a chest complaint, and he faded as spring approached. Suffering with broncho-pneumonia, and fortified in the rites of his faith, Bill Ratcliffe VC died on Tuesday, 26 March 1963.

Following a Requiem Mass at St Oswald's Church, Old Swan, he was buried during a quiet family ceremony in Allerton Cemetery, in the same plot which held his sister Sarah and her husband, John. In attendance were members of his former battalion, including his old friend Sergeant Hugh Higgins.

A stone tablet to his memory was paid for and erected by members of the Transport and General Workers Union, the successor to the Dockers' Union, at their branch office in St James Place, off Upper Parliament Street, and but a short distance from his birthplace. Unfortunately, the tablet was lost when the office was demolished years later.

Bill Ratcliffe's story, however, does not end here. There is a mystery attached to his early days. When he enlisted in 1914, he was quickly recognized as an 'old sweat', a former soldier. 'Private Ratcliffe,' said Brigadier General Bird, 'was an old soldier with the South Africa Medal.' That is, he had served during the Boer War; in fact he did wear the Queen's South Africa Medal on official occasions, together with all his other awards. But there is no record of him in the Boer War rolls.

It has always been assumed he fought in South Africa with 2nd Battalion SLR. But, the battalion remained on station in India throughout the conflict and only a small cadre of fifty men served, and his name is not among them. Bill Ratcliffe was an honest man and would not have deceived anyone, particularly about his military record. The Ratcliffe family history, however, says he enlisted under age and fought under an assumed name in South Africa.

On 22 September 1914, Peter Ratcliffe enlisted as 12237 Private Peter Ratcliffe in 13th Battalion, the Liverpools. He was 36 years of age. But three months later, in December, while undergoing basic training at Bournemouth, the authorities declared he 'was unlikely to become an efficient soldier' and he was granted a medical discharge. He returned to Liverpool; and, determined to do his duty for his country, joined the Merchant Navy and perished on board RMS *Lusitania*.

On his enlistment papers, however, he stated he had been with the colours previously, as 5412 Private Peter Ratcliffe, 1st Battalion, the Liverpools, enlisting in 1899 and fighting in South Africa until wounded and returned to England in 1901. At the height of the recruitment drive in 1914, when the army was crying out for veterans to come forward and assist in the training of the hundreds of thousands of volunteers flocking to the colours, it is doubtful Peter Ratcliffe's Boer War experience would have been ignored; and he certainly would not have been dismissed as someone 'unlikely to become an efficient soldier'.

In 1899, Bill Ratcliffe was 15, and a tall lad for his age. Lured by the colours and prodded by 'Jack Frost', he could have found no better way to enlist under age than by using the name and birth record of a brother six years his senior.

Peter was not a soldier, Bill was. In all probability, it was Bill and not Peter who enlisted in the Liverpools in 1899 and fought in South Africa. If that was indeed the case, then Bill Ratcliffe fought as a member of the mounted infantry of the battalion, and he has the campaigns in Natal and Transvaal to add to his battle honours of the Somme and the Ypres Salient during the First World War. He merited wearing the Queen's South Africa Medal alongside his Victoria Cross, the Military Medal, the British War Medal, the Victory Medal and the two Coronation Medals, 1937 and 1953.

Peter Ratcliffe married Maragaret Melia from Kew Street, off Scotland Road, in 1902 and he lived at 1 Court, 8 House until his death at sea, fathering four children, Mary Jane, William, David and Sarah. Bill's sister Sarah married John Humes, spelled Hulme on the wedding certificate, in the autumn of 1909. Their daughter Margaret, Bill's niece, married Cornelius Walsh just before the outbreak of the Second World War. As 3650251 Private Cornelius Walsh, 1st Battalion, SLR, he served in France with the BEF, and was killed in action on 25 May 1940, north-west of Arras, during the retreat to Dunkirk. He is buried in the Outtersteen Communal Cemetery Extension, Bailleul. His daughter, Noreen Hill, accompanied her great-uncle Bill to London in 1956, and her family live in Liverpool today. Alice Ratcliffe married Thomas Hughes in 1915, but nothing is known of their children, or those of Mary Jane Rowen.

The medals of Bill Ratcliffe VC, the shy and retiring docker and avenging warrior, are in private hands.

Alexander Malins Lafone VC
(1870–1917)

Major Alexander Malins Lafone, 1st County of London Yeomanry, was killed in action on 27 October 1917 and was awarded the Victoria Cross posthumously for gallantry. Aged 47 at the time of his death, he is one of the oldest to have been granted the honour. Such was the impact he made upon the men of his regiment, in life and by his death, that the Sunday nearest to 27 October is known in his honour as Lafone Day, and is celebrated annually by a memorial service in the crypt of St Paul's Cathedral.

He did not die in the carnage of the Western Front, but in one of the side-shows of the First World War, in the land of the Bible. After the fiasco of the Gallipoli Peninsula, the Allies on the Southern Front pushed into Palestine in 1917, aiming to take the seat of Turkish power there, the Holy City of Jerusalem, which had fallen into the hands of the Ottoman Turks 400 years earlier. Its capture would restore the city to the Christian world once more, and signal the final collapse of the Ottoman Empire, a formidable ally of Germany.

The key to Jerusalem was the city of Gaza, situated on the Mediterranean littoral, fifty miles to the south-west. Twice the Allies had tried by direct assault to storm the city, but had been repulsed all along the defensive line which ran for twenty-five miles south-east to the biblical town of Beersheba. Now, on 31 October 1917, General Allenby would feint an attack towards the city while concentrating his main attack on Beersheba: the Turkish left flank could then be rolled up to Gaza, opening the way to Jerusalem.

Seven miles west of Beersheba, the desert town of El Buggar stood on a ridge overlooking the Turkish defences, close to two hills known as Point 630 and Point 720. Nestled into the depression between the two points was the town of Karm, into which Allenby was building his rail link from the west. A week before the attack was to commence, orders were received to occupy the El Buggar ridge day and night to fend off Turkish encroachments; and at dusk on 26 October, the Middlesex Yeomanry relieved the Australian Light Horse on Point 720 and Point 630. Major Lafone, in command of B Squadron, consisting of four troops and two sub-sections of the 21st Machine Gun Squadron, set up his headquarters atop Point 720.

The cone-shaped hill had a small, stone-built house at the summit. To the right of the house, 300 yards away across a shallow depression, was a second rise. The defensive trenches were flimsy and only partially dug, consisting of two rifle pits to the right of the house, a slit trench to the left and a cruciform trench to the rear. Major Lafone deployed his 2nd and 4th Troops in the trenches, together with the Hotchkiss machine guns, and placed a strong picket on the small hill. His other two troops were held in the rear as standing patrols along the El Buggar road. Communications with regimental headquarters would be visual or by dispatch rider, since line telegraphy had not been established on the ridge. Alarm signals at night, requesting reinforcements and artillery support, were red flares at Point 720, and green and white at Point 630.

The night passed quietly for the men in the trenches as they nervously scanned the horizon searching out signs of movement. Then, just before dawn of the morning of Saturday, 27 October, Point 630 came under attack, and green and white flares illuminated the fading darkness while the rattle of sporadic rifle fire broke the silence. Major Lafone ordered his men to stand to and prepare for attack. And as the men hurried to take up positions, he discerned in the half-light a troop of horsemen galloping towards his position. He sent off his distress signal, and when the Turks crested the rise, he ordered his men to open fire. The cavalry were repulsed and dispersed; and a second troop of riders, which had managed to gallop round to the rear unnoticed, were similarly dispatched.

These sorties were a prelude to major assaults on the two high points by the Turks, who were eager and determined to disrupt Allenby's progress. When dawn broke finally, they opened accurate fire with shell and machine gun on Point 720, and Major Lafone sent his runner, Sergeant Broster, to the rear with a message for reinforcements after his first attempts to communicate with headquarters by flare and flag had failed. He realized his small garrison would be overrun in what he surmised correctly was to be a concerted attack by the enemy.

The Turks kept up a relentless fire on Lafone's position for two hours, and a large force of infantry massed and charged the left flank, attempting to carry the hill at bayonet point. But the infantry were easy targets for the Middlesex men, who shot them down in ranks. Major Lafone stood with his men in the rifle pits, calling out his score as he downed one man after another with his rifle. The infantry charge stalled 50 yards from the trenches but not before inflicting 50 per cent casualties on the beleaguered garrison; and as the infantry withdrew, a squadron of Turkish lancers galloped through them, charging the right flank.

No sooner had Major Lafone switched his defence to the right than the infantry regrouped and charged the centre. Under intense fire, the Middlesex men bravely beat back both attacks, but again suffered heavy casualties in the encounter. At half past seven, Sergeant Broster returned with a verbal and written message: Major Lafone was to hold out at all costs and there would be no reinforcements.

He consolidated his lines, abandoning the secondary hill on the right, and prepared to make his stand in the trenches on either side of the stone house, where the wounded were being treated. And as the Turks renewed the attack and developed their firing line, Point 720 was swept with a devastating barrage of shell and machine-gun fire so intense that those defenders unable to find cover in the crowded, shallow trenches instantly became casualties. At nine-thirty in the morning Major Lafone sent his last message to headquarters: 'my casualties are heavy, six stretchers required. I shall hold out to the last, as I cannot get my wounded away.'

The 'Old McCormac' now allied itself with the enemy, rising in a burning arc towards its zenith. The garrison's water had gone to the wounded, and beneath the constant artillery bombardment and the fusillades from 3,000 Turkish infantrymen, the survivors sweated and thirsted and died in the smoking heat of the rocky hilltop. But Major Lafone would not countenance defeat: ignoring the dangers, he strode among his troops, shoulders back, head held high, directing fire, encouraging his men with promises of rescue, laughing and joking with them, invigorating their spirits and asking them to hold on for one more defence.

At ten o'clock, under cover of a pounding artillery and machine-gun barrage, the Turkish infantry launched a massed assault on the stone house. The yeomen fixed bayonets and stood to meet the challenge, alongside their major. Leading by example, Lafone kept up a rapid fire from the shoulder and fended off attackers with his bayonet. After half an hour of steel and point-blank firing, the enemy gave way and were pushed back 30 yards from the stone house. But when they withdrew, the shelling increased in intensity.

The Turks were intent on taking the hill no matter the cost. Another foot charge was made but was met by defeat. The Turks could now see that the defenders were reduced to only half a dozen fighting men, and rather than risk another costly infantry assault, brought on the mounteds. At a quarter past eleven, the Turks were observed preparing for another cavalry charge. Major Lafone ordered the wounded to withdraw to the cruciform trenches in the rear while he remained in the rifle pit to the right of the stone house to cover the withdrawal. He knew he was facing certain death, and he stepped forward manfully to meet it. His last words were spoken to Sergeant Broster: 'I wonder if there is any chance of the infantry getting up in time.'

The Turkish cavalry came on, and Major Lafone walked out into the open to face them, emerging from the dust and smoke like a latter-day David in front of the Philistine horde. Firing rapidly from the shoulder, he downed one horseman after another. His determined defence caused the charge to stall at twenty paces. But, urged on by their officer, the Turks made a final charge and Major

Lafone was overpowered. He collapsed to the ground, mortally wounded, and died where he fell.

For outstanding bravery in the face of overwhelming enemy forces, Major Alexander Malins Lafone was awarded posthumously the Victoria Cross, the announcement being made on 18 December 1917. His citation reads:

> Alexander Malins Lafone, Major, late 1st County of London (Middlesex) Yeomanry. For most conspicuous bravery, leadership and self-sacrifice, when holding a position for over seven hours against vastly superior forces. All this time the enemy were shelling his position heavily, making it very difficult to see. In one attack, when the enemy cavalry charged his flank, he drove them back with heavy losses. In another charge they left fifteen casualties within twenty yards of his trench, one man who reached his trench, being bayoneted by Major Lafone himself. When all his men, with the exception of three, had been hit, and the trench which he was holding was so full of wounded that it was difficult to move and fire, he ordered those who could walk to move to a trench slightly in the rear, and from his own position maintained a most heroic resistance. When finally surrounded and charged by the enemy, he stepped into the open and continued the fight until he was mortally wounded and fell unconscious. His cheerfulness and courage were a splendid inspiration to his men, and by his leadership and devotion he was enabled to maintain his position, which he had been ordered to hold at all costs.

The Middlesex men fought on until there were only three survivors. Helping as many wounded as possible, these men made the dash back to Karm when the Turks swarmed over their positions just before midday. For almost eight hours the courageous yeomen had fought off an enemy force of approximately 3,000 infantry and 600 cavalry. More than 200 Turkish dead were counted on Point 720. On the other rise, Point 630, the garrison was reinforced by fresh troops and fended off the Turkish assaults.

Later that day, the Allies moved up onto the ridge in attack formation and the Turks withdrew from Point 720 to their own lines. Major Lafone's body was recovered, and he was buried 150 yards to the south of the stone house, very close to where he had fallen in the battle. A chaplain to the Royal West Kents led the burial service. Later Major Lafone's body was reburied at Beersheba War Cemetery, on the outskirts of the city, in what is now Israel. His sacrifice was not in vain. The Turkish assault did not interrupt the vital work at the Karm railhead: Beersheba and Gaza were captured as planned; and the victorious Allies marched into Jerusalem on 11 December 1917.

Official word of Major Lafone's death was sent to his next of kin, his brother, Henry Pownall Lafone, Archdeacon of Furness and vicar of the parish of St George the Martyr, Barrow-in-Furness. His colonel also wrote to the Archdeacon: 'He held a post until only three unwounded men remained against vastly superior odds, and was one of the last to fall, but not before he had shown a magnificent example that he was able to hold his post from 3.45 in the morning until 11.30 ... He is deeply mourned by his officers and men, and his squadron is inconsolable. Everybody loved him and his loss is one it is quite impossible to replace.' On 8 January 1918, he received a second letter of condolence, this one from King George V informing him of his regrets that he could not personally confer on Alexander the award of the Victoria Cross.

The roots of the Lafone family are in the south-west of France, in the departments of Gironde, Dordogne and Aveyron. The name is a variant of Delafon, Fond and Lafont, derivatives of the French word *fontaine*, which translates as 'fountain'. During the Reformation, members of the family were Huguenots, followers of the Protestant reformist, John Calvin. At the turn of the eighteenth century, suffering persecution for their beliefs, many fled France to the safety of England.

Alexander's grandfather, also named Alexander, was born in London in 1736, and he was the first Lafone to make the trek north to Merseyside to seek his fortune. He settled in Eccleston, near Prescot, attracted by the prospects of a booming industrial economy and the development of Liverpool as a major seaport. Having established himself as a merchant, he moved into the city, conducting his business from offices in Mount Pleasant. In 1776 he married Mary Marchant by licence at St Nicholas' Church, the parish church of the city of Liverpool, St Nicholas being the patron saint of seafarers.

He fathered five children, and it was his youngest son, Samuel Marchant Lafone, born in 1770, who established the Lafones as a major force in the city's commercial life. He was a broker and merchant, the owner of a counting-house, and the manufacturer of leather goods. As his empire expanded, he moved into leather tanning, operating a tannery from Bevington Bush, off Scotland Road, an enterprise which was to become the mainstay of the family fortunes.

Samuel fathered thirteen children in two marriages. His eldest son made his fortune in Buenos Aires, exporting hides to the family tanning business, and he later established the River Plate Trading Company and the Falkland Island Company. It was left to Samuel's youngest son Henry, born in 1830 at Park Lodge, a fine old house on Lodge Lane, to run the Lafone interests in Liverpool.

Educated at Heidelberg University, Germany, Henry took over the running of the tannery when his father retired. But he was always looking for further opportunities to expand business, and he took up cattle breeding and developed interests in shipping. He lived at 87 Northumberland Terrace, Everton. His first wife, Louisa, died in 1859, a month after giving birth to their first child, Lillian. Four years later, he married Lucy Malins, the daughter of David Malins, of Eccleshalls, Stafford, who owned a brass foundry and was High Bailiff of Edgebaston, Birmingham.

Henry's marriage prospered, but not so his business dealings. By 1865, Henry and Lucy and their two children, Lucy Beatrice and Ella, were living in straitened circumstances at 11 Marine Terrace, Waterloo, and were struggling to make ends meet. Henry's ventures into shipping had been a failure and the family tannery business was almost bankrupt.

As the Union naval blockade of the Confederacy denied Liverpool vessels access to supplies of cotton and tobacco, the city too faced bankruptcy. The British government, however, granted the Confederates belligerent status, making it legal for British companies to trade with them. Liverpool merchants set up bases in Bermuda and the Bahamas, and from them utilized fast sailing vessels to run the Union cordon, carrying in munitions and hauling out cotton and tobacco for transshipment to Liverpool. Investing in several blockade-runners, Henry Lafone's name became famous and infamous on both sides of the Atlantic. But his vessels were unlucky and were taken as prizes. By the end of the Civil War in 1865, he had disposed of a large fortune; and he was no longer in business for himself, but was employed as managing director of a cotton sampling company in Exchange Buildings.

His impoverished state improved somewhat by the turn of the decade, and as his family increased in size he was able to move into a larger home at 4 Crosby Road South, Waterloo. After Lucy Beatrice and Ella came Henry Pownall, Hilda, Alexander Malins, born 19 August 1870, and Violet Grace. But Henry was an independent businessman who had always worked under his own steam, and he did not take well to working for others. When an offer of employment as wharf manager, or wharfinger, in a family enterprise at Butler's Wharf in London was made in 1874, he uprooted and headed south.

Alexander Malins Lafone was 4 years old when he left Liverpool to live in London. As the younger son of the family, he was spoilt and teased in equal measures by his sisters and pampered by his parents, though never over-indulged. There were the usual pets, a dog named Vic was a particular favourite, and several horses, which were stabled to the rear of the family home in Croxted Park, Dulwich. He had a good seat and became an accomplished rider from an early age.

In 1881, Alexander followed his brother, Henry Pownall, into Dulwich College. Not as outstanding academically as his brother, Alexander's forte was athletics, and he excelled in the high jump and in sprinting, representing the college in athletic tournaments. He grew into a tall, gangling young man of 6 feet, 2 inches, and possessed a mop of mousy, brown hair above a pair of startling greenish-blue eyes. He was reserved and reticent by nature and armed himself with a wry sense of humour. But he was also a restless individual, a wanderer, and did not really find a niche in life until he was on service during the First World War.

Graduating from Dulwich in 1889, he intended further studies at Cooper's Hill, the Royal Indian Engineering College at Runnymede, which trained engineers for the Indian Public Works Department. However, he changed his mind and elected to study for two years at the Electrical Engineering Institute in South Kensington. On graduation in 1892, he joined the firm of Marshall and Sons at the Britannia Works, in Gainsborough, Lincolnshire, a huge engineering company manufacturing portable steam engines and agricultural machinery.

He trained for two years as an engineer then opted for India again, taking up the position of Assistant Manager and Engineer to the Jokai (Assam) Tea Company, famed for its Darjeeling and Nilgiri teas. His duties were not onerous, and he had the time in which to ride and hunt, honing skills he already possessed, and becoming an excellent shot with rifle and pistol. He spent an idyllic three years in India: the social life was sparse at times, but he found consolation in reading and summer visits to mingle with other Europeans at the hill-station of Ootacamund, where Paul Kenna VC was married in 1895. He took up pipe-smoking, and was rarely seen without a pipe fixed firmly in his mouth.

Meanwhile, his father prospered on Butler's Wharf; and when Alexander returned from India in 1897, it was to work with his father. He proved a capable and considerate manager, and was, like his father, highly regarded by the workforce. He had the common touch and enjoyed the company of men from all walks of life. But not so with women, with whom he was shy, retiring and often tongue-tied. His sisters adored him and had probably spoilt him for the marriage stakes: he was saving himself for someone of their kind.

Henry Pownall, after Dulwich and Trinity College, Cambridge, was ordained a minister in the Church of England in 1890, and was given the living in Ambleside, in the Lake District. With one of the family a clergyman, perhaps it was inevitable that Alexander would consider the army as a career one day. The opportunity arose when the Boers declared war. He enlisted in the newly formed Imperial Yeomanry, signing on for a year's service as volunteer 8352 Private Alexander Malins Lafone in the 49th Company, 9th Battalion, Montgomeryshire Imperial Yeomanry. An excellent shot and fine rider, he was quickly promoted to sergeant, and helped in the training of those less proficient. Kitted out in a woollen Norfolk jacket, breeches and gaiters, lace boots and a felt hat, he landed in Cape Town, South Africa, on 6 April 1900.

On the journey to Africa, he carried with him the sad tidings that his first cousin, Captain William Boucher Lafone, Devonshire Regiment, had been killed in action at Wagon Hill, Ladysmith on 6 January. He was deeply distressed by the death, and his spirits were further depressed after spending several weeks in the squalor of the disease-ridden congregation camp at McKenzie's Farm at Maitland, on the outskirts of Cape Town. And they were not to be revived over the next eight months on patrol across the veld, supporting the regular army. It was monotonous duty and there was little contact with the enemy. His morale and that of the yeomanry plummeted further during the summer when, under orders from General Kitchener, he was tasked with the burning of Boer farms, a duty which he, in common with Donald Farmer VC, found both distasteful and unsoldierly.

On 18 August 1900, at the height of the farm-burning campaign, he was wounded in the right eye while on patrol west of Pretoria. He was hospitalized for several weeks and was grateful when he was repatriated to England, arriving home early in the New Year. He received the Queen's South Africa Medal and three clasps. His original term of enlistment had been for one year or for the duration of the war, and once fully recovered, he rejoined the Imperial Yeomanry, being commissioned as a second lieutenant in the Hertfordshire Imperial Yeomanry on 25 April 1901.

However, he resigned this position in June, and in August, was granted a second commission, this time with the 1st County of London (Middlesex) Yeomanry. But he did not return to South Africa, and began work with his father again on Butler's Wharf. And with the end of hostilities the following year and the reorganization of the yeomanry regiments, he was promoted to captain in the newly named Middlesex (Duke of Cambridge's Hussars) Imperial Yeomanry on 14 July 1902.

Henry Lafone's success at the wharf had restored the family fortunes, and he was living with his wife at the prosperous address of 59 Onslow Square, Kensington. Close to retirement, he hoped Alexander would replace him as wharfinger. But, in 1903, Alexander quit the wharf and entered the Colonial Service. He was posted to Nigeria as Assistant Resident in Kabba Province.

The break was sudden and took his father by surprise. His abrupt departure suggests a failed romance. It was not unusual at the turn of the last century for young men, thwarted in love, to decamp abroad and lose themselves in the remoter parts of the empire where they could nurse their sorrows in solitude. Perhaps Alexander did find a woman with whom he could share his life, but was heartbroken when his advances were rejected.

He threw himself into his career and progressed so quickly that after two years he was promoted to Resident: a lifelong career in the Colonial Service beckoned. But it was not to be: he was struck down with malaria, which was endemic to the region, and was forced to give up his post. Family history says he suffered recurrent attacks following the initial infection and treatment in England was considered necessary. He convalesced at his parents' home, now at Court Lodge, Knockholt, in Kent, but was knocked off his feet again when his mother died on 22 November 1910. She was buried in the village graveyard of St Katherine's Church.

After this loss, Alexander returned to London and found work in the City, becoming a director of several companies and partner in the brokerage firm of F.A. Roberts, of Leadenhall Street. He lived the life of a well-to-do Edwardian bachelor, but could not find a woman to capture his heart. He kept up his part-time military career and, following the War Office reforms of the army in 1908, when the Middlesex Imperial Yeomanry was renamed the 1st County of

London Yeomanry, Middlesex (Duke of Cambridge's Hussars) Territorial Force, he was promoted to major in 1911.

Major Lafone was a gentleman soldier. He received no formal military training, and did not serve in the regular army or attend for officer's school at the Royal Military College. His only military experience was as a volunteer in South Africa. Nevertheless, he was a good soldier. A natural leader of men, he was highly intelligent and did not possess the usual officer mentality of 'them and us'. He was able to communicate easily and readily with his men, very often employing his well-known sense of humour, and he earned the respect and affection of all who served under him. He became a father-figure to many of the younger men in the unit, 'dear old Laffy' as he was known, inspiring them to do their best, and welding together a highly efficient fighting force at the weekend camps when the regiment trained in the business of war. And it was at one of these gatherings, at Moulsford Camp, in Berkshire, on Bank Holiday Monday, 3 August 1914, that Major Alexander Lafone and the 1st County of London Yeomanry were ordered to prepare for war.

As part of the London Mounted Brigade, Major Lafone assembled with his regiment at Churn in Wiltshire, where, on 2 September, it was made part of the 2nd Mounted Division, under the command of Major General W. Peyton. Brigadier General Paul Kenna VC led his Notts and Derby Mounted Yeomanry Brigade into the new divisional formation. In November, the division moved to the Norfolk coast to equip and train, and to learn the tactics of trench warfare, before being posted to the Southern Front.

In August 1915, Major Lafone fought on the blazing slopes of Scimitar Hill, Gallipoli; and after service in Egypt with the Suez Canal Defence Force, he landed in Salonika, Greece, and confronted the Bulgarian Army in Macedonia for eight months until June 1917. He then returned to England on leave, but too late to see his beloved father who had passed away in May. He spent several weeks at Knockholt, dealing with his estate, and it was not until 5 October 1917 that he rejoined his regiment, at Khan Yunis, Palestine. Here, he was drafted into the Yeomanry Mounted Division of the Desert Mounted Corps under General Allenby, and moved up to Beersheba, towards Point 720.

Alexander Lafone VC was not the only member of the family to make the ultimate sacrifice during the First World War. Henry Pownall's son, his nephew, Captain Eric William Lafone MC, 12th Battalion, Durham Light Infantry, served on the Western Front. Badly wounded at Pozières during the Battle of the Somme, he was awarded the Military Cross and the Croix de Guerre for his courage. But, in October 1917, the Durhams were transferred to the Southern Front to buttress the Italian army in the face of renewed attacks by Austro-Hungarian forces. At the Battle of Asiago Plateau on 15 June 1918, Captain Lafone was killed in action. He is buried in the British War Cemetery, Granezza, in Vicenza Province, Italy.

During and after the Second World War, Major Lafone's regiment underwent several reorganizations and rebirths. In 1961, it became 47 Signal Regiment (Middlesex Yeomanry), a Territorial Unit of the Royal Corps of Signals, with a role of support troops to Supreme Headquarters Allied Powers Europe, at Rocquencourt, France. It was here that Lieutenant Colonel S. Williams, commanding the regiment, suggested to his opposite number in the Turkish Armed Forces that the Turkish government should present to the regiment a cavalry lance in recognition of the gallant stand made by Major Lafone on Point 720.

In July 1965, Major General E. Alpkaya of the Turkish army presented the lance to the regiment at a ceremony at Camp de Frileuse, in France. In return, Lieutenant Colonel Williams presented a sword to the major general, which was inscribed thus: 'Presented by the Middlesex Yeomanry to the Turkish Cavalry with mutual respect for the bravery of Major A.M. Lafone VC, on 27 October 1917.'

Major Lafone's Victoria Cross is held in the Lower Hall at Dulwich College, alongside a framed portrait and a copy of his citation. He is remembered on the Regimental Memorial in the crypt of St Paul's Cathedral. In St Katherine's Church, Knockholt, where his parents are buried, the memorial plaque to Major Lafone VC contains a line from 'Horatius', penned by Thomas Macaulay almost eighty years earlier, and which could have been written for him: 'And how can man die better than facing fearful odds.'

Hugh McDonald McKenzie VC
(1885–1917)

Three countries and two army units claim Hugh McDonald McKenzie VC DCM as one of their heroes. Brought up in Scotland, he emigrated to Canada, and, at the outbreak of the First World War, was sent to France with the Princess Patricia's Canadian Light Infantry (PPCLI). After winning the Distinguished Conduct Medal with that unit in 1915, he transferred to the Canadian Machine Gun Corps (CMGC) in 1917 and won the Victoria Cross. Both the PPCLI and the CMGC admit him as one of theirs, just as Canada and Scotland both declare him one of their sons. But Hugh McDonald McKenzie was born in Liverpool, and the city has first call on this gallant soldier, whose life began and ended in tragedy.

His father, James, was the son of a shepherd from Perthshire who eschewed the hardships of rural life for the bright lights of the city. He left home to labour in Cupar and later Dundee, where he was employed as a confection packer in the factory of James Keiller and Company, manufacturers of marmalade and jam. While lodging at 6 St Peter Street, he met Jane McDonald from Inverness, whose father Hugh was a shipwright. Jane had followed her mother, Agnes, into domestic service in Dundee, where she lived and worked at 24 Pirie Street. James and Jane married on 13 June 1877, and almost immediately moved across country to Greenock, where they found accommodation on Main Street and began a family.

Greenock was Scotland's major west coast port, twenty-two miles downstream of Glasgow, on the south bank of the Firth of Clyde. A shipbuilding town of great renown, it also boasted fourteen sugar refineries wherein West Indian muscovado was processed into sugar and syrup to meet the demands of the nation's sweet tooth. James McKenzie found work as a sugarhouse labourer, toiling twelve hours a day in a hot, sticky environment. But he was earning far more than he had done in Dundee, and, with money in his pockets, he could cast around at his leisure for better paid jobs.

This he did, and by the time Robert, James and Isabelle were born, James McKenzie had quit the sugar refinery to work as an engine driver for the local railway company. Baby Jean was born in January 1884, and later that year the McKenzies left Scotland and headed south to Liverpool. They took up residence at 62 Hunter Street, behind the Walker Art Gallery, where Hugh McDonald McKenzie was born on 5 December 1885.

In Liverpool, James McKenzie joined the Merchant Navy and began calling himself a marine engineer. He had no previous experience at the sea and no formal training in engineering, though he probably picked up the basics during his time as an engine driver. More than likely, he was a motorman in the engine room, under the supervision of a marine engineer, responsible for oiling and helping to maintain motors and small engines. The fact he moved his family to Liverpool suggests it was his home port and that he crewed on the small coastal freighters or passenger ferries operating from Liverpool to north Wales, the Isle of Man and Ireland. He would be ashore on a regular basis to see his wife and children after a trip away of two or three days' duration. But the family sojourn in Liverpool was short and ended tragically: in rough seas in the Irish Sea on 16 November 1888, James McKenzie was lost overboard and drowned. His body was never recovered.

Following the death of her husband, Jane McKenzie, mother of five young children, and pregnant with a sixth, was deprived of all financial support; and with no family in the city to assist, her only recourse was to return to Scotland. Her parents, Hugh and Agnes McDonald, were both dead, and the only living relative was her aunt, Jane McDonald, who lived at 13 Blackpark, Muirtown, in Inverness. It was to her aunt's she decamped with her children in 1889; and it was there that Hugh McDonald McKenzie was brought up. His brother, Alexander, was born in Muirtown in the summer of 1889, never knowing his father. A seventh child, Nora, was born to Jane McKenzie in 1893.

The family prospered in Inverness: Jane found work in the town, as did the elder children, and within a short time the family were able to move into their own home at 128 Croft Cottage. Hugh McKenzie was educated at the local school in Leachkin Road and left at the age of 12 to work as a farm labourer. He grew into a fine specimen of a man, 5 feet, 7 inches tall, with a lean, muscular physique and the fresh and ruddy complexion associated with outdoor work. He had brown hair and grey eyes and was a popular young man in the district, taking an active interest in local sports, and excelling in wrestling.

In 1905, Jane McKenzie moved the family to Dundee, where she had worked as a domestic servant as a lass, living at 23 James Street. Next door, at No. 25, lived the McGuigan family. A daughter of the family, Marjory, caught young Hugh's eye, and soon captured his heart. He found work as a carter in Dundee with the Caledonian Railway Company, transporting goods in horse-drawn carts to and from the railhead at Dundee. Some of the engineers and staff of the Caledonian were members of the Engineer and Railway Volunteer Corps, a militia unit; and it is thought that Hugh, through their example, was inspired to enlist. When the War Office created the Territorial Force in 1908, he volunteered to serve for four years with the Royal Garrison Artillery in Dundee and two years with the Royal Field Artillery Special Reserve.

He kept up his sporting interests and was a member of the Dundee Amateur Boxing and Wrestling Club, which had rooms and facilities at Dudhope Castle, situated in parkland overlooking the city. Concentrating on his wrestling, he made a name for himself on the local circuit. Reports say he was the North of Scotland Wrestling Champion for his weight and age in 1908, and he filled his trophy cabinet with silver cups and a gold medal. In addition, he became an instructor at the club and brought on younger talent, helping to establish the club as one of the best in Scotland. This experience as a teacher, of bringing out the best in others, would prove invaluable when he went to war on the Western Front.

Marjory McGuigan was the love of his life, and they made secret plans to marry: there was strong family opposition to the match from both sides, she being a Roman Catholic, he a Presbyterian. But the lovers saved their money and purchased tickets, probably for the Greenock sailing, and when the time was right, packed their bags and eloped, crossing the Atlantic in 1910 to Montreal, where they married. They rented a home at 297 Gertrude Avenue, Verdun. Hugh found work with the Canadian Pacific Railway, in his old calling of carter, a teamster in North American jargon, a job he held until he enlisted in the army when the First World War began. By that time, he was the father of two children, Alexander and Elizabeth, though his marriage to Marjory had broken down.

He attested to the Canadian Overseas Expeditionary Force on 21 August 1914 in Montreal, and was inducted as 1158 Private Hugh McKenzie to the Princess Patricia's Canadian Light Infantry. Like Lord Strathcona's Horse, the PPCLI was a privately raised regiment, the Montreal businessman, Captain Andrew Hamilton Gault, a veteran of the Boer War, having put up $100,000 to raise and equip it. The regiment was named after Princess Patricia of Connaught, granddaughter of Queen Victoria, and daughter of the Duke of Connaught, Governor General of Canada.

Such was the speed and efficiency with which Hamilton Gault, assisted by Lieutenant Colonel Francis Farquhar, organized recruitment and equipment, that the regiment was able to hold its first parade on 23 August. Only five days later, Hugh McKenzie kissed his children farewell and waved adieu to Marjory, hoping, perhaps, that his absence would make her heart grow fonder, and boarded the *Megantic* bound for Southampton. However, the sailing was delayed by German U-boat activity in the Atlantic, and later cancelled; and, it was not until the end of September that the regiment sailed aboard the *Royal George*, landing in England on 18 October, the first Canadian fighting force to arrive in Europe.

The regiment was put through its paces at Morn Hill, Winchester, impressing with its efficiency and *esprit de corps*, and towards the end of November was passed fit for duty in Flanders. Hugh managed a short leave to Scotland and was reunited with his mother and sisters in Dundee for a few days, when he confided his marital problems. Dashing back to the bivouac, he barely had time in which to collect his rucksack before the PPCLI crossed from Southampton to Le Havre on board the *Cardiganshire* on 20 December, spending Christmas at Blaringhem, France, before being marched up to the front and into the Ypres Salient.

The PPCLI became part of the hard, cutting edge of colonial troops which the Allies deployed to incise German resistance in all of the major offensives on the Western Front, at Ypres, on the Somme and at Arras, and the men suffered as a consequence. For three years, up until his death in 1917, Hugh McKenzie survived the fighting unscathed while his friends perished, and his only complaint was a bout of dysentery which necessitated a stay in hospital not long after his arrival in France. He was one of the stalwarts of the PPCLI, and his intelligence, fighting skills and leadership qualities were recognized from the outset, at St Eloi, south of Ypres, in March 1915, when the regiment had its first face-to-face encounter with the enemy, and helped to stem a major offensive. Following the baptism of fire, he was promoted to corporal in the machine-gun section; and two months later, in the latter stages of the Second Battle of Ypres, his courage under fire was rewarded with two medals for gallant conduct.

On 8 May, the regiment was in makeshift trenches at Lake Bellewaarde, three miles east of Ypres, when the Germans renewed a stalled offensive to the north, towards Frezenburg Ridge. The first the PPCLI knew of the attack was when the trenches were enfiladed and pummelled by artillery fire from the right. With very little protection, the Canadians stood their ground, but, as the fight developed, Corporal Hugh McKenzie and his comrades found themelves under fire from three sides as the front began to waver and German troops penetrated the battered defences. The regiment regrouped to hold the southern shoulder of a wide breach, and stoutly resisted further enemy incursions aimed at rolling up this flank.

Casualties were heavy: high explosive shells finally demolished the last vestiges of cover and when machine-gun fire raked their exposed positions, the men were siting ducks. But intensive and concentrated fire from Corporal McKenzie and the machine-gun sections halted the infantry advance. The Germans responded with another curtain of shells; and the infantry pushed up again, but the PPCLI would not give way and kept the enemy at bay.

Head down, eyes fixed directly ahead, Corporal McKenzie battled on through the morning, leading by example and refusing to give ground. He rallied the men and kept them organized as a fighting unit. But, early in the afternoon, a shell exploded close to his machine-gun position, killing and wounding several of his squad and burying everyone and everything in a pile of muddy debris. He dug himself free; and, realizing his position was now untenable, he disabled his weapon, picked up the wounded and made his way along the line to safety.

The artillery barrages had destroyed all means of communication between the PPCLI front line and brigade headquarters, and for the remainder of the day and into the night, McKenzie worked as a runner between the front and headquarters, carrying messages and orders. The devastation to the lines was such that there was no cover as he dashed back and forth under fire, but grimly he stuck to his task until the PPCLI was relieved in the lines just before midnight.

For exceptional dedication to duty at Bellewaarde Lake on 8 May 1915, Corporal Hugh McKenzie was awarded the Distinguished Conduct Medal. The award was gazetted on 14 January 1916. His citation reads:

> For conspicuous gallantry. His machine gun having been blown up by a shell and the whole crew killed or wounded, Corporal McKenzie displayed the utmost coolness in stripping the wrecked gun of all undamaged parts and bringing them safely out of the trench, which by then had been absolutely demolished. Having no machine gun, he volunteered to carry messages to and from Brigade Headquarters under terrific fire and succeeded. His devotion to duty has always been marked.

The PPCLI went into billets at Hooge Château after the fight and moved further to the rear to Busseboom, to be re-equipped and reinforced by a draft of new faces. In September, he was promoted to sergeant and sent to Camiers Camp, part of the huge, reception complex at Étaples, for further training in machine-gun tactics. There, he received news that the French had honoured him for his bravery in May with the award of the Croix de Guerre, which was gazetted on 24 February 1916. But, despite the glad tidings, he was sombre and depressed, unable to concentrate or think clearly.

He had kept up regular correspondence with Marjory since leaving Canada, but had received few replies in return and no hint of how their relationship stood. Then a friend, Clement Howard, had written to say Marjory was engaged in an extra-marital affair and had placed their son in a Montreal orphanage. A second letter now informed him his daughter Elizabeth had been made to risk the perilous transatlantic voyage to Scotland and was now living with his mother. In October 1915, he was granted compassionate leave and travelled to Dundee to see Elizabeth.

The visit was fraught and distressing: as if a faithless wife and the forced separation of his children were not enough to cope with, he was met on arrival at his mother's home with the news that one of his brothers was missing in action. Robert, serving at the front as a driver in the Army Service Corps, was fine. But, young Alexander, a private in the Cameron Highlanders, had not returned to his unit following a German attack. The Red Cross would later report him a prisoner of war, and he returned to Scotland after hostilities ceased.

He could but comfort and reassure Elizabeth. There was nothing he could do to resolve the issues short of travelling to Canada to confront his feckless spouse and remove his son from the orphanage, but the much larger troubles on the Western Front precluded this, and he would have to wait until after they were settled before he could resolve his personal situation. Summoned back to battle, he rejoined his comrades in the trenches at Dranouter, near Ypres, seething, sombre and despondent. But, he realized he would have to suppress his feelings and give his full attention to the task in hand and channel his angst towards the enemy if he was to survive the war and return to Canada to obtain redress: one slip in concentration during a fight, one brooding lapse, would spell doom.

In his absence, there had been a major reorganization of Canadian forces in Europe, and from January 1916, the PPCLI, together with the Royal Canadian Regiment, the Royal Highlanders of Canada and the Edmonton Regiment, made up 7th Canadian Infantry Brigade, 3rd Canadian Division. In addition, the brigade was to have its own machine-gun unit, the 7th Canadian Machine Gun Company (CMGC), made up from the most experienced machine-gun sections of the four regiments.

In June, on Mount Sorrel, where Sergeant David Jones also did duty, he kept himself focused and distinguished himself in the face of the German onslaughts; and continued to be when serving on the Somme, at Flers-Courcelette, Thiepval and Le Transloy. His fighting spirit and expertise as a machine-gunner merited promotion to company sergeant major with 7th Company. And when the Somme fell silent in November, and as the regiment prepared to move back north, he became warrant officer, 2nd Class, and was sent off to Camiers again for additional training. The following January, he was gazetted as lieutenant in the PPCLI and transferred to A Company of the machine-gunners.

Delighted with his new prospect, he found he was gaining ground on the other front, in the personal arena. In February, he applied to stop his monthly allowance of $20 to Marjory on the grounds of her infidelity, and had been relieved of some of his anger and anxiety with the news from friends in Canada that she had reclaimed their son from the orphanage and was now caring for him at home. In addition, letters from his mother, giving details of his daughter's progress and happiness, heartened him, and helped restore some balance to his life.

His first taste of battle as an officer came in April, during the Arras offensive, at Hill 145, better known as Vimy Ridge, a name synonymous with Canadian courage and grit. Rising from the western edge of the Douai plain, six miles north-east of Arras, the escarpment known as Vimy Ridge climbed to a height of 450 feet above sea level and ran north for approximately eight miles to the commune of Givenchy-en-Gohelle, south of Loos. Forward, the ridge over-looked the Allied positions west, north and south, and the Douai plain to the rear. It was the hinge of the German defensives on the Western Front, protecting the newly constructed Hindenburg Line to the south and the trench system running north into Flanders, and was one of the most heavily fortified sectors of the Western Front.

Starting on 2 April 1917, the Allies opened up with what was up until then the heaviest artillery bombardment of the war, 'the week of hell', as the Germans called it, and Vimy Ridge was pulverized by 1,000,000 tons of shells. On Easter Monday, 9 April, amid a flurry of snow and freezing sleet, four divisions of Canadian troops went over the top. By early afternoon, most of the Ridge was in their hands and thousands of Germans had been killed and taken prisoner. The following morning, the 'pimple', the high point, had been taken; and two days later the victory was complete. Muddy, bruised and fatigued, Lieutenant Hugh McKenzie and the men of the PPCLI stood atop the bluff and gazed eastwards, across the rolling plain of Douai, the first Allied soldiers to do so in more than two years of fighting.

The great success of the Canadians on Vimy Ridge only brought more demands for their fighting abilities, for their grim tenacity in difficult situations, and they were afforded little rest before being called into action again. In the summer of 1917, Hugh McKenzie fought at La Coulette, at the River Scarpe and the River Souchez, and at Avion; and it was not until the autumn, that the exhausted and battle-weary Canadians were allowed time out to rest and recuperate, and to rebuild their numbers. They would need to: ahead lay Passchendaele.

Early in June, the Allies fought the Battle of Messines Ridge in the south of the Ypres Salient, the prelude to the Third Battle of Ypres. But it was not until 31 July 1917 that the Battle, the 'race to the coast', commenced. It was a long, drawn out, stop-go offensive, the rainy weather as much as the poor planning and indecisive leadership responsible for its prolongation. The latter stage of this disastrous campaign, from October until November, is known to history as the Battle of Passchendaele, the bloody, muddy fight for the tiny Belgian crossroads village, described by Winston Churchill as a 'forlorn expenditure of valour and life without equal'.

The land over which the troops attacked was reclaimed swamp land, soggy and boggy even without rain. The initial Allied artillery bombardment tore up the land and destroyed the drainage system; and heavy rains throughout August transformed no man's land into an impassable terrain of oozing mud, one in which even tanks became bogged down, and in which exhausted men, stumbling, slipping and falling, drowned in their hundreds. The attacks aimed at Passchendaele were called off in late August, and were not resumed until drier weather arrived in late September. Some gains were made in early October, but when the rains returned, the offensive stalled.

On 10 October, as the 3rd and 4th Canadian Divisions were preparing to move forward into the lines near Passchendaele, Lieutenant Hugh McKenzie took a short leave, travelling to Scotland for what was to be his final reunion with his daughter and family. It was a far happier visit than his last, and he was able to relax and put his feet up while indulging and pampering Elizabeth. No doubt he hoped and prayed that Passchendaele would be the final break-through the generals expected it to be and would signal the end of the war and the final resolution to his own problems. He was only partially right: the battle would not end the war but his marital difficulties would be over, if not in the manner he hoped for. Perhaps he had some foreboding of his fate: with some prescience, he placed his Distinguished Conduct Medal and Croix de Guerre in safekeeping with his mother before returning to Flanders, and also entrusted her with his will, scribbled out two years earlier on a page torn from his note-book, bequeathing her all his back pay.

By 17 October, he was back in Belgium. Nine days later, the fighting recommenced with an attack designed to advance the line just 500 yards; and Lieutenant McKenzie found himself struggling through a surreal landscape of blackened tree stumps and twisted corpses, knee-deep in the quagmire of no man's land, inching forward in the mist and rain, shell hole by muddy shell hole, towards Bellevue Spur. At the cost of 12,000 Allied casualties, the advance made 200 yards before it was called off. On 30 October, the heavens opened again and rain, almost as heavy as the enemy barrages, pelted the men and the ground, swamping everyone and everything in a deluge through which another attack began. More than 28,000 men of the 3rd and 4th Canadian Divisions climbed from the waterlogged trenches and slogged along both sides of the Ravebeek River up to Meetcheele Spur and the outskirts of Passchendaele village.

The PPCLI was in the vanguard of the move towards the spur, and Lieutenant McKenzie commanded four machine guns of 7th Company. The Germans were deeply entrenched, their lines protected by mutually supporting pillboxes which the initial Allied bombardment had failed to destroy. Under devastating artillery and machine-gun fire, the attack progressed slowly and became bogged down in the clinging mud while casualties mounted. The success of the entire offensive hinged on the attack the PPCLI were making along the route to the spur; and it now hung in the balance as the Canadians were confronted by heavily fortified pillboxes and machine-gun nests atop the hilly terrain and placed squarely across their path.

Ahead and to his left, Lieutenant McKenzie observed that all the officers and most of the non-commissioned officers of a PPCLI unit had been mown down by machine-gun fire and that the survivors could not advance further in the teeth of such murderous resistance. But they would not retreat either, and the men were standing their ground, waiting for someone to take charge and show them the way forward. Placing a corporal in charge of his guns, he took command of the leaderless men and organized two parties to circle round the flanks of the pillbox that had caused all the casualties to attack it from the rear.

McKenzie then led the remainder of the PPCLI unit in a direct frontal attack up the slimy slope to the pillbox so as to draw away fire.

The ploy was a success. The machine guns concentrated on McKenzie and his men, enabling one of the flanking parties, led by Sergeant George Mullin, to get in behind the machine-gun post. Mullin charged the pillbox, letting fly with a couple of hand grenades, then climbed on top of the concrete housing and shot dead both gunners. But seconds before he did so, a burst of fire from one of the guns brought down Lieutenant McKenzie in mid-stride: he fell dead to the muddy ground, shot through the head, a few yards in front of the pillbox. Sergeant George Mullin cleared out the pillbox and took several prisoners. Slowly but surely, the advance continued again.

For gallantry in the face of the enemy, Lieutenant Hugh McKenzie DCM was awarded a posthumous Victoria Cross, which was gazetted on 13 February 1918. His citation reads:

> Hugh MacKenzie, DCM, Lieutenant, late 7th Canadian Machine Gun Company, Canadian Machine Gun Corps. For most conspicuous bravery and leading when in charge of a section of four machine guns accompanying the infantry in an attack. Seeing that all of the officers and most of the non-commissioned officers of an infantry company had become casualties, and that the men were hesitating before a nest of enemy machine guns, which were on commanding ground and causing them severe casualties, he handed over command of his guns to an NCO, rallied the infantry, organised an attack, and captured the strong point. Finding that the position was swept by machine-gun fire from a pillbox which dominated all the ground over which the troops were advancing, Lieutenant MacKenzie made a reconnaissance and detailed flanking and frontal attacking parties, which captured the pillbox, he himself being killed while leading the frontal attack. By his valour and leadership this gallant officer ensured the capture of these strong points and so saved the lives of many men and enabled the objectives to be attained.

So fractured and piecemeal in scale had the Allied offensive become because of the atrocious weather, ground conditions and enemy retaliation that it was the actions of individuals such as Lieutenant Hugh McKenzie and Sergeant George Mullin which had the most significant impact on the success of the attack at the end of the day. Following the capture of the pillbox and McKenzie's sacrifice, Meetcheele Spur was taken and held. And, on 6 November, Passchendaele was captured. But for the individual bravery of McKenzie and Mullin, the result may well have been different.

The body of the gallant Lieutenant Hugh McKenzie was recovered by his best friend, Lieutenant Neatly, who oversaw the burial during a lull in the carnage, marking the grave with a wooden cross. But as the fighting raged, the grave marker and the grave, along with countless others, were lost to the mud.

The 3rd and 4th Canadian Divisions lost 15,000 men killed, wounded and missing at Passchendaele. In total, the Allies suffered 500,000 casualties, all for a territorial gain of four and a half miles. The 'race to the coast' never materialized. Passchendaele was, as Churchill said, a needless waste of life. For Lieutenant Hugh McDonald McKenzie VC DCM, who bravely gave his life, the environs of the village was to be his last resting place. His name is recorded on the Menin Gate Memorial at Ypres.

Major J.G. Weir, who commanded 7th Company, wrote to Hugh's mother in Dundee, informing her of his death. 'He did not know fear, and was always outstanding even amongst the most courageous. He had hosts of real friends who loved and admired him, and his influence was always for the good. . . . In all my experience out here I have never seen a better officer nor a more likeable officer than your son.' He offered also a second version of the action: 'Hugh instantly went forward, shouting, "Come on, boys, we'll take it." He succeeded in taking the first objective but he had only gone a short distance towards the second when he was shot through the head and killed instantly. The men, however, carried on, and took the second pillbox.'

Marjory McKenzie received a telegram from the Canadian War office at her home, 1021 Clarke Street, Montreal, on 5 November, informing that her husband was missing in action, presumed dead. A week later a second message confirmed this. Hugh's death had a profound effect upon her. She sought consolation in her son, and atonement, perhaps, for her behaviour: at the end of hostilities and after several letters begging forgiveness of Hugh's mother, she brought Elizabeth back to Canada and became a mother again, concerning herself solely with her children's happiness. They started life anew in North Bay, Ontario, where she remarried with their blessing in January 1920. When she died, Elizabeth took possession of her father's honours.

However, tragedy continued to strike the McKenzie family: Hugh's son, Alexander, served with the Canadian Army during the Second World War, and survived the conflict only to be killed in a road accident shortly after being demobbed. Elizabeth took up residence in Amherstburg, Ontario. On 24 May 1955, fire raged through her home, killing her sister-in-law and her three children. Her father's Victoria Cross was also destroyed. In 1970, the PPCLI Museum contacted her about the whereabouts of the honour, and hearing of its loss, organized an official replacement, which was presented to her. Shortly before her death, she donated all her father's medals to the Canadian War Museum.

Today, the replacement Victoria Cross, the Distinguished Conduct Medal and Croix de Guerre of Hugh McKenzie, together with his campaign medals, are held by the PPCLI Museum in the Military Museums, Calgary.

Cyril Edward Gourley VC
(1893–1982)

The Smithdown Road area of Liverpool was once arable land and grazing pasture overseen by Penketh Hall and the village of Wavertree. From the mid-Victorian era, it was developed for housing to accommodate the growing population of the city, and nowadays it is a major route, running south–east for three and a half miles from Upper Parliament Street, near the city centre, to Penny Lane on the outskirts. The hall has long gone, and the village is now a suburb, but for many years the old and the new coexisted. The Ashcrofts, a long-established farming family, and the Gourleys, newcomers to the area, lived at either end of the developing thoroughfare.

Edward Ashcroft was born in Wavertree village in 1806, and he farmed sixty-five acres in the Penny Lane area. A bachelor for most of his life, in 1863, at the age of 57, he married Emma Hope, thirty-three years his junior, who came of farming stock from Much Dewchurch, Herefordshire. The couple lived on a new housing development at 12 Prince Alfred Road, Wavertree, where their four children, John, Martha Ann, James and Emma were born.

Martha Ann was educated privately at an exclusive boarding school in Tattenhall, Cheshire. When she returned to Liverpool to live in 1885 at the age of 18, her mother hoped she would make a suitable match, and marry a man of property and discernment. But Martha Ann would not be rushed and would marry for love rather than position. Some months after attaining her majority, and much to her mother's disappointment, she met and fell in love with a young Irishman, Galbraith Gourley, from the other end of Smithdown Road. Galbraith was a son of the land, his father, Irvine, farming thirty acres across the Fermanagh–Tyrone border, and he was born in Irvinestown, County Fermanagh, in August 1865. But, as the youngest of five sons, he had to look elsewhere for a livelihood.

Galbraith and his elder brother, John, were enterprising young Ulstermen. They landed in Liverpool in 1889, took a house in Smithdown Road, close to Upper Parliament Street, and set about making their fortunes in the grocery trade and finding wives. The charming and industrious Galbraith Gourley won over all objections and married Martha Ann Ashcroft on 16 March 1891. They lived at 55 Earle Road, which he converted into a grocery shop. John married Emily Wright a month later, and likewise turned his new home at 49 Lawrence

Street into a store. The two brothers then established a joint venture, Gourley Brothers, at 43 Lawrence Road, and within a decade their business prospered and expanded so rapidly that they were running seven grocery shops in the Smithdown Road area and a huge warehouse in Dove Street nearby.

When Galbraith and Martha started a family, they moved home to 6 Victoria Park, Wavertree, to be closer to her mother. Cyril Edward Gourley was born there on 19 January 1893, and was the second eldest of a family of five boys and one girl, Irvine, Reginald, Eunice, Roland and Alfred. At the turn of the century, Galbraith moved his family away from the hustle and bustle of the city, across the Mersey to the peace of the Wirral Peninsula, purchasing a new home, Arncliffe House, 39 Westbourne Road, where Cyril spent his formative years and developed a keen interest in horses. He would later say that it was the horse that prompted him to enlist in the artillery militia as a young man.

The Gourley boys were educated at Calday Grange Grammar School, one of the oldest schools on Merseyside. Cyril was an outstanding pupil academically, and was the brains of the family. In 1910, he won the Edward Rathbone Entrance Scholarship to Liverpool University, at a time when university education was restricted to the sons of the very rich. Three years later, he was one of the first students to graduate in the new degree of Bachelor of Commercial Science, gaining honours in Economics, French and Commerce. Surprisingly, he did not follow his father into the grocery trade, but decided on a career with the well-known Liverpool shipping firm, the Ocean Steamship Company, the Blue Funnel Line, owned by Alfred Holt, which was the leading British shipping company sailing to China. The line was unrivalled for the high quality of its vessels, management, crews and shore staff. It was known locally as the 'China Company', not only because of the China trade, but also because of the large numbers of Chinese lascars employed: the growth of Liverpool's China Town, the oldest in Europe, stems from this policy.

A train journey across the Wirral Peninsula to Birkenhead and a change to the Mersey Railway Tunnel Line carried Cyril Gourley to James Street in the city centre, and a two minutes' walk brought him to India Buildings, Water Street. Working from the main office of Alfred Holt and Company, he began to learn the shipping business, dealing with the trade in tea and silk. He was a modern man with a university education and was full of new ideas and theories which he was eager to apply. Always courteous, he unintentionally ruffled feathers with his management style which appeared a little abrupt to older, more staid members of the firm when progressive theory collided with deep-rooted tradition; and he came to be seen as an unconventional, if not eccentric, individual. It was a characteristic he adopted and would maintain throughout his life. He progressed well but slowly in his profession, and travelled regularly to the Far East on company business.

Just before the outbreak of the First World War, and like many young men employed in the office, he joined the Territorial Force, enlisting as 681886

Private Cyril Gourley in the 4th West Lancashire Howitzer Brigade, Royal Field Artillery (RFA). His background and education should have merited an officer's commission, but he was an unassuming, if not diffident, young man when with the unit, content to listen and watch rather than lead. The brigade, which had its origins in a Volunteer Artillery Corps raised after the Crimean War in Liverpool from employees in the commercial sector, comprised the 7th and 8th Lancashire Howitzer Batteries, and had its headquarters at the Grange, a large house on the corner of Botanic Road and Edge Lane, part of which is now the museum of the Liverpool Scottish.

He indulged his love of horses with the 'terriers', and attended the Saturday afternoon training sessions, and gave up one evening a week for instruction at the barracks. At the beginning of August 1914, he was making arrangements to attend his first annual camp with his comrades over the Bank Holiday weekend when he found himself mobilized for war. As a 'terrier', he was a volunteer and was not obligated to serve overseas, the principal role envisaged for the Territorial Force in an emergency being home defence. However, like the vast majority of 'terriers', Cyril Gourley willingly signed away his right to remain at home, resigned his position with Blue Funnel, and headed south to Sevenoaks in Kent, where the brigade began training as part of the divisional artillery of the 55th West Lancashire Division.

The three infantry brigades of the 55th Division were broken up piecemeal and sent over to France, while the artillery brigades remained in England. Cyril Gourley was not posted overseas until 28 September 1915, when he served briefly with the 2nd Canadian Division at Ypres before being returned to 55th Division the following January in the Hallencourt area, east of Albert. The divisional artillery was reorganized, the howitzer batteries ceasing to exist, and Gourley's 7th Battery was redesignated D Battery of the 276th West Lancashire Brigade, RFA, deploying 18-pound guns. His brother, Irvine, who enlisted at the same time, served with the 278th Brigade. For the remainder of the war, the two Gourley brothers would provide artillery support for the divisional infantry, in whose ranks was Private Arthur Procter.

In February 1916, the division moved into lines south of Arras, between the hamlets of Wailly and Bretencourt. No major confrontations took place along this part of the front, but small-scale actions, raiding parties crossing no man's land in search of intelligence, occurred frequently. Usually these raids were preceded by a brief artillery barrage, and 276th took its turn in pounding the German trenches. One such raid, near the village of Ficheux, would result in another Liverpool hero, Private Arthur Procter, winning the Victoria Cross when his company from the 5th Liverpools fell victim to the 'friendly fire' which Gourley's battery, among others, rained down on them.

At the time of the Ficheux raid, Cyril Gourley had been promoted and wore the single chevron of a bombardier. He had shown he was a competent soldier and able leader of men, but when he was persuaded to apply for a commission, which his education certainly merited, he was turned down every time because of his poor eyesight and hearing. These refusals rankled and he was convinced there were other agendas being followed: if he could see and hear well enough to be a bombardier, what additional levels of hearing and sight did he have to attain to become an officer? In his own inimitable and eccentric way, he would exact retribution for these rebuffs in 1918.

He saw action on the Somme in the summer and autumn of 1916, most notably at Guillemont, Flers-Courcelette and Morval, before being transferred in October to the Ypres Salient, where the division took up positions near Wieltje, and prepared for General Plumer's attack on Messines Ridge, the prelude to the Third Battle of Ypres, Passchendaele. By 20 May, Plumer had more than 2,500 guns in position; and the following day they opened the preliminary bombardment against the Messines defences. The barrage continued unabated until just before three o'clock on the morning of 7 June. Exhausted after seventeen days of continuous action, Cyril Gourley and his comrades slumped to the ground beside their guns for a respite before the most intricate part of the battle plan was opened.

The British gunners did not always have matters their own way during the barrage. The German artillery hit back and Cyril Gourley and D Battery had a narrow escape: a high-explosive shell landed near the gun position, and though no one was wounded, the explosion caused a fire in the brushwood camouflage screen above the ammunition dump. The fire spread quickly and began to envelop the shells. Cyril Gourley was first to react to the danger, risking serious injury to drag away the burning screen and extinguish the blaze. For bravery in the field, Cyril Gourley was awarded the Military Medal in July. He was still without a commission, however, though his hearing and eyesight had improved sufficiently to merit his promotion to the rank of sergeant.

When the Germans withdrew from the Somme in the spring of 1917, they took up positions behind the Hindenburg Line, a vast defensive entrenchment of fortifications five miles deep, bristling with barbed wire, concrete emplacements and bunkers, which stretched for 100 miles from Lens, near Arras, to the River Aisne in the south. The Germans considered it impregnable, and their battle-weary troops, including those from the Third Battle of Ypres, were sent there to rest, recuperate and refit. Behind the *Siegfriedstellung* section of the line in the north stood the city of Cambrai, the hub of the German supply routes for the Western Front.

The British planned to launch a surprise attack against the *Siegfriedstellung* on a six-mile front near Cambrai and breach the impregnable defences, moving on to surround the city before widening the front and breaking out, all before the strong German reserves could be brought up. The 55th Division moved into the front line between the villages of Lempire and Ronssoy, south-west of the city, and readied itself for battle. In great secrecy, 1,000 guns and 476 tanks were concentrated behind the narrow front, and on 20 November 1917 the attack was launched.

The offensive opened with an intensive, predicted-fire barrage which caught the Germans unawares. This was followed by a rolling barrage placed 300 yards in front of the advancing infantry and tanks. On the first day, the impregnable *Siegfriedstellung* was penetrated and gains of up to four miles were made. But by the second day, the attack had failed to envelop Cambrai. With few fresh troops to maintain the impetus of the attack, and with the tanks under heavy fire from the enemy artillery, the offensive was halted temporarily to consolidate the gains, while the field guns were brought forward to more advanced positions.

Sergeant Gourley MM and D Battery moved forward to positions east of the village of Epehy, and north of Lempire, close to Little Priel Farm. In front, stood the 6th Liverpools at Eagle Quarry. As the captured territory was consolidated, the Germans began to hit back and launched a heavy bombardment on the British lines on 28 November. The barrage lasted two days and was the prelude to a massive infantry assault, supported by aircraft, which machine-gunned the British lines. Now it was the turn of the British to be surprised: the Germans attacked swiftly in small groups rather than in waves, deploying light infantry units, stormtroopers, which bypassed strongly defended positions and made for thinly-held sections of the front. The direction of the assault was across both divisional and battalion boundaries and command structures collapsed rapidly as the defenders became mixed up and were thrown into confusion.

The first blow fell on the 55th Division, which was soon in trouble. The exhausted men were bewildered when they were confronted suddenly by swarms of determined stormtroopers. The artillery batteries, which responded to the attack and fired off continuous salvoes, soon came within range of the advancing infantry; and once their positions were identified, the enemy big guns zeroed in. Two hours after the initial attack, calls were being made for reinforcements all along the line, and hundreds of prisoners were taken as the defences crumbled.

D Battery came under heavy fire from the German guns. Lieutenant Ridealgh, in charge of a two-gun section at Little Priel Farm, was badly wounded by flying shrapnel, and he was carried off by some of the gunners for urgent medical treatment. As the enemy came on, overrunning the infantry lines in all directions, D Battery gunners fired over open sights, but their efforts could not stem the advance. The German retaliation was merciless, and shells rained down on the gunners, thinning their ranks and forcing some to take refuge in a dugout. With Lieutenant Ridealgh's guns in danger of falling into enemy hands, the breech blocks were removed, and the gunners decamped to the safety of battery headquarters.

When Major Hudson MC heard that Lieutenant Ridealgh was wounded and his two guns had been abandoned, he ordered Sergeant Gourley to take charge at the farm and bring the two guns into action again. Gourley collected to-gether a group of men, among them Sergeant Thornley and Gunner Hartley, and a couple of signallers. With the breech blocks in hand, they slithered and crawled their way to Little Priel Farm. However, the position was still under heavy fire, and they had to seek cover until the barrage moved on.

The intensity of the shell fire gradually reduced as the morning wore on and the artillery ranged over other targets. During a lull, Gourley and his squad regained the guns and re-seated the breech blocks. A signaller was sent forward to contact the remnants of the 6th Liverpools, who were making a stand, and with their help, enemy positions were identified and the information relayed back to Sergeant Gourley.

Using one gun at a time, Gourley opened up on enemy concentrations near Pigeon Quarry and Meath Post, and kept up a continuous fire for more than an hour. At noon, he received intelligence that the Germans were now sweeping down from these positions towards Holts Bank, directly in front of, and to the north of, the farm. Coolly and calmly, Sergeant Gourley began registering targets in that direction, knowing that the enemy was almost at the gates.

Enemy aircraft machine-gunned the position and redirected the artillery to attack the farm, while stormtroopers brought rifle fire to bear from the left flank. The motley crew was further depleted under the renewed attack, and one gun was put out of action when the crew were bowled over by an exploding shell. Gourley manhandled the second gun from its pit and began firing over open sights at the Germans, who at times got within 300 yards of his gun. With the assistance of Gunner Hartley, and all the time under heavy fire, he fired off twenty rounds before being forced to retire to a dugout. He returned to the gun with one of his men several times during brief pauses in the attack and kept the gun firing before retiring to safety again. At two o'clock in the after-noon, he was joined by Lieutenant Biggart, and once more the gun was manned. With Biggart acting as loader, Gourley kept up a continuous fire into the German ranks as they swarmed down from Holts Bank towards the farm, firing off twenty rounds while being shelled and fired on from the air and the ground.

Gourley and his men were driven off finally and had to take refuge in a gun pit. But again, from time to time, he crawled back under fire to the gun with one of his men and fired off several rounds at the enemy, on one occasion engaging, and destroying, a machine gun. But by four o'clock, the position became untenable, and Gourley and his exhausted squad slipped back one at a time to battery headquarters.

'He took charge of the section for four hours with complete competence and unlimited courage,' reported Major Hudson MC:

> In addition ... his behaviour in keeping his detachments together was
> heroic. Whenever the guns had to be left, he would not take cover himself
> until he was sure all his men were safe. On one occasion when the

detachments were driven away and he could not find Sergeant Thornley, he walked across in the open and searched all dugouts and all possible places with absolute disregard of machine-gun bullets all around him, until he found him in a detached dugout some distance from the others. Also, he voluntarily with Gunner Hartley alone kept one gun in action at a most dangerous period.

For bravery in the face of the enemy, Sergeant Cyril Edward Gourley MM was awarded the Victoria Cross. His citation reads:

Number 681886 Sergeant Cyril Edward Gourley, MM, RFA (West Kirby). For most conspicuous bravery when in command of a section of howitzers. Though the enemy advanced in force, getting within four hundred yards in front, between three hundred and four hundred yards to one flank, and with snipers in rear, Sergeant Gourley managed to keep one gun in action practically throughout the day. Though frequently driven off he always returned, carrying ammunition, laying and firing the gun himself, taking first one then another of the detachments to assist him. When the enemy advanced he pulled his gun out of the pit and engaged a machine gun at five hundred yards, knocking it out with a direct hit. All day he held the enemy in check, firing with open sights on enemy parties in full view at three hundred to eight hundred yards, and thereby saved his guns, which were withdrawn at nightfall. He had previously been awarded the Military Medal for conspicuous gallantry.

That evening, with the German offensive driving back the 55th Division, the two guns were manhandled down to the road to Lempire, where they were met by limbers and taken away to safety. Sergeant Gourley saved his guns. Little Priel Farm was overrun by the stormtroopers during the night, but was retaken the following morning.

'Cyril has done something very great this time,' wrote Irvine Gourley to his parents a few weeks later, 'much better than last time but you will hear about it later.' Irvine, a year older than Cyril, had also taken part in the Cambria offensive with the 278th Brigade. Cyril did not write to his parents to explain what he had done, but simply posted off to them the card he had received from his commanding officer which notified him that he had been recommended for the Victoria Cross.

On 5 January 1918, while the division was undergoing retraining at Bomy, Sergeant Gourley, no longer impaired by faulty hearing and eyesight, was finally granted a commission, as a second lieutenant, RFA. Notification of the award of the Victoria Cross came in the *London Gazette* of 13 February, when the division was on the march to take up positions near Givenchy. Once in position, Gourley was granted home leave to receive the award and to see his family.

News of his homecoming spread quickly throughout Merseyside and was widely reported in the local press; and in Hoylake and West Kirkby the local dignitaries hastily began dusting off robes and wiping clean china services to prepare for civic receptions to take place in the afternoon of Saturday, 2 March. Unfortunately, Cyril Gourley VC MM, did not arrive on Merseyside until the Sunday, according to his parents, and the events had to be postponed until the following week, much to the disappointment of all concerned.

Cyril was essentially a shy and modest man, who did not like or appreciate public acclaim. There is a hint in one of the newspaper reports in the *Liverpool Courier* that he did in fact return home in time to attend the celebrations, but that he got cold feet and would not face the clamour. He did not emerge into the public spotlight until Tuesday, when, accompanied by his parents and sister, Eunice, he was honoured at Liverpool University by the Vice-Chancellor, Sir Alfred Dale, and the student body.

Roared on, cheered and applauded into the hall by the undergraduates, Cyril Gourley VC MM was abashed and tongue-tied. Having been welcomed by the vice-chancellor, who reminded the gathering that his Victoria Cross was the fifth to be earned by former students of the university, Cyril was invited to make a speech. Blushing, he got to his feet and nervously declined to do so; the vice-chancellor, calling for another cheer and round of applause, concluded the celebration. The students carried their hero shoulder high from the hall and sent him on his way to a meeting with the Lord Mayor of the city. The next day, the *Liverpool Echo*, which had christened Arthur Richardson VC 'the shy VC', now named Cyril Gourley VC MM 'the bashful hero'.

Second Lieutenant Cyril Gourley received his Victoria Cross from the hand of King George V at Buckingham Palace on Saturday, 16 March, in a cere-mony that caused a great deal of embarrassment to the top brass in attendance. In reprisal for what he considered to be an unwarranted delay in granting him a commission, he stood to attention before his monarch dressed as a sergeant, rather than as a lieutenant in the RFA. There was a great deal of muttering and coughing and harrumping over this breach in etiquette from the assembled 'geraniums', as the red-flashed staff officers were known to the rank and file. But Lieutenant Gourley VC MM blithely took it in his stride: he had, after all, won the award as a sergeant; and with his eyesight impaired, he had misread his instructions on how to dress for the occasion.

He was greatly relieved to escape the fuss and the public's attention and return to the front at the end of March. There, he knew what he was dealing with and what was expected of him. And he did not have long to wait before his services were called upon again. At Estaires, during the Battle of the Lys, also known as the Fourth Battle of Ypres, his guns were in constant action when the Germans were fought to a standstill during their final, major offensive; and following the action at Hazebrouck, he took part in the advance through the Artois region, finishing the war near Tournai, alongside Arthur Procter VC.

The 55th Division moved up to Brussels after the Armistice, and was disbanded in the spring of 1919. Cyril remained in uniform for another four months and in May he was promoted temporary captain, RFA. He returned to Merseyside the following month and was demobilized. For his services during the war, he received the 1914–15 Star, the British War Medal and the Victory Medal.

Back home, he took time to contemplate his future. He would not return to work with his former employers, Blue Funnel. The company had made no contact with him during the celebrations marking his return in March 1918, and appeared reluctant to have him back on board, which was particularly galling as most employers on Merseyside endeavoured to re-employ former workers who had fought during the war. When it came time for him to earn a living again, he made application to Lever Brothers, the soap manufacturers of Port Sunlight, where he was made most welcome. Not only was it a local firm, but one he was familiar with: throughout the war it was impossible to pick up and read a newspaper without being faced with one of its advertisements, 'The cleanest soap for the cleanest fighters' being the most prominent.

The company was still expanding, not only within Britain, but also worldwide, and he was given a position in the export department, then called the Marketing Advisory Service. He brought to this post the same diligence and intelligence he had shown when with Blue Funnel and became a great success as a salesman. It was largely due to his efforts, to his quiet courteous manner, which, at times could be insistent, and in what must have been the largest sales round in history, that Lever Brothers established markets in the Balkans and Central and South America. For thirty years, Cyril Gourley VC MM travelled through these regions and laboured assiduously to build up the brand name. He also made many good friends on his rounds – but it is doubtful if any of them were aware of the heroic deeds which had won him the Victoria Cross in 1917.

He rarely spoke of his award, but he must have been proud of it and what he had accomplished in his own modest way, and he made a point of attending Victoria Cross celebrations and anniversaries to meet other holders and share experiences. He was present at the afternoon Garden Party at Buckingham Palace in 1920, and met King George V again in 1924 at Wavertree Playground, close to where he had been born, along with Arthur Procter VC, during the review of the 55th West Lancashire Territorial Division on the afternoon of Saturday, 19 July.

Despite his travels abroad, he continued to live at home with his parents and his brother Irvine, with whom he had a very close relationship, cemented in part by their shared battlefield experiences. And, like Irvine, he gave no thought to marriage: he had been inundated with proposals following his award, but had ignored them all, and was content with the single life of a bachelor within the bosom of his family. In 1925, the family moved to a large house, Hill Close, in School Lane, West Kirby, and while living there, he was approached by the district council with the suggestion that School Lane should be renamed Gourley's Lane in his honour. However, he politely refused to allow this; and it was only after his death that the council was able to make the change.

During the Second World War, Cyril Gourley, like Donald Farmer, did duty as a fire-watcher during the blitz when the Luftwaffe attempted to destroy the Merseyside docks. In 1952, he moved to the south of England, living at Grayswood House, Haslemere, Surrey, with his mother, Irvine and spinster sister Eunice. He continued with his very quiet and sheltered life, which was interrupted only once when he was pressed to make another speech in March 1958, on the occasion of his retirement. Mr Morrell, a Director of Lever Brothers, presented him with a silver salver and two decanters; and after describing him as a gentleman in the true sense of the word, asked him to speak. In his usual, blushing manner, Cyril Gourley VC MM barely whispered his thanks.

In retirement, he took on the project of restoring the grounds and gardens of his new home; and most days, regardless of the weather, he could be found out and about on the property, repairing walls and fences, plodding away, doing whatever was needed to be done. Denis Rose, who met him just before his death, recalls he interviewed Cyril at the end of a muddy lane, not far from the cowsheds, and that he was attired in a ragged mackintosh, work trousers and a pair of old army plimsoles. He was never a man for occasions.

When his mother died, Cyril brought her body to West Kirby to be buried with Galbraith at Grange Cemetery. Irvine passed away in 1972, and Eunice and Cyril lived out their days together in Grayswood House. Cyril Edward Gourley VC MM passed away in his sleep at the age of 89 on 31 January 1982. He left instructions with Eunice, who outlived him by a year, to have his body returned to West Kirkby, and he was buried with his parents in the family plot.

He is remembered with a plaque in the Royal Artillery Chapel, Woolwich, a photographic memorial at Grayswood College, Chiddingfold, Surrey, and in the permanent exhibition of local heroes at Birkenhead Town Hall. In 1919, the Cyril Edward Gourley VC Scholarship was established by trust deed and a subscription of £1,500 to provide an annual scholarship award to Liverpool University for students from Calday Grange Grammar School and grammar schools in the area of West Kirby and Hoylake.

In addition to the Victoria Cross, the Military Medal and his campaign medals, Cyril Edward Gourley also received two Coronation Medals, George VI in 1937, and Queen Elizabeth II, 1953, and also the Silver Jubilee Medal of 1977. All his medals are on display at the Royal Regiment of Artillery Museum, Woolwich, London.

Arthur Evans VC
(1891–1936)

Arthur Evans is one of four men to have won the Victoria Cross under an assumed name. He enlisted in the 1st Battalion, King's (Liverpool) Regiment, as 11930 Private Arthur Evans in 1914. But four years later, as 41788 Corporal (Lance Sergeant) Walter Simpson, 6th Battalion, Lincolnshire Regiment, he won the Victoria Cross at Etaing in France. Notice of the award to Walter Simpson appeared in the *London Gazette* of 30 October 1918. And at Vincent Barracks, Valenciennes, on 6 December 1918, he received the Victoria Cross from the hand of King George V.

Evans was a remarkable man: intelligent, adventurous and absolutely fearless, he inspired confidence and respect among the officers and men with whom he served, and engendered deep affection and loyalty in his family and friends. His only real home was the army. He was an affable, handsome individual, 5 feet, 6 inches tall, with brown hair and blue eyes, and he weighed in at 149 pounds with the compact, muscular physique of a Welterweight boxer – though he was a fighter, rather than a boxer, as he proved during the First World War. But he was also something of an enigma, as his name change and service record attest.

He led a peripatetic existence during the First World War, moving at will, apparently, from battalion to battalion. It is doubtful whether any soldier of the conflict did duty with so many different units. Evans claimed he served with five, his sister Eleanor says six, the National Archives place him in a seventh, while Sid Lindsay made the intriguing assertion that in addition to all this army time, he also spent a year in the Merchant Navy.

It is not known for certain when Evans/Simpson joined the 6th Battalion, the Lincolnshire, but he was with that unit at Whitsuntide of 1918 when he visited Eleanor in Bolton on leave; and, on returning to the front, he left her home with a prophetic valediction: 'Nothing will do for me now except the VC. I will bring home the VC and peace.'

Commencing in the early hours of Thursday, 8 August 1918, the 'Hundred Days Offensive' was the final 'Big Push' against the Central Powers on the Western Front. It ended at the eleventh hour, on the eleventh day, of the eleventh month, when Germany capitulated and the First World War came to an end. Lance Sergeant Walter Simpson won the Victoria Cross during that push, in the dash towards the Drocourt–Quéant Switch, known to the Germans as the *Wotanstellung*, an outwork of the northern sector of the Hindenburg Line, east of Arras.

During the spring and early summer of 1918, 6th Battalion had been in action near Loos, but towards the end of August it moved south to Arras, tasked to support the left flank of the Canadian 4th Division. In the early hours of 2 September 1918, it was positioned on the west bank of the River Cojeul, ahead of the Canadians on the opposite bank, who were to attack towards the town of Etaing, where the river ran into the River Sensée; and the Lincolnshire was ordered to keep in close contact with them during the advance by moving forward along the west bank.

A and C Companies of the Lincolnshire took up positions in dugouts ahead of the battalion; and a small patrol from C Company, consisting of Second Lieutenant Barrett, Lance Sergeant Simpson and four other ranks went forward to reconnoitre the ground ahead. Simpson led the party through a small stand of trees, Galley Woods, without encountering any opposition. But, on emerging from the trees, he spotted an enemy machine-gun post and a sentry 400 yards ahead on the opposite bank of the river. Lieutenant Barrett decided to investigate. Where the patrol stood the river was 20 feet wide and too deep to ford, and Simpson volunteered to search out a suitable crossing place.

There was good brush cover on the bank, and Simpson crawled forward undetected beyond the sentry to a point where he could cross. He stripped off his uniform, and armed with a revolver only, forded the river. As the German sentry gazed off to the south watching for the advancing Canadians, Simpson crept up from the rear and shot him dead. A second German at the post tried to rush Simpson, but he killed him also. In his stride, he then dashed into the dugout behind the machine gun where he found four more of the enemy, who threw down their weapons and surrendered immediately.

From the opposite bank of the river, Lieutenant Barrett spied two more of the enemy attempting to escape from the rear of another bunker; and he ordered his men to open fire. The two fleeing Germans were quickly brought down. Simpson then sent his prisoners across the river to Barrett via a wooden causeway to the rear of the bunker. Leaving them in the custody of two of his men, Barrett crossed the river with the other two to join Simpson.

Surveying the terrain ahead, Lieutenant Barrett could see no signs of enemy activity, and he ordered Simpson forward for further reconnaissance along the bank of the Cojeul. Some 70 yards from the machine-gun post, Simpson came across a slit trench. Stealthily, he infiltrated the line but found it empty, and he waved for the patrol to come on. A second and third trench in the distance caught his eye, but they too appeared deserted. And when Barrett brought up the men, he set off again to scout them.

He had advanced only 20 yards when he spotted a blur of movement ahead and dropped to the ground. Peering through the underbrush, he saw there were Germans in the lines; and before he could communicate a warning, they attacked with machine-gun and rifle fire. The earth around him was pounded with flying lead and the covering of shrub was torn apart. Lieutenant Barrett was shot in the thigh and collapsed to the ground.

Forced to hug the ground by the withering hail, Simpson wriggled and slithered on his stomach back the way he had come, reaching the slit trench and his comrades without injury. As Barrett was unconscious he took command. Designating the two men as bearers, he armed himself with a rifle and gave covering fire while they hauled and dragged the unconscious officer through the thick brush to the wooden causeway. Once they were under cover there, Simpson retreated from his own position and made the perilous dash under fire to join them.

He dispatched Private Boughton to the opposite bank to find and bring back the other two men of the patrol and the German prisoners to help carry the wounded officer to safety. Meanwhile, he and Private Charles Alletson returned fire on the Germans, some of whom were now creeping forward in small groups, and they stood their ground until Barrett was ferried to safety. Then he ordered Private Alletson to the opposite bank and kept up the covering fire alone. Only when all the men were secure on the west bank did he make his escape and lead the patrol back to the battalion's position. Second Lieutenant Barrett survived his wound, but Private Boughton was wounded in the final retreat and died later in hospital.

For conspicuous bravery in the face of the enemy, Lance Sergeant Walter Simpson was awarded the Victoria Cross. His citation reads:

Walter Simpson, Number 41788, Corporal (Lance Sergeant) 6th Battalion, Lincolnshire Regiment. For most conspicuous bravery and initiative when with a daylight patrol sent out to reconnoitre and to gain touch with a neighbouring division. When on the west bank of a river an enemy machine-gun post was sighted on the east bank. The river being too deep to force, Sergeant Simpson volunteered to swim across, and, having done so, crept up alone in the rear of the machine-gun post. He shot the sentry and also a second enemy who ran out; he then turned and caused four to surrender. A crossing over the river was subsequently found, and the officer and one man of the patrol joined him, and reconnaissance was continued along the river bank. After proceeding some distance machine-gun and rifle fire was opened on the patrol, and the officer was wounded. In spite of the fact that no cover was available, Sergeant Simpson succeeded in covering the withdrawal of the wounded officer under most dangerous and difficult conditions, and under heavy fire. The success of the patrol, which cleared up a machine-gun post on the flank of the attacking troops of a neighbouring division and obtained an identification, was greatly due to the very gallant conduct of Sergeant Simpson.

The award of the Victoria Cross to Walter Simpson was published in the *London Gazette* on 30 October 1918. But before the news reached the front line, he was involved in a second daring feat of arms, almost as meritorious as the first. Following the assault on Etaing and the breaching of the Drocourt-Quéant Switch, the 6th Battalion continued to support the Canadians. Simpson took part in the fierce fighting for the Canal du Nord, behind which the retreating Germans had rallied. And by the beginning of October, the battalion had advanced from the canal to lines south-west of the village of Aubencheul-au-Bac, approximately five miles to the north-west of Cambrai, preparing to descend on the town during the Second Battle of Le Cateau.

Orders were received at battalion headquarters that Aubencheul-au-Bac was to be taken by 7 October, the day before the battle was to commence. At ten o'clock on the night of 6 October, A and C Companies of the 6th Battalion set out to capture the village and if possible to establish outposts along the Canal-de-la-Sensée. The night was dark and misty, the terrain unknown, but stealthily the two companies converged on the village without mishap. Fortunately, the enemy patrols had been withdrawn.

Lance Sergeant Simpson led a platoon from C Company to scout the lie of the land in front of the canal. But, in the pitch darkness, the platoon stumbled upon a heavily defended enemy outpost. Simpson reacted quickly: before the Germans could draw a bead on the intruders, he charged the position followed by his men; and in a short, sharp exchange, ten Germans were killed and several wounded without casualties to the patrol. He had the foresight to take a prisoner and bring him in for interrogation. The captive belonged to a special party of pioneers detailed to cut through the bank of the canal and flood the surrounding countryside to slow the Allied advance. With this information to hand, the Allies were able to invest the canal zone with sufficient men to avert the flooding.

For his courageous leadership and initiative, Lance Sergeant Simpson was awarded the Distinguished Conduct Medal, which was gazetted on 2 December 1918. His citation reads:

For great courage and initiative near Cambrai. He was in charge of a platoon acting as a fighting patrol on the night 6/7th October 1918, with instructions to clear the country north of the Château of Aubencheul-au-Bac to the Canal-de-la-Sensée. A strong enemy post was encountered. He promptly rushed the post killing ten, wounding several, and taking one prisoner. The prisoner secured afforded most valuable information. He has shown excellent leadership and the utmost disregard of all danger.

Simpson and the 6th Battalion remained in the thick of the fighting until the end of the war. From Aubencheul-au-Bac the battalion fought along the Cambrai–Valenciennes Road, before breaking away to the east, towards the Maubeuge–Mons Road, and crossing the frontier from France into Belgium near Aulnois. On 10 November 1918, the battalion advanced into the town of L'Ermitage; and the next day, following the announcement of the Armistice, moved peacefully and joyfully into billets at Quevy-le-Grand, five miles south of Mons. Home beckoned.

But the dole queue also was beckoning to the thousands of brave servicemen returning to Britain at the end of hostilities, even men honoured with the Victoria Cross. The regiment he had served so gallantly, however, did not let down Walter Simpson VC: he was given a lifeline and remained in uniform with the Lincolnshire, working as a regimental clerk. He reverted to his real name, and the *London Gazette* of 31 March 1919 published an amendment to his award: the name of Walter Simpson was stricken from the record and replaced with Arthur Evans.

It was not until 19 November 1921 that he was transferred to the reserve and was discharged from the army. Out of work but with money in his pockets, he was given a home by Eleanor in Bolton, where he stayed until the summer of the following year, contemplating his future. This arrived in the form of employment as a clerk in a branch of Lloyds Bank in Wimbledon, London. Packing his bags, he headed south to new horizons, and found digs locally at 20 St George's Road. And, as luck would have it, he found a wife at the same address. He courted Ellen Maud Whitaker, from Brentford, Middlesex, the daughter of Thomas Whitaker, a journeyman brass moulder and finisher. The couple married at Kingston Register Office on 9 April 1924.

But his luck did not come in threes. Just before his marriage, he became a bank messenger with direct access to cash at the British Empire Exhibition Branch of Lloyds in Wembley. On the night of 9 July 1924, Arthur Evans VC was arrested; and on 28 July he appeared before Wealdonstone Police Court, charged under the Larcency Act of 1916 with the theft of £500 from his employer, a crime punishable by a term of imprisonment not exceeding five years.

He elected to be dealt with summarily in a lower court, the police court, nowadays the magistrates' court, and submitted a statement in defence: he had been led astray and duped by a second party whom the bank trusted, and he had not gained financially from the theft. Lloyds Bank gave the impression it had been reluctant to prosecute, but that the sum involved had forced its hand. The prosecution claimed Evans alone had taken the money, which had not been recovered, but added he had voluntarily alerted the authorities to its loss and had readily admitted his guilt. Several testimonials to his previous good character were submitted to the Bench, together with details of his exceptional war service. Justice was done; and as a first offender, he was 'bound over to be of good behaviour for twelve months in the sum of £10'.

The matter did not end there, however. Called upon in his defence, that very same honourable war record was responsible for his public disgrace. A lesser man in his position would have received no publicity, but the scandal of a dishonoured hero was widely reported in the media. He lost his good name and his job; and, with his reputation in tatters, his prospects of work at a time of high unemployment were nil. His world in ruins, he decided to emigrate and start anew.

Mrs and Mrs Arthur Evans arrived in New Zealand in January 1925, taking up residence in the town of Tauranga on the Bay of Plenty, in the north-east of North Island. The New Zealanders saw only a hero, and he had no problems finding work. Armstrong Whitworth and Company was a British firm contracted on several huge engineering projects for the government in Wellington, and hired him as a clerk during the contruction of the east coast main trunk railway line. Six months later, however, the lure of the colours drew him back into uniform: he attested to the New Zealand Army on 1 July 1925, and was made welcome with the rank of staff sergeant with Southern Command, based in Christchurch.

Staff Sergeant Arthur Evans VC became part of a cadre of approximately 500 men of the Permanent Force, full-time soldiers responsible for the training of the New Zealand Territorial Force, which numbered 20,000. Back in his element and doing what he did best, instructing and leading men, he served for a year in Greymouth, on the west coast of South Island, before transferring to Blenheim in the north-east; and as sub-area sergeant major he served with the 'terriers' of the Nelson, Marlborough and West Coast Regiments. Ellen Maud was also content, settling in and making a home, and the happy couple tried for a family.

On 25 November 1927, Arthur quit the Permanent Force. His resignation and subsequent move to Australia were for health reasons: the New Zealand climate did not suit him, and he was afflicted and incapacitated with chest problems and stomach pains. He moved to Sydney in 1928, and lived in the eastern suburb of Randwick; and it is thought he reverted to his old trade of clerking.

His health improved in the drier climate of Australia, so much so that after four years of intermittent illness he felt encouraged to return once more to the colours. On 17 October 1932, he enlisted as 311052 Private Arthur Evans VC in the newly formed Australian Tank Corps. Once again, he was back in the milieu where he found the greatest pleasure, wearing a uniform among men he understood, men he could teach and lead, and sharing in the rough and tumble of army life. Within weeks of enlistment he was promoted to sergeant, and six months later, he became staff sergeant.

What is more, after nine years of trying for a family, he and Ellen Maud were blessed with a son, Arthur George, born in 1933. In that year, life could not have been better for Arthur Evans: a loving wife, a son to dandle and listen to his adventurous tales, a secure position in the army and a host of new friends. The black clouds, however, were now descending rapidly, and the First World War fingered another casualty across time and distance.

Arthur Evans VC was discharged from the Australian Tank Corps because of ill health on 13 March 1934. The stomach pains that had afflicted him for several years were diagnosed as carcinoma of the bowel, induced by a mustard gas attack he suffered seventeen years earlier. In January 1936, he was admitted to the Prince of Wales Hospital in Randwick, and after many tests and several operations, the medical staff could offer only comfort. He clung bravely to life, displaying yet again the raw courage and determination that had made him such a hero in France. Sergeant Fuz, a fellow sergeant in the Tank Corps, made regular visits to his bedside, and reported it was Evans that usually cheered him up rather than the other way around. On 1 November 1936, Arthur Evans VC died from cardiac failure, complicated by carcinoma of the bowel. He was 45 years of age.

On 3 November, thousands of people lined the streets of Sydney as his coffin, drawn on a gun carriage and preceded by the band of the Royal Australian Artillery, passed on its last journey to the train that would carry it to Rookwood Crematorium. Seven Victoria Cross holders formed an honour guard, and a firing-party from the Australian Tank Corps fired a volley with revolvers over the grave as the ashes of Arthur Evans were laid to rest by his wife and son.

There the story of Arthur Evans VC should have ended. But, behind the scenes, his elder brother James lobbied successfully for the return of the remains to England. A year later, Arthur Sullivan VC, a member of the Australian Victoria Cross contingent attending the Coronation of King George VI, carried them to Lytham St Anne's, Lancashire, where James was living. At Lytham St Anne's Park Cemetery on Monday, 29 March 1927, the ashes of Arthur Evans VC were reburied with full military honours in the grave of his brother John, who had died in 1933. James Evans and his son Noel led the mourners, accompanied by Anne Evans, widow of John Evans, and Sarah McCann, aunt and godmother to Arthur Evans VC. Sadly, the tale continued: twelve days later, Arthur Sullivan VC died in London, when he slipped and fell in Birdcage Walk. After a military funeral, his ashes were carried home to his wife, Dorothy, in Sydney by the returning Australian contingent.

Arthur Evans was born on 8 April 1891 at 33 Caradoc Road, Seaforth, the son of Robert and Eleanor Ann Evans; and Arthur Evans was born on 8 April 1891, at 67 Landseer Road, Everton, the son of Ada and Arthur Ryland Evans. Both births were recorded in the Registration District of West Derby, Liverpool. Some of the confusion over the birthplace of Arthur Evans VC – the authoritative *Register of the Victoria Cross*, for example, has him born in Everton – and the errors in his army service record stem from this coincidence of births.

Arthur Evans VC was born in Seaforth. His father, Robert, came from Wigan and lived for a time in Wales before moving to Liverpool to work as a timekeeper on the docks. In 1879, he married Eleanor McCann from Everton, daughter of Samuel and Ellen McCann who both hailed from Antrim, Northern Ireland. The young couple lived for several years with Eleanor's widowed father, at 16 Myrtle Street, Birkenhead, where their first three children were born.

Sarah did not survive infancy, and second-born Eleanor became the eldest, and the historian of the family. John Robert, known in the family as Jack, came next, followed by James Arnold. In 1890, the family moved across the Mersey to Seaforth, where Arthur and Alice Evans were born, and where, in 1914, several battalions of the Liverpools were to be raised.

All accounts of the early life of Arthur Evans are derived exclusively from an interview given by Eleanor Evans to the *Bolton Journal and Guardian* on 1 November 1918, following the announcement of the award of the Victoria Cross to Lance Sergeant Walter Simpson. He had named Eleanor, who was living at 99 Davenport Street, Bolton, as his next of kin. His younger sister Alice also lived in Bolton, at 48 Church Street, together with John and James, who were then serving with 11th Battalion, the Liverpools. Because of the difference in surnames, Evans and Simpson, and wishing to remain loyal to her brother and to preserve the secret of why he was fighting under an assumed name, Eleanor referred to her heroic brother throughout the interview as her 'stepbrother' Walter Simpson.

According to Eleanor, when he left school in 1905, his father placed him in an office job in Liverpool. But young Walter was of a restless, adventurous disposition, and the pace of the office routine did not suit him. He quit his job and joined the Royal Navy as a stoker, but was invalided out after breaking a couple of ribs in an accident. Recovering from his injuries, he tried his hand in the Merchant Navy as a trimmer and fireman. But on his first trip he jumped ship in New York and travelled across America before heading down to Central America, where he worked on the construction of the Panama Canal, overseeing a 1,000-strong gang of labourers. Tiring of that experience, he moved on in company with a Scotsman and an Australian to explore the jungles of Central and South America, where he contracted malaria, and had to be carried to the coast by native bearers for treatment.

After convalescing, he ventured to Cuba and back to America, living in Detroit and Buffalo and Niagara Falls, taking any job he could find in order to finance his travels. In 1912, he headed home and took a berth on a four-masted sailing ship out of New York, sailing to England via Australia, a journey which took a year to complete. Arriving in Liverpool at the end of 1913 after an absence of six years, he found his family had moved to Bolton, where his enterprising father had found work as an accountant in a cotton mill shortly before his death in 1910. Walter lodged with Eleanor for several months and then joined the 1st Battalion, the Liverpools, three weeks before the outbreak of the war. He was wounded in action in 1915, and before winning the Victoria Cross served with five other regiments, was gassed in 1917 and mistakenly reported as killed in action the following year.

Arthur Evans VC never spoke to the media, nor did he ever put pen to paper to record his exploits. Despite his problem with the bank, he was an honest man, and would not have intentionally misled anyone. Eleanor's account, based upon what she knew and what she heard from her brother, and allowing for one or two embellishments, is a good approximation to the truth. However, the detail she gives of his army service is at odds with the version he himself was to give when he attested to the New Zealand Army in 1925, and which recent research has confirmed.

Enlisting under his real name in 1st Battalion, the Liverpools, three months, rather than three weeks, before the outbreak of war, Arthur Evans saw action with the BEF at Mons, the retreat to the River Marne, the stand-off at the River Aisne and the First Battle of Ypres. He was, therefore, a member of that elite group of fighting men who are known to military history as 'the Old Contemptibles'. As detailed in his army papers and copied to his New Zealand attestation papers, he was in receipt of what is popularly, but incorrectly, known as the Mons Star, the 1914 Star, with clasp and rose, which was given only to 'the Old Contemptibles'. The rose was worn on the medal ribbon to distinguish it from the later 1914–15 Star.

The same papers also show he was promoted to Lance Corporal with the Liverpools and was wounded in action at the Battle of Festubert in May 1915. He was also mentioned for honourable service in the dispatches of General Sir John French of 22 June. But, after hospitalization for the wound in Manchester, he left the Liverpools. Sid Lindsay claimed he deserted the regiment to join the Merchant Marine, but the records show he immediately re-enlisted under the name of Walter Simpson in the Devonshire Regiment. Why he did so and why he used a *nom de guerre* has never been discovered. In total, he served, as he said, with five regiments only, and being placed in a sixth and seventh, in particular the 32nd London Regiment, can be accounted for by his having the same birthdate as the Arthur Evans born in Everton.

From the Devonshire Regiment, he transferred to the 243rd Training Reserve Battalion. But, by the autumn of 1916, he was with 3rd Battalion, the Lincolnshire Regiment, and saw home duty in Ireland in the wake of the Easter Rising. No date is given in his papers for his final transfer, but in 1917 he moved from the 3rd to the 6th Battalion, the Lincolnshire. He had come full circle: having fought in the First Battle of Ypres with the Liverpools, he was to take part in the Third with the Lincolnshire.

On 9 October 1917, as the Allied troops slogged forward through the flowing mud aiming for Passchendaele, the heavily fortified village of Poelcapelle blocked their path and became the focus of attack. The 6th Battalion, the Lincolnshire, did not participate in the assault on the village but remained in support trenches for two days under continuous artillery attack. Some of the German shells that landed in the trenches contained the chemical agent known as mustard gas. And Arthur Evans fell victim to this insidious killer. After Poelcapelle, he was a dead man walking.

He was taken out of the lines, and so severe were his injuries he was re-patriated to England, to Bath, for treatment. Outwardly, he healed; and after convalescence he was granted leave over the Whitsuntide holiday of 1918, which he spent in Bolton with Eleanor, before returning to the front to win the Victoria Cross. Though lethal in only 1 per cent of cases, and while the acute effects of temporary blindness and skin blistering could be successfully treated, the mustard gas was carcinogenic, and many soldiers who suffered exposure to the agent were to die years later from a variety of cancers. Arthur Evans VC was such a victim. His death in Australia in 1936 was attributable to the gas attack at Poelcapelle.

Arthur Evans VC was a heroic soldier and a very able leader of men. A fearless adventurer, by the age of 22 he had travelled the world and witnessed one of the twentieth century's greatest engineering achievements, the con-struction of the Panama Canal. He fought valiantly on the Western Front, for which he received the honours of the Victoria Cross, the Distinguished Conduct Medal, the 1914 Star, with clasp and rose, the British War Medal and the Victory Medal. He was also human, and made mistakes, one of which could have sent him to prison, and which led him to forsake the city and country of his birth. He died, in a sense, in exile. His consolation was a loving wife and a son, and the respect of all who knew him.

Nothing is known of his son, Arthur George. There were rumours that Ellen Maud returned to England with her son following the death of her husband, rumours which apparently received confirmation with the transfer of her husband's ashes to England in 1937. But she has not been heard of since that year. The medals of Arthur Evans VC are in private hands. It is believed his Victoria Cross retains the original inscription, and is made out in the name of Walter Simpson.

Frank Lester VC
(1896–1918)

Frank Lester and George Hall were inseparable pals during the First World War: they transferred at the same time to their battalion, fought alongside each other, went home on leave together and, on 21 March 1918, were both wounded in action. They made a compact that if one was killed the survivor would contact the other's family to explain what had happened. Tragically, their contract was stillborn: reunited at the front after hospitalization, they were killed on the same day, on the same battlefield, a month before the Armistice was announced. Corporal Frank Lester died in the village of Neuvilly, France, knowing that the life of his best friend, like his own, had been forfeited that day. His unselfish courage in that tiny French hamlet was acknowledged with the award of a posthumous Victoria Cross.

The origins of the Lester family are in the Potteries, in the six towns of Tunstall, Burslem, Hanley, Stoke, Fenton and Longton, which nowadays make up the city of Stoke-on-Trent, Staffordshire. A local pottery industry utilizing native clay and coal had developed in the seventeenth century, producing earthenware known as creamware. But, with the introduction of china clay from Cornwall, the region was transformed by the genius of Josiah Wedgwood into a hub for the production of high-quality, decorative porcelain, which became renowned throughout the world.

The opening of the Trent–Mersey canal in 1777 brought some of Wedgwood's booming production to Liverpool, which had, since the 1750s, been one of the world's leading centres for printing patterns and decorations on pottery. However, the city was not content simply to provide decorative prints for china from elsewhere and sought to develop its own distinctive Liverpool school of pottery and porcelain. Several potteries sprang up on Merseyside, but it was the Herculaneum Pot Works in Toxteth that led the enterprise, producing fine-quality earthenware and porcelain tea and dinner services, punch bowls, jugs, mugs, plates and figurines, all thrown by experienced potters brought in for their expertise from the Potteries. The Herculaneum was successful for many years and had good markets locally and in America. But, under pressure from cheaper rivals, it began to founder, and even the further introduction of skilled craftsmen from the six towns failed to halt the decline, and so the kilns were finally extinguished in 1841. Other, smaller potteries continued working for several years, but the industry would eventually disappear from Liverpool.

John Lester was born in Stoke in 1809. A potter by trade, he was one of the hundreds of journeyman potters who came to work in Liverpool. He married Ann Pitt from St Helens and settled nearby to bring up a family of four sons. Three of them, Henry, John and Richard, followed him into the pottery trade, and the fourth, George, was apprenticed as a watchmaker, a booming cottage industry in that part of Lancashire at the time.

George Lester married Elizabeth Davies, a midwife from St Helens, in 1864, and lived for a time in Whiston and later Huyton. He fathered ten children, most notably, John, Robert and Lillie. The Lesters were a robust, Nonconformist family, and worshipped at the Congregational Church in Huyton, not far from where they resided at 37 Richardsons Lane. George's eldest son, John, born in 1868, was an active churchgoer throughout his life; and his son, Frank Lester VC, was to follow his example.

By the time John Lester was born, not only was the pottery industry in sharp decline, but his father's trade, that of watchmaker, was also failing, due to the collapse of the markets in America; and there were precious few opportunities for apprenticeships in the area. John found work as a general labourer after leaving school, and later worked alongside his uncle Richard, who had forsaken pot-making for glass-making, as a stoker in the furnace room of Pilkington Brothers of St Helens, glass-makers *sans pareil*. He courted Ellen Heyes, who was born in June 1870 in Aughton, near Ormskirk. She was the daughter of Henry and Lucy Heyes, and as a young girl she worked as a dressmaker. When her father died, her mother took her to live at 225 Baker Street, Huyton, a short walk from John Lester's home.

The couple married in the summer of 1892, and their first child, Edwin, arrived in September the following year. Frank Lester was born on 18 February 1896 in West View, Huyton Quarry. John Lester's younger brother, George, worked as a market gardener after leaving school; and perhaps it was his example that led John to try his hand in the same business. After the birth of his sons, he relocated the family, including his widowed mother, Elizabeth, across the River Mersey to 28 Rudd Street, Hoylake, and began working as a market gardener.

At the time, Hoylake, situated on the north-east coast of the Wirral Peninsula overlooking the Irish Sea and the Dee estuary, and home to the historic Royal Liverpool Golf Club, was undergoing rapid growth: its population would increase fivefold in ten years following the advent of the railways. Merseysiders sought the dual delights of a spa town on the coast and an unspoilt, rural hinterland, and John Lester found a thriving market.

John and Ellen Lester had four more children in their new home: Lucy, George, who did not survive infancy, John, known to the family as Jack, and Ruth. The Lesters were a very close-knit, Christian family, with strong ties to the Church. Parents and children excelled in music, and mother and father were excellent vocalists and members of the choirs of the local Congregational Church and the Hoylake Temperance Society. Young Frank's forte was the organ, which he learnt to play at an early age.

The children were educated at Hoylake National School in Trinity Road and passed through without remark. Frank was an average student, more inclined towards the practical than the academic, and he set his mind on a trade in carpentry. He joined the 1st Hoylake Company of the Boys' Brigade, the uniformed youth movement founded in Glasgow in 1883 by Sir William Alexander Smith, and dedicated to the upbringing and development of boys in a Christian environment. Frank was a member of the brigade for several years, and he was to learn and develop many of the skills which would hold him in good stead as a soldier and leader of men during the war. Apprenticed as a joiner to a local firm, F. Thomas, at Oxton, after he left school in 1910 aged 14, he continued membership in the Boys' Brigade, and his talent as an organist was put to good use most Sundays in the Irby Methodist Chapel, known locally as the 'Tin Tabernacle', because of its construction from corrugated iron sheets. In 1912, when John Lester moved the family to Mill Hill Road, Miller's Hay, in Irby, a small village four miles south of Hoylake to accommodate his growing business, Frank gave up his apprenticeship to work with his father as a market gardener.

Like his father, he was a strapping man more than 6 feet tall, with broad shoulders and a strong physique developed by working long hours in the fields. With his sociable disposition he made friends easily and had about him a presence, an air of authority and command, which made him stand out in a crowd. He became a familiar figure in the Wirral and across the river in Liverpool at the wholesale vegetable, fruit and flower market in Cazneau Street. Three times a week during the spring and summer, on Tuesdays, Thursdays and Fridays, he would load his father's cart with produce, hitch up the horse and by half past two in the morning would be on the road, crossing the Wirral Peninsula to the floating landing stage at Woodside. There he met up with other producers heading to the city. The tang of the salt air from the Mersey would be lost in the aroma of freshly dug vegetables and the sweet fragrance of thousands of blossoms, which the flower growers of Greasby were carting to market. They would board the luggage boat, the ferry which took vehicular traffic, and before dawn they were on their way to the Pier Head.

In 1847, the first floating landing stage, which rose and fell with the tide, was built at what became known as the Pier Head on Mann Island, allowing ferries to berth at any time. It was later developed into a huge floating structure, for many years the largest in the world: at the northern end was Princes Landing Stage, where the great liners of the Cunard, White Star and Canadian–Pacific fleets berthed; the south end, George's Landing Stage, marked the Pier Head, and here the local ferries tied up. In the 1880s, a floating roadway was constructed to George's Landing Stage, which permitted vehicles access to the stage and the cross-river ferries.

Frank Lester would lead his horse and cart from the luggage boat and onto the stage, then up the floating roadway and through the city centre and into Scotland Road. He would cross into Cazneau Street and the wholesale market, which extended into Collingwood, Great Nelson and Great Homer Streets. He would try to arrive before six o'clock in order to obtain a good pitch, and he would remain until all the produce was sold. It is possible he did business with Arthur Procter, who was working at the time as a wholesale buyer for Wilson Brothers; both men were living on the Wirral side of the Mersey.

When war broke out, Frank Lester's work as a market gardener was classified as a reserved, or starred, occupation, a job deemed essential to the upkeep of the home front, and he did not immediately volunteer his services to the war effort. His cousin George from Huyton was the first of the Lesters in uniform, and the family's first casualty. His death was a great blow to Frank, who had been his friend since childhood.

George Lester enlisted in the 1st Battalion, Lancashire Fusiliers, and fought in Gallipoli, landing on W Beach, Cape Helles, when the battalion won six Victoria Crosses 'before breakfast'. George survived the fighting on the peninsula, but following the disaster of Scimitar Hill in August, the last battle of the campaign, he, like Albert White, was left to fend for himself in the harsh winter that engulfed the peninsula, while the generals discussed their next move.

Towards the end of November, every gully and ravine, every trench and fortification, was turned into roaring waterways and torrents, lethal man-traps following heavy rain and blinding snowstorms. On 27 November 1915, the Lancashire Fusiliers in Gully Ravine reported 4 feet of surging water raging through their lines; and twenty men, among them Private George Lester, were carried away in the rapids and drowned. He is remembered on the Helles Memorial, Gallipoli, and on the war memorial in Huyton.

Frank Lester enlisted on 30 March 1916 in the 10th (Reserve) Battalion, South Lancashire Regiment (SLR). From his first day in uniform, he made a huge impression on both officers and men. His physical stature, his presence, his air of confidence, and, in addition, his natural ease with men and the ability to give and take orders, legacies of the drill and discipline with the Boys' Brigade, were looked on most favourably by his superiors. He was marked down as a man who could be of great assistance in the training of new recruits; and he was sent to Chelsea Military School to train as an instructor. There, he lived up to expectations and proved himself, qualifying as a sergeant instructor and passing out with the highest honours.

While he trained and studied at the Military School, universal military conscription was introduced in May 1916, which applied to all men, single or married, between the ages of 18 and 41. This sudden surge in the numbers of men needing basic instruction and training overwhelmed the regimental system, and at the beginning of September 1916, the regimental reserve battalions were reorganized and designated as Training Reserve (TR) units. Frank Lester's battalion became the 51st Battalion, TR. He lost his regimental distinctions, dropping the regimental cap badge and shoulder titles, and wore in place a general service button on a red disc on his cap, and the letters TR on his shoulders.

He joined the new unit at Prees Heath Military Training Camp in Shropshire, close to the town of Whitchurch, and spent most of his time as an instructor there, and meeting his friend George Hall. The camp had been set up in 1915 on commandeered common land, part of which was transformed into a small-scale front line. Trenches and dugouts were constructed similar to those on the Western Front, and the new recruits trained and, at times, lived, in them. The training was very tough, for nothing could possibly replicate the harshness of trench warfare the men would have to face overseas, and the instructors drove the recruits relentlessly through their paces in an effort to prepare them.

From Prees Heath, Frank Lester moved to a larger camp, Kimmel Park, near Abergele, North Wales, and after several weeks of duty there, he decided to give up his role as instructor. He could have seen out the war there, for his services were invaluable to his superiors. However, he felt he could do more to help the war effort by fighting on the front line, as his cousin and brother had done, following in the footsteps of the men he had trained. In June 1917, he applied for a transfer to a fighting unit, and joined 10th (Service) Battalion, Lancashire Fusiliers. George Hall, who lived at 222 New Chester Road, Port Sunlight, a few miles from the Lester home in Irby, had just completed his basic training at Prees Heath, and, having kept in contact with his former instructor, joined the battalion at the same time.

At the turn of the year, Frank Lester was reduced in rank, the norm when being posted overseas, and journeyed across the Channel, joining the Battalion as 51674 Private Frank Lester. With his pal George, he went into trenches near the village of Havrincourt, five miles to the south-west of Cambrai, in front of the formidable defences of the *Siegfriedstellung* sector of the Hindenburg Line. The two chums arrived in time to be battered and wounded during the course of 'Operation Michael', the first of four attacks of General Erich Ludendorff's Spring Offensive, the last gamble by the Germans to defeat the Allies before the human and *matériel* resources of the United States could be deployed: General 'Black Jack' Pershing would arrive in Liverpool on 8 June 1917 aboard RMS *Baltic* to lead his American doughboys against the Central Powers.

On 21 March, reinforced by sixty divisions released from the Russian Front, Ludendorff unleashed his army along a ten-mile front. Specially trained German stormtroopers attacked swiftly under a heavy but brief artillery barrage, and, bypassing any strongly held positions, infiltrated in small detachments all along the front line, followed by the bulk of the infantry. Frank Lester and the 10th Lancashires held a section of the front at Havrincourt, which was invested by the stormtroopers; and when the German infantry attacked, the line wavered as fire was brought to bear from the front, the rear and the flanks. Ground was lost at first, and then regained in fierce fighting, and Frank Lester and George Hall were both wounded. But they kept on fighting. The front was in chaos and ceased to exist: units were overrun, men became detached and were disorientated and confused, many of them losing their way to stumble into captivity. That night, orders were given to fall back.

For the next week, the Allies continued to withdraw, and they retreated, five miles, then ten, then fifteeen, back through the old Somme battlefields, fighting rearguard actions near towns and villages which had been won at such huge costs in 1916 – Le Transloy, Flers, Courcelette, Fricourt, Guillemont. All the way back they came, all the way to Albert, where the line steadied and was stabilized, and where the 'Michael' steamroller was eventually brought to a grinding halt.

At Albert, 10th Battalion Lancashire Fusiliers took stock: Frank Lester and George Ball were two of only 300 men from a strength of 1,000 to answer roll call. And because of their wounds, they were shipped off to one of the RAMC hospitals in Rouen, Normandy, for treatment. Frank made a full recovery and returned to his unit temporarily and gained promotion to corporal. However, the battalion was in the reserve lines, awaiting replacements after sustaining so many losses; and in July, he was returned to England, where he was stationed at Cromer, in Norfolk.

It is not known for certain what he did at Cromer, but it is thought that his previous experience as instructor was called upon, and that he assisted in the final training of some of the reinforcements destined to refill the ranks of the battalion. By the time he returned to the front in September, the 'Hundred Days Offensive' had been launched, General 'Black Jack' Pershing's American Expeditionary Force was now in action, and the German Army was being pushed back on all fronts, back to the Hindenburg Line again.

The town of Cambrai, a major railhead and supply depot for the Hindenburg Line, and the town of Le Cateau to the south-east, had been in the Allies' sights in March, prior to the 'Spring Offensive'. Now, in September, as the Allies stoked up the 'Hundred Days Offensive', their capture was once more on the agenda. Frank Lester and the battalion were tasked with the capture of Gouzeaucourt, to the south-west of Le Cateau, and on 9 September, under a rolling barrage, the men went into action. At first, inroads were made against the defences, but then the wounded animal that was the German Army turned and snapped at its pursuers before the gains could be consolidated; and Frank Lester once more found himself backtracking in the face of determined opposition. It would be another nine days before the village fell, when, during a lightning strike, the battalion threw back the Germans, who now appeared dispirited, as if they had given up the fight.

Corporal Frank Lester and Private George Hall had been in the thick of the action on both occasions at Gouzeaucourt, and luckily neither had been wounded. The offensive was halted for two weeks while the Allies brought up men and *matériel* for the final thrust against the Hindenburg Line. In the trenches, as the nights grew longer and colder and Christmas approached, the sentiment among the men was that it would be this Christmas, the Christmas of 1918, which would see an end to hostilities. Confidence was high: the German Army did not want to fight any more, and it would be all downhill from now on. But a wounded animal is at its most dangerous when cornered.

In the first week of October, the Allied offensive resumed. The 10th Battalion advanced from Gouzeaucourt and penetrated the Hindenburg Line in the Gonnelieu-Banteux sector. In the north, Cambrai fell on 8 October; and, two days later, Le Cateau succumbed. Corporal Frank Lester and his jubilant comrades crossed the Cambrai–Le Cateau Road at Inchy, and the following day the village was captured. From Inchy, the drive would continue to the River Selle, to throw back the fleeing Germans against the Belgian frontier. In the evening, while the men cleared out the remnants of the German defenders and consolidated their lines, orders came through that the battalion would move out from Inchy and continue the advance against Neuvilly in the morning.

Neuvilly was a mile and a half to the north-east of Inchy. The River Selle ran through the middle of the village, and two bridges gave main access across to the centre and the railhead, beyond which the ground in the east rose steeply in a series of terraces, each divided from the other by a vertical bank. The Germans were well entrenched on the terraces, and the approaches to the bridges were strongly fortified with barbed wire and pillboxes.

Two battalions, the 12th Manchesters on the left and the 9th Duke of Wellingtons on the right, would lead the assault against Neuvilly. The 10th Battalion would supply B and D Companies to support the Manchesters, and the other two companies, A and C, would back up the Wellingtons. Corporal Frank Lester of A Company would follow the Wellingtons to the east of the village centre after crossing the river, to secure the railway station before attempting to clear out the rising terraces.

In the early hours of Saturday, 12 October, A Company began moving up from Inchy towards the assembly positions in front of the village, passing through the ruins of Rambourlieux Farm, from where German artillery batteries had pounded Major Ernest Alexander VC and his men on the heights of Le Cateau in 1914. At five o'clock, the artillery barrage commenced, and an hour later the assault began. On the left, the Manchesters were held up initially at one of the bridges, but after a fierce fire-fight made short work of the defenders and crossed the river to begin clearing out the village from the west.

On the right, the Wellingtons, having taken their bridge, moved on to capture the railway station, but were encountering strong opposition from a narrow street of houses and a factory as they pressed forward to the terraces. The fighting was close and ferocious, and the enemy sold every yard dearly: the wounded army was turning yet again to snap at its pursuers.

The fighting raged through the morning and into the afternoon. Lieutenant Roderick Graham commanded a section of A Company, 10th Battalion, consisting of Corporal Frank Lester and six other men, in support of the Wellingtons while they tried to advance house-to-house along the street which was swept with machine-gun fire. Snipers from the upstairs windows of several of the dilapidated houses were taking a heavy toll of the attackers also, and progress was slow. It is believed that George Hall was shot down by a sniper at this time.

As the Wellingtons inched forward, Lieutenant Graham supervised mopping-up operations in their rear. Corporal Frank Lester advanced on one of the houses which had been bypassed by the Wellingtons, and charged through the back door. He was confronted by two Germans. They made a dash for the front exit and he shot dead both of them. But, as Lieutenant Graham followed behind with the men, the house began to crumble and collapse, and the rear entrance was blocked off by falling masonry. There was no way out of the house for the men except through the front door, which gave onto the street alive with flying lead and steel.

Opposite, amid the rubble of a house, a small party of men had taken refuge from the machine-gun fire. One by one, as they tried to find cover, they were being picked off by a sniper. From the ruins of the house, Corporal Frank Lester sized up the situation and spotted the sniper. Without a thought for his own safety, he acted. 'I'll settle him,' he shouted, and dashed out into the street to confront the sharpshooter.

He charged the position and shot dead the sniper. But, as he did so, he was fired on by a second sniper, and he fell, mortally wounded. 'Remember me to all at home, and tell them I did my best,' he told his comrades as they nursed him in his last moments. He could not entrust his dying words to his chum, George Hall, for he had been killed earlier. His final message was carried home to his father by another friend.

For gallantry under fire in the face of the enemy, Corporal Frank Lester was awarded the Victoria Cross posthumously. His citation reads:

Frank Lester, Number 51674, Private, late 10th Battalion, Lancashire Fusiliers (Irby, near Birkenhead). Date of Act of Bravery: 12 October 1918. For most conspicuous bravery and self-sacrifice during the clearing of the village of Neuvilly on 12 Oct. 1918, when with a party of about seven men under an officer, he was first to enter a house from the back door, and shot two Germans as they attempted to get out by the front door. A minute later a fall of masonry blocked the door by which the party had entered. The only exit into the street was under fire at point-blank range. The street was also swept by the fire of machine-guns at close range. Observing that an enemy sniper was causing heavy casualties to a party in a house across the street, Private Lester exclaimed, 'I'll settle him', and dashing out into the street, shot the sniper at close quarters, falling mortally wounded at the same instant. This gallant man well knew it was certain death to go into the street, and the party opposite was faced with the alternative of crossing the fire-swept street or staying where it was and being shot one by one. To save their lives he sacrificed his own.

The following day, with only part of Neuvilly in Allied hands, the 10th Battalion was taken out of the front line and returned to Inchy, where it remained until 17 October, when the attack was resumed on the village. Three days later, Neuvilly and the terraced heights were finally captured. Corporal Frank Lester's body was recovered, and was interred later in row B, grave 15, at the Neuvilly Communal Cemetery Extension, three miles north of Le Cateau.

Notification of the award of the Victoria Cross appeared in the *London Gazette* of 14 December 1918. On 30 December, John Lester received a formal letter from King George V expressing his sincerest regrets that he could not bestow the Victoria Cross on his son. An invitation to attend at Buckingham Palace to receive the Victoria Cross was also extended. On 22 February 1919, Mrs Ellen Lester received her son's award from the king in the ballroom of the palace. She returned home grief-stricken. Not only had she lost a nephew, George, and a brave son, Frank, but her eldest boy, Edwin had also given his life in the conflict.

Edwin had enlisted in the 1/4th Battalion, the Cheshire Regiment, which formed at Birkenhead in August 1914. He served, like his cousin George, on Gallipoli, but had survived the terrible winter conditions. He saw action in Egypt, in Sinai, was promoted to corporal, and then took part in the first two assaults against Gaza, in Palestine. But while preparing for the third attack, he died of syncope in the trenches in July 1917. News of his death reached the Lester family a few weeks after Frank had re-enlisted as a fighting man. He is buried in the Beersheba War Cemetery.

Frank Lester VC, and his brother Edwin, are remembered throughout the Wirral. The war memorials at West Kirby and for the parishes of St Bartholomew, Thurston, and St Chad, Irby, carry their names, as does a special page in the Book of Remembrance at Chester Cathedral, and the gravestone of their parents in Holy Trinity Church, Hoylake. Denis Rose produced a display honouring and commemorating the life of Frank Lester VC at the Wirral Museum, Birkenhead Town Hall, and with John Ellison the remembrance plaque at Irby Public Library.

After the war, Frank's father continued to work as a market gardener until his death in 1941. He lived to see his four sons buried. In fact, only one of his children outlived him. George died in infancy, Edwin and Frank both perished in the war, and Jack was killed in 1929, in Thingwall Road, Irby, when his motorcycle struck a loose horse. His younger daughter, Ruth, died in 1931, ten weeks after giving birth to a son, William Lester Grey, Frank Lester's nephew, who now lives in Oxford.

The surviving daughter, Lucy, who passed away aged 88 in 1989, married Thomas Wilson in 1924. He served his time as a pattern maker in Cammell Laird's shipyard in Birkenhead and fought during the First World War with the Royal Naval Air Service. After the war, he went to work for John Lester as a market gardener, and met Lucy. The couple had two children, Edna Lucy and Frank, who was named after his brave uncle. Frank Wilson, too, worked as a market gardener for many years until he took employment with the local council authority as a district pools inspector. He married Maureen Harmer in 1962, and they have two sons, Stephen and Andrew. Retired now, he lives next door to his sister in Greasby, who occupies the house their father built.

Shirley Ross was born in Anfield. Her grandmother was Lillie Lester, younger sister of Frank's father, John. During the Second World War, to escape the blitz, her family moved to Whiston, and later to Huyton, where Shirley grew up in Crossvale Road, not far from where Frank Lester VC was born. She trained as a chiropodist and lived in West Derby, from where she worked in private practice in Liverpool and Chester. She married Alan Ross and they retired to live in Irby. A second cousin to Frank Lester VC, she lives in Irby, not because of its association with him, but simply because she loves the area. Until quite recently, Shirley Ross and Frank Wilson lived within a few miles of each other without either of them knowing of the other's existence and the family connection.

On 18 April 2002, Frank Lester's Victoria Cross, together with other effects and ephemera relating to him and to Edwin Lester, were put up for auction by Frank Wilson through the auction house of Morton and Eden. 'The family were all very proud of him,' said Frank Wilson. 'But it had got to the stage where the medal had become a liability. When you talk of the value involved, we couldn't afford to insure it and if you put it in a bank vault you don't see it so what's the point in keeping it? Reluctantly, we decided to sell it.'

Frank Lester's Victoria Cross was knocked down to the Michael Ashcroft Trust, the holding institution for Lord Ashcroft's collection of 146 Victoria Crosses. The Trust plans to open the collection to the public when a suitable location can be found.

Appendix

Patrick Mylott VC (1820–77)

Patrick Mylott was born in Hollymount, in the parish of Kilcommon, County Mayo, Ireland, in May 1820. At the age of 19, on Saturday, 18 May 1839, he attested at Ballinrobe to the 63rd Regiment of Foot as 1440 Private Patrick Mylott. He served for seven years in Burma and India and was granted a transfer to the 84th Regiment of Foot as 2542 Private Patrick Mylott on 1 January 1847. He fought throughout the Indian Mutiny with the 84th. Under Rule 13 of the Royal Warrant, he was elected to the award of the Victoria Cross by the rank and file of the regiment for several acts of gallantry between 12 July and 25 September 1857, during the siege and first relief of Lucknow.

The 84th Regiment returned to England in 1859. On 4 December of the following year, while stationed at Manchester, Patrick Mylott VC applied for and was given a voluntary discharge from the army. In his army papers he stated that he would take up residence in Warrington, where his Victoria Cross pension was to be paid.

Sir O'Moore Creagh VC, who, until 1920, compiled *The VC and DSO Book*, which, like the work of Canon William Lummis MC, chronicled the lives of Victoria Cross holders, noted that Patrick Mylott VC died on 7 December 1877, but did not say where. And, until quite recently, that was all that was known of the man following his discharge from the army. However, several years ago, a death certificate was uncovered at the General Register Office which stated that a Patrick Mylett died on 22 December 1878 in the Liverpool Workhouse on Brownlow Hill, the same institution in which John Kirk VC had passed away thirteen years earlier.

In 1837, it became compulsory in Britain to register births, deaths and marriages, and in 1841 the first national census was taken. Mylott is an English name, but it is found in Ireland, and common variants are Mylett, Millet and Milot. Registrars and census officers wrote down names as they heard them, and had no means of checking whether the correct spelling was used when respondents, such as Patrick Mylott VC, were illiterate. An individual's name could appear in various official records in a variety of different forms, for example, Mylott, Millet, Mylett or Milot; Dowling or Doolan.

Historians researching the life of Patrick Mylott VC therefore assumed that Patrick Mylett was in fact Patrick Mylott VC, his name having been misspelled on the death certificate; and so Liverpool claimed another Victoria Cross hero.

The fact that Patrick Mylett was 64 when he died, which gave him a birth year of 1814, six years before Patrick Mylott VC was born, was not considered relevant.

Patrick Mylett was buried in a pauper's grave in Anfield Cemetery, and the site of the grave was lost over the years. In 1994, a headstone was erected at the cemetery to honour him. However, while preparing the paperwork, the original burial work order and burial record from 1878 revealed that Patrick Mylett was in truth William Patrick Mylett. The headstone was thus inscribed William Patrick Mylott VC. But, there are no records of Patrick Mylott VC ever having the Christian name William.

The body of Patrick Mylett was claimed from the Liverpool Workhouse by his son-in-law, Robert Hardman, who lived with his wife Bridget and children at 2C Duckworth Street, off Fontenoy Street. Robert Hardman had married Bridget Millet, the daughter of Patrick and Mary Millet, on 5 December 1861. Patrick Millet is Patrick Mylett. Recent research shows that Patrick Mylett or Millet was born in Mayo in 1816, that he married Mary and had a child Bridget before leaving Ireland. He travelled to Liverpool in the late 1840s, where he found work. Once established in the city, Mary and Bridget joined him, and the family lived off Fontenoy Street, very close to where Robert Hardman grew up. According to census records, Bridget Millet, sometimes Bridget Mylett, was born in Mayo no earlier than 1841, and no later than 1844. Between 1841 and 1844, Patrick Mylott VC was stationed in Burma and India and could not have fathered a daughter in Ireland. In addition, his service record shows him as a single man without a wife or children.

Patrick Mylott VC received his annual Victoria Cross pension of £10 in four quarterly instalments. Payments to him were recorded in the Victoria Cross Pensions Book, which can be viewed in the National Archives. The pension book correctly shows that Patrick Mylott VC left the army on 4 December 1860, and that pension payments were made to him until his death on 27 December 1877, when they ceased. The record does not indicate in which town or city the money was paid, or where he died, only that his Victoria Cross pension was cancelled on that day. And the date is very close to that given for Patrick Mylott VC by Sir O'Moore Creagh. Patrick Mylett died on 22 December 1878, a year later.

Patrick Mylott VC had no known connections with the city of Liverpool. In all known documentation he never used the name William. On discharge from the colours he stated he would live in Warrington where his Victoria Cross pension was to be paid. The names Millet and Mylett are recorded in the Warrington area in the 1871 national census. The Victoria Cross pensions book notes his death occurring on 27 December 1877, and no further pension payments were made to him after that date. Patrick Mylott VC is not William Patrick Mylett, who died in Liverpool in 1878 and is buried and honoured in his stead at Anfield Cemetery.

The last resting place of Patrick Mylott VC has yet to be identified; and until it is found, Liverpool cannot claim Patrick Mylott VC as one of her heroes. The location of his Victoria Cross is not known.

Charles Anderson VC (1826?–99)

Charles Anderson won the Victoria Cross on 8 October 1858 at Sundeela, Oudh, during mopping-up operations following the suppression of the Indian Mutiny. Together with Thomas Monaghan, he saved the life of his commanding officer, Lieutenant Colonel Seymour, who had fallen wounded when attacked by more than twenty-five sepoys. The award was gazetted on 11 November 1862.

Very little is known about Charles Anderson VC. Canon William Lummis MC, whose research into the lives of the early Victoria Cross winners was continued and developed by David Harvey into the most thorough and voluminous account of all the Victoria Cross heroes, *Monuments to Courage*, could say only that Charles Anderson VC had a connection with Waterford, Ireland. And all that Sir O'Moore Creagh VC could offer was the belief that he spent his later years in Waterford.

He is believed to have died at Seaham Harbour, County Durham, on 19 April 1899, when a Charles Anderson, aged 70, who worked as a miner, was found dead at the bottom of a cliff. However, there is no overwhelming evidence to suggest that this Charles Anderson was in fact the same Charles Anderson who won the Victoria Cross in India.

Neither Canon Lummis MC nor Sir O'Moore Creagh VC discovered his year or place of birth. Nowadays, most Victoria Cross references give him a birth year of either 1826 or 1827, and Liverpool as his birthplace. And the city certainly claims him as one of her native sons. However, no evidence has been uncovered to support the belief that he was a Liverpudlian by birth.

Until very recently, the only known public record of Charles Anderson VC was his brief service history: he attested to the 2nd Dragoon Guards, the Queen's Bays, in Dublin on 11 December 1845, was promoted to corporal in 1858 after winning the Victoria Cross and was discharged from the army with that rank at Colchester on 28 June 1870, having been with the colours in England, Ireland and India for twenty-five years.

On 30 March 1851, a cadre of the 2nd Dragoon Guards was enumerated at Leeds Cavalry Barracks during the national census. Among the respondents was Private Charles Anderson, formerly a clerk, aged 24, born in Dublin, Ireland. His birth year was 1827. The regimental rolls for the 2nd Dragoon Guards are incomplete, but recent research shows only one man by the name of Charles Anderson was serving with the 2nd Dragoon Guards at the time; and that this same man sailed from Liverpool with the Regiment on 25 July 1857, and arrived in Calcutta, India, in the last week of November. The Queen's Bays, with a strength of 710 officers and men, was one of the first heavy cavalry regiments to serve in India, and moved out from Calcutta to participate in the suppression of the Mutiny and mopping-up operations in Oudh, most notably at Sundeela. Private Charles Anderson won the Victoria Cross during this campaign.

Further investigation reveals that Private Charles Anderson was born in Dublin in 1827, the son of James Anderson, and that he grew up in the Suffolk Street area of Dublin, close to Temple Bar on the south bank of the River Liffey. His only known connection with the city of Liverpool appears to be when he embarked on a troop transport ship, either the *Blenheim* or the *Monarch*, at the port for passage to Calcutta on 25 July 1857 as a private in the Queen's Bays.

Further research is needed to firmly establish his antecedents. But the recently discovered census record of 1851, together with the only other known public record of him, his army service history, indicate he was a native of Dublin, not Liverpool: when he decided to join the colours in 1845, he enlisted in a regiment which was on station close to where he was living and where he had been born and brought up. And that place was Dublin.

The Victoria Cross of Charles Anderson VC is held by 1st Queen's Dragoon Guards Museum, Cardiff Castle, South Glamorgan.

Bibliography and Sources

Books

1914, Lyn Macdonald (Michael Joseph, 1987).

Arras & Messines, Gerald Gliddon (Sutton Publishing, 1998).

The Autobiography of Donald Dickson Farmer VC (unpublished).

The Boer War, Thomas Packenham (Weidenfeld & Nicolson, 1979).

The Book of the VC, A.L. Haydon (Andrew Melrose, 1906).

Cambrai 1917, Gerald Gliddon (Sutton Publishing, 2004).

The Final Days, Gerald Gliddon (Sutton Publishing, 2000).

From Cutlasses to Computers, W.R. Cockcroft (S.B. Publications, 1991).

The Great Mutiny, Christopher Hibbert (Allen Lane, 1978).

The History of the Lincolnshire Regiment, C.R. Simpson (The Medici Society, 1931).

Irish Winners of the Victoria Cross, Richard Doherty & David Truesdale (Four Courts Press, 2000).

The Lafone Family, Sue Sayers (J.S.J. Publishers, 1999).

Liverpool Heroes, Sid Lindsay, Bill Sergeant, Ann Clayton (Noel Chavasse VC Memorial Association, 2006).

My Mystery Ships: Rear Admiral Gordon Campbell VC DSO (Hodder & Stoughton, 1928).

The Naval VCs, Stephen Snelling (Sutton Publishing, 2002).

Our Bravest and Our Best, Arthur Bishop (McGraw-Hill Ryerson, 1995).

Passchendaele 1917, Gerald Gliddon (Sutton Publishing, 1998).

Raj, Lawrence James (Little, Brown & Company, 1997).

The Reason Why, Cecil Woodham-Smith (Constable & Co., 1953).

The Register of the Victoria Cross, Nora Buzzell (This England, 1988).

The River War, Winston S. Churchill (Longmans, Green & Co., 1899).

Rorke's Drift, Adrian Greaves (Cassell, 2002).

The Seven VCs of Stonyhurst College, H.L. Kirby & R.R. Walsh (THCL Books, 1987).

The Sideshows, Gerald Gliddon (Sutton Publishing, 2005).

Somme, Lyn Macdonald (Michael Joseph, 1983).

Stories of the Victoria Cross, Frank Mundell (The Sunday School Union, 1898).

Symbol of Courage, Max Arthur (Sidgwick & Jackson, 2004).

The VC and DSO Book, O'Moore Creagh and E.M. Humphris (eds) (The Standard Art Book Company, 1920).

VCs of the First World War, 1914, Gerald Gliddon (Alan Sutton Publishing, 1994).

VCs of the Somme, Gerald Gliddon (Gliddon Books, 1991).

The Victoria Cross at Sea, John Winton (Michael Joseph, 1978).

Victoria Cross Heroes, Michael Ashcroft (Headline Review, 2006).

Archives

Dulwich College Archive

General Register Office

Harrow School Achive

Liverpool Records Office
Liverpool Shipwreck & Humane Society
The Military Historical Society of the National Army Museum
The National Archives, Kew

Journals, Magazines and Newspapers
Bolton Evening News
Bolton Journal and Guardian
Gunfire Magazine
Inverness Courier
Journal of the Australian War Memorial
Journal of the Victoria Cross Association
Liverpool Daily Courier
Liverpool Daily Post
Liverpool Echo
Liverpool Express
London Gazette
Lytham St Annes Express
New York Times
RCMP Quarterly, Autumn 1999
Stonyhurst Magazine, 2005, 2006
Sunday Mirror
The Times
This England, Summer 1983

Internet sources
www.bmd.nsw.gov.au
Through this website, birth, death and marriage certificates can be obtained for residents of New
   South Wales.

www.ancestry.com
This website provides search facilities for those seeking birth, death or marriage certificates for
   family members.

www.1914–1918.net
The Long, Long Trail – the history of British forces during the First World War.

www.findagrave.com
Paul F. Wilson's site for burial places of Victoria Cross holders.

www.victoriacrosssociety.com
A site for all enthusiasts of the Victoria Cross.

Index